MOI
TODDLER
DISCIPLINE

MW01172277

2 BOOKS IN 1

Parenting Toddlers in the Digital Age

&

Toddlers' Discipline

The Ultimate Survival Guide for Parents: Effective Strategies on How to Talk So Tots Will Listen

Written by

Nicola Davies

ISBN: 9798693309470

First Edition: 4th October 2020

10 9 8 7 6 5 4 3 2 1

Get Your Audiobook
Absolutely Free.

Sign up for free on Audible with any email and get your audiobook that you can listen to in your car, bus, train or when your travel.

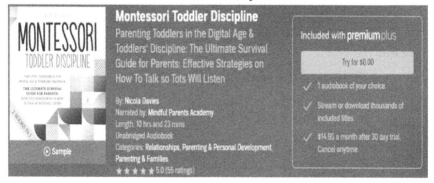

CONTENTS

We're here
because of you

If you have found any value in this material, please consider leaving a review and joining the Author's Mission to give the most resourceful start to all children around the world

By scanning the QR-Code below ♥

★ ★ ★ ★ ★

PARENTING TODDLERS IN THE DIGITAL AGE

Montessori Strategies for Thriving ToT(s). Survive Sleep Deprivation with a Curiosity Led Routine, Nurture a Developing Mind with a Mindful and Positive Discipline

Preface

This book is part of a series of manuscripts from the Mindful Parent Academy. This growing collection contains books that tackle various aspects of the life of modern parents with its inevitable challenges and unfathomable joys. All our books are driven by a compassionate, none judgmental and positive approach that aim to support parents in their journey into parenthood, 'the most difficult job that comes without instructions but with plenty of expectations and demands'. At the heart of the Mindful Parent Academy there is a mission that is to shift the current trend that sees parents either feeling guilty and worried for spending too much time with their children to the detriment of their career. Or vice versa, a world where parents cannot spend enough time with their kids because of the strains put on them by their adult life and their job commitments. At the Mindful Parent Academy, we believe that any parent around the world should be put in favourable conditions in order to enjoy the right to be fully involved in this wonderful period of their child's life while being supported by the larger society. It is not a coincidence that in any given culture, in any part of the world, family (whoever this includes) is what drives people's actions and interests.

Stressed by the demands of modern life and sleep deprived, often parents of the digital age risk to miss out on the absolute magic and delights of their child's early stages of life by leaving their toddlers to indulge in their favourite and hypnotising digital content. However, the period such as toddlerhood, is increasingly recognised as the foundation for a happy, resilient and confident adult life later on. A delicate period where parents can really lay down the foundations for a healthy life long relationship with their children based on common values, rules and respect for each other.

Our mission is to build a world that gives back to the family its core role as the foundational institution that sustains society and that provides wellbeing for all of its members. Our revolution starts here and now. It starts by wanting to be capable of looking after the little people that constitute the future of our human society. This starts by equipping parents with the right knowledge and activities that will allow you to think strategically about your toddler's development. Be able to follow their curiosity by providing tailored activities for every stage of their toddlerhood without continually investing in new toys.

This also includes the tools and strategies to implement effective tactics to discipline today's toddlers to let them thrive and reach their full potential despite all the digital temptations and distractions. At the Mindful Parent Academy, we support the Montessori Method as one of the most reliable teaching approaches that fosters children's development and stimulates their curiosity in an age-appropriate way. This should also help to manage your child's 'absorbent mind' and help them to sleep deeply and soundly. However, at the Mindful Parent Academy we believe that it is not just about the kid. Actually, we believe that there cannot be a flourishing tree without sturdy roots and that 'you cannot pour from an empty cup'. Therefore, whatever your circumstances, No Matter What, you must first look after your own well-being.

And without guilt. We would like to introduce to you ways of keeping yourself mindful and positive with your children even when seriously sleep deprived, emotionally drained and juggling between the many demands of life. Keep yourself sane by finding time to look after yourself whatever that means in a given day: listening to your favourite podcasts on headphones while doing the dishes, repeating positive mantras while changing dirty nappies, doing on-line (and possibly live) exercises classes for mums (dads can join too), reflect and write down the rules and values that you most care about and discuss them with other relevant carers so to agree, updating your gratitude list, read a paragraph (or even a line) of your favourite book before falling asleep, give yourself permission to cry and let it go, going to the woods or for a walk on your own even when it's starting to rain, singing nursery rhymes with your kids at the top of your voice and join in with the actions, connect yourself and your kids to nature even by just watering the plants or repotting them to bigger pots, dancing with your kids like no one is watching, and much, much more..
At the Mindful Parent Academy, we have your well-being at heart. You must try every possible way to keep yourself calm, happy, connected and sane while the demands put on you as a carer and provider are never ending and your energy and patience are fluctuating. Enjoy your reading.

Introduction

This book combines the Montessori Method for children with the mindful and positive discipline approach for parents. The Montessori Method was developed over 100 years ago by Maria Montessori, the Italian physician and educator. Montessori has developed a practical framework for the application of her theory. Her creativity in this regard is a significant explanation for the long-lasting and pervasive influence of her work. It should be borne in mind, though, that Montessori intended her approach to be considered an open-minded, not a predetermined program. She believed in creativity in the classroom, and her entire approach to teaching was in the spirit of continuous exploration focused on the child's insight.

Montessori is not an unknown term in the world of education. Even though parents may not know what Montessori all is about, they must have already heard of it. One of the best things about Montessori is that children can learn through this method even in the comfort of their own home.

When it comes to applying the Montessori Method and its principles at home, there are some things you must do. This method is not just about the materials and activities. Here are some tips to guide you:

Prepare the Environment.

When it comes to the prepared environment of Montessori, keep in mind that there is always a place for everything, and everything must always be in its place. Assign one of the rooms in your home as your child's Montessori learning environment. If there are Montessori schools in your area, go ahead and visit them to have a better idea of how to arrange this room. Otherwise, you can add some child items in every room of your house, such as, a small kitchen in your kitchen for the child to mimic you, a peg for your child at the entrance of your house to hang their coat when enter the house, and so on.

You may also go online and search for Montessori classroom ideas on Google or Pinterest. But please do not think you need to invest in new toys or forniture, just keep it simple and follow the ideas described later on in this book. Either way, having a visual image of what Montessori classrooms must look like will give you a better idea of how to arrange the room/s you have assigned in your own home. One thing to keep in mind though, is to make sure that everything is child-sized and at your child's level so that he will not keep asking you for assistance when he wants to take something.

Plan All the Materials and Activities to Include in Your Child's Environment

After planning the environment, it is time to think about the materials and activities to place inside that environment. You can go online to search for a complete list of Montessori materials in each of the learning areas. Then you can either purchase similar materials (actual Montessori materials are very expensive) or create them on your own. For instance, you can easily create sandpaper letters and numbers using thick cardboard and sandpaper.

Arrange these materials and activities according to their areas of learning and make sure that all of them are accessible to your child. You may want to include a combination of easy materials and those which are a bit more challenging or unfamiliar to your child. Also, you may want to rotate these items regularly, so your child does not get bored. If you see that she is not interested in some activities or she has already mastered others and she is not using them anymore, take these materials out and replace them with new ones.

Focus on Life Skills

Activities and materials which teach life skills are the easiest ones to replicate. Children need to learn life skills early on. With these skills, they learn how to care for themselves and their environment. This sets children up to become capable and considerate adults when they grow up. Providing the proper materials to teach these skills even makes your life as a parent a lot easier! Soon, your child will start volunteering to help you around the house because he already knows how to do these chores.

Of course, you must always match the activities and materials to the abilities and age of your child. Introducing activities which are too difficult for children is never a good idea. Your child will not be able to do these activities. If you force him, this might weaken his self-confidence and his willingness to continue with the rest of the activities you have prepared.

Help Your Child Learn Concentration and Inner Motivation

These skills are essential if you want your child to get the most out of the Montessori Method. For a child to master a skill, concept, or activity, he must concentrate while doing it. If you have prepared the environment well, your child will be able to concentrate on the activities you have prepared for him. This means that there should be no distractions such as gadgets, electronic devices, and random toys which do not have a purpose inside the room.

Also, avoid giving your child rewards when he does something good or gains proficiency in something. Try to observe your child when he realizes that he has finally been able to master a puzzle or a practical life activity. You will see a sense of accomplishment in your child. This is much more valuable than extrinsic rewards because this sense of accomplishment becomes the driving force within your child to keep on going to master the other activities in his environment.

Take on the Role of a Montessori Teacher

Finally, learning how to facilitate the Montessori Method for your child is also essential. Rather than teaching everything to your child, allow him to discover, explore, and choose the materials and activities on his own. If your child asks for help, oblige. If not, observe.

You may also step in if your child picks up material and cannot figure out how to use it. Again, he will probably ask you to help him out. These are the best and most appropriate times to step in when it comes to the Montessori Method. Then when your child celebrates his mastery of a skill, celebrate with him! There is nothing more satisfying than to see your child grow, develop, and improve at his own pace and through his efforts.

Montessori is truly a wonderful learning approach. Whether it is done in school or at home, children love learning through this method mainly because of how it has done. Now that you have learned all the basics about Montessori, you may start planning how you will apply this in your home. Then step back and watch your child learn in the best possible way!

1

What We Need to Know About Toddlers' and Their Brain Development?

I t is pretty amazing when you realize that right when your child is born into the world that they become aware of their surroundings, even though they may not be able to determine what is precisely happening properly. The precious beauty of the toddler stage is you get to watch firsthand as your child learns to explore the world that is around them. These are the ages in which they truly begin to build an understanding of people and objects, as well as learning with their bodies, home, and world functions.

While there are interesting changes physically within your toddler that you can see on the outside, there are even more drastic developments occurring within their rapidly expanding brains as they learn how to take in and interpret the world around them. As they are making strides in observing and successfully interacting with objects and people, their brains become more and more capable of processing, storing, and utilizing vital information.

Toddler and Their Brain Development

Ages 1–2 Years

- ✓ They can feel proud and accomplished when they have completed something independently.
- ✓ They understand the difference between "me" and "you."

- ✓ They can recognize objects that are familiar to them.
- ✓ They are capable of matching similar objects.
- ✓ They enjoy short and simple story time.
  - Storytime for kids means getting to snuggle up next to Mom and/or Dad, look at cool pictures, and hear interesting sounds as parents read. Your kids are learning the following:
  - Stories have both a beginning and an end.
  - Books can tell stories.
  - Reading properly involves doing so from left to right.
  - How the books work from the beginning then to how the story works.
- ✓ They can understand and respond to words and commands.
- ✓ They start to imitate the words and actions of adults.
- ✓ They highly enjoy dancing to music.
- ✓ They recognize what the term "no" means and begins to use it properly.
- ✓ They can recognize who they are in the mirror or other reflections.

Ages 2–3 Years

- ✓ They have learned to count "1-2-3."
- ✓ They have the capability to inform others of their actions.
- ✓ They can identify themselves in the mirror with their name.
- ✓ They can put together simple 3- to 4-piece puzzles.
- ✓ They are more than capable of stacking rings on peg toys in order of size.
- ✓ They play pretend with dolls, stuffed animals, or other toys.
- ✓ They can group objects by categories (food, clothing, and animals).
- ✓ They can name off objects in books or magazines.
- ✓ They respond effectively to simple directions.
- ✓ They understand simple stories.

Cognitive Red Flags to Be Aware

If you take note of some of the following things by the time your child reaches the ages of 18–24 months, you may want to speak with your doctor.

Ages 1–2 Years

- ✓ They require the need for constant, undivided attention to stay at an activity.
- ✓ They constantly go from one activity to another and is unable to stay absorbed in an activity for very long.
- ✓ They are interested in feeling or watching toys rather than playing, interacting, or using them.
- ✓ They never imitate other individuals.
- ✓ They do not grasp the function of common objects ("find something to eat" instead of "find a cookie").
- ✓ They begin to understand empathy.
  - Toddlers are beginning to make connections between not only their feelings but also the feelings of others. This is crucial in building relationships and friendships now and in the future.
  - Do not put an emotional band-aid over them when they feel bad or sad about something they did or something that has occurred. Your child must learn how to cope by adequately identifying with their emotions. Reassure them that it is okay that they feel the way they do.

Ages 2–3 Years

- ✓ They need undivided attention to stay within an activity.
- ✓ They move from one activity to another.
- ✓ They continue using mouth toys and have no interest in playing with toys.
- ✓ They are not able to understand the function of common objects.
- ✓ They are unable to practice basic categorization successfully.
- ✓ They have no interest in wanting to participate in pretend play.

Strides in Independence

By the time your little one has spawned into walking and slightly talking human beings, they are already making strides in gaining their independence. With the realization that they can do quite a few simple tasks on their very own, they tend to venture to do their things. It is crucial to give your child plenty of room and opportunities to grow.

- ✓ When it is necessary, be firm with your toddler. When you need them to abide by your rules and in your way, ensure that you are communicating this to them quickly and deliberately, yet calmly as well. For example, once your child is properly restrained in the means of their car seat, you can inform them of the reasons why they are buckled into one, include the dangers but do not frighten them with gory details.
- ✓ Tell your little one "yes" whenever you possibly can, if you are sure, they are not in any grave danger or injuring or drastically harming themselves.
- ✓ Patience is key and curbing the need to assist your child will come with practice. But let them use their eating utensils and let them pull down their pants. They will learn!
- ✓ Ensure that you include them when it comes to chore time. Show and let them hold the dustpan. Give them a rag or duster to get down and dust things at their level.
- ✓ Make plenty of room in your hectic schedule for your toddler to do certain things at a pace that is comfortable for them. If they want to dress by themselves, let them. If they want to attempt to put on their shoes, by all means! Just remember that leaving your house will inevitably take longer until they get the hang of these tasks.

From Birth to 3 Years of Age

The roots of the youngsters' development are set during the initial three years of their life. Montessori considers this period one of a "profound embryo," in which the youngster observes, does, and experiments. This procedure is accomplished by the youngster's "retentive psyche," which joins relations, feelings, pictures, language, and culture through their faculties and by the straightforward reality of living. These educational encounters shape their mind, their framing systems of neurons that have the capability of remaining with the individual for all their life. From birth to 3 years of age, the Montessori training is also focused on the improvement of talking that facilitate development and autonomy, gives the kid confidence, and permits them to find their underlying capacities and their place inside a network.

The Five Principles

Rule 1: Respect for the Child

Regard for the Child is the most significant rule hidden behind the whole Montessori Method (not basic practice in the mid-twentieth century). Regard is express by not interfering with their fixation. Additionally, regard is express by allowing students to settle on decisions, to get things done for themselves, and to also learn for themselves. The most important instruction for the Montessori adult is to respect all pulpils and learn to observe without judgment.

Rule 2: The Absorbent Mind

Montessori training is based on the rule that, essentially, by living, kids are continually gaining from their general surroundings. Through their faculties, youngsters continually assimilate data from their reality. They understand it since they are thinking creatures.

Rule 3: Sensitive Periods

The Montessori teaching method considers certain periods when youngsters are progressively prepared to gain proficiency with specific abilities. These are delicate periods when is essential for the youngster to persevere to gain the skills. These delicate periods change for every youngster. Through their perception, Montessori educators must distinguish delicate periods in their pulpils and give the right assets to kids to thrive during this time.

Rule 4: The Prepared Environment

The Montessori Method proposes that youngsters learn best in a situation that has been set up to empower them to get things done for themselves. Continuously kid-focused, the learning condition ought to elevate opportunity for youngsters to freely investigate materials. Instructors ought to set up the learning condition by making materials accessible to kids deliberately and autonomously.

Rule 5: Auto training

Auto instruction, or self-training, is the idea that kids are fit for teaching themselves. This is one of the most significant convictions in the Montessori Method. Montessori instructors give the motivation, the direction, and the support for youngsters to teach themselves.

Arranged Environment

The Montessori approach gives an appealing and deliberately arranged condition to exploit the pinnacle time of affectability toward learning. It is particularly intended to address the kid's questions and animate his interest. Quality, simplicity, attempt, and sensible request are fundamental traits of homeroom materials if kids are to be attracted to investigate and gain from them.

The Prepared Environment is equipped with a studied arrangement of self-showing instructive materials that fulfil the youngster's ability while shielding the person in question from pointless disappointment. The kid is allowed to participate in "unconstrained action" with most extreme freedom from the grown-ups and with the advantage of friends who can likewise help in the learning.

Numerous Montessori exercises, particularly at toddler level with the most solid students, are intended to cause the child to notice the tactile properties of items: size, shape, shading, surface, weight, smell, sound, and so forth. Step by step, toddlers figure out how to focus cautiously, seeing even more unmistakably little subtleties in the things around them. They have started to watch and value their condition. This is key in helping the kid find hows and to learn.

Self-rule

Opportunity is a pre-imperative condition for learning. A free youngster is one who is building up their latent capacity and wants to work out issues; yet he is fit for requesting and accepting heading when important. Opportunity does not suggest that youngster may fiercely do whatever, at whatever point the person in question needs; it alludes to the demonstration of duty and sensibly picking one's game-plan, among many offered, whitin a characterized set of limits.

The Montessori Method accepts that every youngster is completely fit for instructing oneself and appreciates learning through development and experience of opportunity when their rights are regarded. The desire of the grown-ups is not forced on them.

If they knew the words, even small kids would state, "assist me with figuring out how to do it without your help!"

Order

Order is the second pre-imperative condition for learning; it is the inward, individual drive to make and keep up an inside feeling of direction and inspiration. Control alludes to the capacity to direct one's conduct intentionally and worthily by utilizing the Prepared Environment.

Montessori depends on significant regard for a kid's character, where the individual in question works from the free decision and is permitted a portion of autonomy—this structure the premise of internal order. The youngster builds up their positive conduct with the assistance of the Montessori materials to enough stimulate and challenge themself. Dr. Montessori noticed some alleged "disorderly" kids were sensible and able people, disappointed by an absence of legitimate incitement in their condition and insufficient chance to accomplish it. As such, they were exhausted. She noticed that little youngsters became more joyful and progressively self-controlled after a timeframe when those necessities were met inside a Montessori situation. They met testing, rousing tasks, which retained their energies, however, brought about a personal feeling of accomplishment.

Basic Thinking

Montessori centers on instructing and learning for comprehension, and bravely holding onto fails as normal strides in the learning procedure. The Montessori Method instructs kids to fundamentally think, not just to retain, criticize, and overlook. As opposed to giving replacements heaps of right answers, Montessori instruction continues posing the correct inquiries to lead the learner to find the responses for themselves from the materials. Learning turns into its prize, and every achievement power a craving to find significantly more.

Kids will figure out how to reinforce their social and enthusiastic turn of events. Kids figure out how to bargain and be aware. Preschool gives a domain to youngsters to investigate, increase a feeling of self, play with friends, and assemble fearlessness. Kids learn they can achieve assignments and settle on choices without the assistance of their folks.

Brain development is continuous and begins even before the child is born. So, children need to improve their mental skills and talent. The Montessori playschool helps to improve child mental abilities, not only by limiting them to coloring and blocking buildings. They satisfy a child curiosity and help them find out what they like best. This could provide clear instructions for parents and teachers to steer their education in the right direction. Montessori schools focus on developing a child natural talent. Talent and art lessons are part of the curriculum. There is also room for physical development. Children are given playtime in which they can develop their physical abilities through outdoor games. This can improve a child's health.

The Montessori play school introduces a child into society. Here the child learns to socialize with other children and becomes a social being. The early involvement of disciplines and methods can make them responsible citizens. The Montessori school aims to teach a child good manners and habits so that they can grow as worthy individuals. The right combination of play and study is good for the general development of your children. Research shows that Montessori education is far superior to traditional or non-Montessori schools. The principles of this form of education emphasize a safe and stimulating environment in which the child can grow at his own pace, and teachers follow the self-directed learning process.

Deep-rooted Learners

Even though much has been said about the academic accomplishments of Montessori youngsters, the worth lies in the self-authority and love of discovering that kids accomplish. Montessori schools are intended to enable every child to find and build up their exceptional gifts and potential outcomes. Youngsters learn at their pace and in ways that work best for them; the objective is to be adaptable and innovative, intending to every pulpil in a way that mirrors this way of thinking.

Montessori sets an example for a lifetime of good work propensities and awareness of other's expectations by permitting kids to build up a significant level of freedom and self-restraint. Students figure out how to invest wholeheartedly in doing things cautiously and well for the sole purpose of self-satisfaction.

Each youngster is brought into the world with an inclination to learn, with a profound love for impersonation and perseverence of deliberate work, and with one instinctive point: their self-improvement. Dr. Montessori accepted that training is a forever groundwork and should assist kids with building up a solid self-idea and an inspirational demeanor toward learning while securing the essential examination abilities which will serve them all through life.

2

The Importance of Early Years

Getting it right during your child's earliest years will have a crucial impact on their future life chances. The emphasis tends to be placed on children's results throughout their time in compulsory education, with 61% of parents believing school is the most important learning period for children.

However, little is said about the stage from birth to five years, where the important foundations are laid for all further skills learned.

Early Brain Development

During the period from birth to five years, rapid and intense growth of your child's brain will be seen and clearly can only happen once in a lifetime.

So how are brain cells developed? When your child receives positive interactions, and when they are deeply involved in play experiences that interest them, the synapses form connections between one neuron's head to another neuron's tail.

During the early years, this process happens at the double the rate of an adult brain, allowing children to learn things more quickly than is possible in adulthood.

As can be seen, this period of creating synapses is critical for learning new things. Without practice and repetition, certain skills will disappear. For example, to create lasting skills in your child, such as learning to talk, their exposure to rich, meaningful language and words and the opportunities they must practice must be constant for it to be retained. Such things as reciting nursery rhymes or reading stories will enable connections to be made and then strengthened on hearing the words again and again.

Working with your child during the prime time of their brain development is a privilege. Whatever the approach used, we ensure we fully capture this brief but unique opportunity to nurture, support and encourage the formation of your child's brain circuitry.

We achieve this through positive interactions and the use of age-appropriate resources that are carefully planned to support your child's individual learning journey.

How is My Child Learning Through Play?

Through play, your child will make sense of the world around them and can discover, explore and experiment all through the medium of play.

It is learning through doing, creating those experiences through first-hand knowledge. There is never usually one outcome from this; as the activity evolves and adapts, it can lead to many outcomes.

The Montessori Method sits beautifully alongside this play-based learning approach, as in the Montessori curriculum, children also learn through doing. Learning should never feel like 'work' but should instead feel like a fascinating and exciting journey of discovery!

Speech and Language Development

Children who have a strong vocabulary have a better start to their education and even enhance their life chances. This is a fact. Vocabulary directly links to attainment in all phases of schooling, and building that vocabulary is most important during the early years.

Did you know that children who are read to every day until the age of five will have heard over a million more words than their non-reading peers?

Imagine the words that you read in books but rarely use in day-to-day life, words like shimmering, glimmering, and glinting, for example. Now imagine that your child will have access to those words when they are trying to describe a beautiful lake, they saw at sunset to you, as opposed to another child trying to describe the same scene without those words to hand; how much comfortable will your child description be?

Your child will need to hear a word a massive 500 times before they know, understand, and start to use it correctly. Hopefully, you can see how vital speech and language are to all aspects of learning and life in general and why we need to take it so seriously at such a young age.

As this is such a hugely important area, it forms a big part of our work in the early years. Skilled educators work very hard every day to fill children's 'word bank' with as much rich language as possible.

To support this important work, we would like to encourage you as parents to play an active part in developing these vital skills.

Here Are Our Top Tips

Read to your child every day. If you do nothing else for your child but this, you will have done enough.
Hold a running commentary on life in general—tell children what you are doing and what they are doing—for example, 'mummy is putting up a shelf, you are watching me from your highchair.'

Name things for your child when they point things out or point things out to them yourself—'look, this is a shiny green leaf.'

Avoid using baby language—use 'dog' not 'doggie,' 'thank you' not 'ta.'

Repeat and mirror language, even babies babbling.

Show you are interested in what your child has to say by using eye contact and getting down to their level.

When Will My Child Write Their Name?

The Journey to Writing

Pencil control is one of the most complex skills to introduce to children. Therefore, we have considered how we support this. For a child to hold and use a pencil correctly by the time they leave the nursery to go on to school, there are many stages in which we provide a wealth of opportunities and experiences for the children to participate in, starting with our youngest children in the Baby Room.

Children need to develop control over their whole body and make as many large movements as possible, which will then enable them to gain control over the very small movements that are needed to write. Here are some of the experiences we provide, all of which can be further promoted at home.

Children Aged 0-1 Year

'Tummy Time'

It is essential to provide plenty of opportunities for babies to spend time on their tummy with books, treasure baskets, gloop, and natural and interesting play items for them to explore this along with supporting the development of neck, shoulder, and core strength, prepares the arms and hands for fine motor skills and supports early hand-eye coordination, both fundamental to the development of pre-writing skills.

Crawling

You should also encourage crawling for as long and as often as possible. This develops the arches in the palm of the hands, enabling the grasping of different sized and shaped objects. The arches direct the skilled movement of fingers and control the power of grasp.

Crawling also helps to promote your child's bilateral skills—the ability to use both sides of the body at the same time—supporting the essential skill of holding the paper steady with one hand and writing with the other.

Large Motor Movements

Upper body strength and stability ensure effective arm movement and good postural control, which allows the hands to be used effectively when working on tabletop tasks such as writing and cutting with scissors.

The children have lots of opportunities to develop their upper body strength by rolling, catching, and throwing balls, music and movement, and obstacle courses.

Messy Play

Sensory play promotes the development of fine motor skills by encouraging the manipulation of materials, telling the brain where the hands are as they perform a task. The brain then coordinates these sensations to make small changes for precise coordination and muscle control.

Montessori Nurseries use a vast range of media including paint, gloop, play dough, shaving foam and water to enable the children to begin making their marks and discover different ways to manipulate the materials.

Children Aged 1-2 Years

Developing Hand Preference

We provide many opportunities for children to practice activities that require a 'stable hand' and an 'active hand.' These include—pegging items on a line, washing the table, spreading butter on bread, pouring water from a jug, mixing items in a bowl, and using bottles with pumps in the water tray.

Crossing the Midline

Without this skill, children may not be able to complete a line of writing without either swapping the pencil to the other hand or turning their body to reach towards the opposite side.

We provide opportunities such as: tearing paper, popping bubbles, catching balloons, washing bikes in the garden, sweeping the floor, and passing items round in a circle.

Children Aged 3-4 Years

Finger Isolation

The ability to move each finger independently—it is important to develop a child's dexterity further. It contributes to developing an efficient pencil grasp, as well as promoting the skills to type on a keyboard, tie shoelaces and successfully manipulate buttons and zips.

The children have lots of opportunities to access tweezers, chopsticks, pegs and tongs, to pick up and transfer items such as pom-poms and beads.

Thumb Opposition

This refers to the ability to turn and rotate the thumb for it to touch each fingertip of the same hand. This is the main skill required to operate tools effectively and comfortably.

We encourage this by squeezing foam balls, hiding small objects inside tennis balls with a slit cut in them—requiring children to squeeze to open and shake the contents out, turkey basters and pipettes to squirt water in the water tray or to blow pom-poms across a table.

3

See It from Their Point of View

In the process of mastering how to talk to your kids and understand them better, it is important to pause for a moment and think about how your child thinks. Whether your child is two years old or 14 years old, there is power in trying to see things from their point of view. For a two-year-old, everything is still new to them. They are trying to understand this world, and they are gradually getting their vocabulary right. For a teenager, everything around them might make sense in their way of understanding things. You may have experienced what your teenager is experiencing now. But does this mean that they also understand what they are going through? Sometimes parents forget that their kids are learning things that they do not know. Therefore, taking their point of view is the best way of understanding them and helping them to grow and to become the individuals you would want them to be.

Numerous benefits can be gained when a parent understands the significance of perspective thinking. The good news is that both the parent and the child stand to benefit. When a parent "thinks like a child," they are in a better position to see their children from their lenses. This means that they can recognize what is going on with their children.

If parents take a walk with their kids emotionally, they will be more informed about how they feel. Instead of pushing your child to say what is wrong with them, you will translate that they are having a difficult time managing their emotions. They also want to be heard, just like you and me. For that reason, providing your presence rather than ignoring them could help. With time, your child will be more convinced that you care about them. Thus, they will not hesitate to tell you what is going on.

Parenting is a challenge, yet an enjoyable experience worth going through. Parents do their best to understand their kids. However, most of them fail because they judge their kids based on their knowledge. Instead of allowing a child to live their life, a parent may want to force their child to engage in certain activities that they might not like. Some parents simply assume that they are good parents just because they provide everything for their young ones. Parenting is not just about meeting the needs of your children. In fact, emotional needs and other invisible needs take precedence over basic physical needs. If a child's emotions are not being listened to, they might turn out to be stubborn with all sorts of negative behaviors.

Your observation should also include taking time to see how your child socializes with others. Maybe your child prefers to stay indoors. Find out why this is the case. If they are too playful, you should also study them to ensure that you know them better. The point of observation is to enhance your awareness about your child. Who is he or she? What do they like? What are their hobbies? Do they love to socialize, or are they shy and withdrawn?

With the advent of technology, communication has greatly improved. It is now possible to share our ideas with millions of people at the touch of a button. Similarly, you can catch up with your friends and relatives in different geographical locations. However, these technology perks should not blind us from seeing the harm that some of these devices have caused. Parents spend a lot of time on their gadgets instead of actively listening to their children. Today, a parent will shush their child, claiming that they are busy checking their e-mail or texting on social media. Honestly, this is not a good lesson to teach your child about communication.

Spending quality time with your kids does not mean that you sacrifice your work life. It only means that you should spare some time to listen and play with them without allowing anything else to distract you. This will make a huge difference toward understanding them and helping them cope with challenging life situations that come their way.

It is important to understand that you can only know your children better if you give them your undivided attention. If you are going to juggle several duties at a time with the notion that it is good to multitask, it will be daunting for you to connect with your kids on a deeper level. Make your kids feel special, and you will be surprised how they open to you. It is as simple as that. Parents only waste a lot of time, sometimes focusing on unnecessary things when they are interacting with their kids.

Another thing is that environment plays a crucial role in the upbringing of children. The environment here does not necessarily mean the physical environment that your child is exposed to. It also refers to the individuals they choose to hang out.

We have talked a lot about listening to your kids. To create a stronger bond with your child, you must listen to their stories. Get your kids to talk by initiating interesting topics that resonate with them. Your child might not be able to tell their stories clearly; however, you should actively listen to them. This will convince them that you are interested in what they are saying. They will surely open and help you know them better.

Imagine you are talking to your child about how their day was. Instead of querying about the friends they played with, you could say, "Which games did you enjoy playing? This is an open-ended question that will motivate your child to keep talking. It is from such conversations that you will know more about your child, what they like, and what they do not.
Just like you are reading this book, it is worthwhile that you educate yourself about the varying stages of child development. Knowledge is power. Keeping yourself informed about how to talk to your kids can help you to get to know them better and raise them to become productive in society.

How Your Kid Sees the World

What would you see if you saw the world through your child's eyes? There is no doubt that you will see things from a whole different angle. One thing for sure is that kids see a world that is filled with opportunities. Every day is seen as a new day to them. Adults would see this differently as they would think about the deadlines that they have to meet. Kids lack this mentality and that is why they tend to have more fun than adults.

Moreover, a child will see anyone as a potential friend. Kids find it easy to interact with strangers. They are not judgmental, and this makes it easy for them to make friends with new people who come their way.

The fact that kids view the world differently can make it unpredictable to figure out what they want or what they are dealing with. Let us consider a few examples of how kids perceive the world around them.

Have you ever bought your child a present and asked them not to open it? If you have done this before, then you can attest to the fact that kids are impulsive. Children cannot wait for the right time to have something that they want. When a kid craves for something, the last thing they want to hear from you is that they cannot have it. Kids lack the self-control that adults have. Often, when you ask a kid to do something later, they will want to do it right away.

Imagine your child asking you to go out and play with their friends. Perhaps you have visitors at home, and you want your kid to stay indoors and bond with the visitors. Interestingly, these are the priorities that you are thinking about. Your child has other plans. They want to go out to play.

Consequently, denying them the opportunity to play at that very moment will only frustrate them. They will resort to crying as a way of getting your attention and allowing them to go and play. But the funniest thing is that if you allowed your child to go to play outside and asked them to be back soon, they would be bored quickly and come back home.

Using the example above, you should try to see your child's point of view before making any decisions about whether they should go out. Ultimately, you will make the right decision that will make both of you happy.

Another incredible attribute about kids that you should be aware of is that they are super-attentive. Have you ever wondered why something you tried to whisper to your friend did not go unnoticed by your child? Your child might have been busy playing with their toys, but the moment you talk about cookies, they will turn their heads and ask you about what you just said. Since they are sure about what they heard, they will insist on getting what they want.

The advantage of being super-attentive is that it can help your child to learn quickly. However, there is a disadvantage linked to it. Their attentive nature will often annoy you when your child does not listen to you. The truth is that they are attentive to something that interests them. As such, if you cannot present them with something that captures their attention, you might conclude that they are intentionally ignoring you. You must see the world through your child's eyes for you to understand them better.

If you find that your child misbehaves while trying to get your attention, you should ignore them. This shows your child that what they are doing is unacceptable and that it does not warrant your attention. You should also make sure that you do not find yourself rewarding your child for behaving badly. For example, when you were on an important call and your child screams, you should not hang up and listen to them. This only gives them what they wanted—your attention.

Knowing your child depends on how you interact with them even when they do not use words. You should pay attention to their body language and non-verbal cues that could help you to recognize what they need. A few signs here and there can help you communicate better with your child and prevent miscommunication issues that will frequently frustrate you.

4

A Parent's Greatest Burden

One of my greatest frustrations as a parent (if not the greatest) has been the constant management of so many conflicting needs and desires. My kids need me (each in different ways), my partner needed me (nearly as much as the kids), the house needs me (the family makes sure of this), my work needs me (my passions make sure of this), and of course, my bank accounts need me too. Mixed in among the constantly changing and boldly expressed needs all around me are a mess of desires, relentless as laundry and just as impossible to ignore.

My parent load, if you will, has felt so heavy through the years that removing my own needs and desires from the mix often seemed the only way to stay afloat. Reasoning that I was strong enough to endure, I denied the existence of most of my needs and desires, seeing them as extravagances I did not have time to consider.

Had you asked me twelve years ago what I needed (before my tipping point), I'd likely have responded (with a convincing smile), "Who, me? Oh, I'm good. I don't need anything." I would then have changed the subject back to my kids or my projects or whatever the current crisis. Even after I realized that this mind-set was making me miserable, it took a good while for me to quit apologizing for "being a burden" when asking for help or expressing a personal preference.

These oh-so-common stories—that our own needs and desires as a parent (and as an adult) are less important or worthy than everyone else's, and that we owe the world an apology for taking up space and being human—not only speak of our level 3, self-imposed oppression but they also cultivate exactly the opposite effect that most of us are going for.

Quite simply, when we fail to recognize and honor our own needs and deepest desires, everyone pays.

If I am not getting enough sleep because the house needs attention, I'm not only saying "the household needs are more important than my well-being," but I'm also likely to be grouchier with my family on little sleep. If I say yes to yet another engagement when I am already maxed, I am not only saying, "coming across as helpful and agreeable is more important than meeting my needs," but I'm also setting myself up for feelings of resentment that tend to have a ripple effect. If I drive all over town so that my children receive the best in extracurricular activities despite the stress it causes me, I am not only saying to them, "your quality of life is more important than mine," but I am also sending them messages about what it means to be a parent, an adult, and a caring person. I am defining my value and worthiness for them.

Still not convinced that your needs matter as much as theirs do? Think of it this way: Every time you deny your own needs for the sake of those around you, you are teaching your daughters and sons how they should expect to be treated (and treat themselves) should they one day become parents. In the same way, every time a mother puts herself last, they are modeling the worthiness of mothers for your sons. The same sons who will grow up to respect and revere their children's mother or not.

We Teach People How to Treat Us, Largely Based on How We Treat Ourselves

Your kids need you to matter to you. How else will they learn to matter to them? Here is a simple mantra that is saved me time and again in moments when self-denial seems like the most reasonable route:

Treat Yourself as You would Have Your Children Treat Themselves

Adopting this perspective can be a complete game-changer. It's also okay if you're not there yet. It takes time to become comfortable, admitting that we have needs and valuing ourselves enough to prioritize meeting those needs. I used to see all self-focus as selfish and my full investment in others a reflection of my endless generosity. But with every twist and turn in my parenting journey, particularly the uphill climbs and slippery slopes (of which there have been many), it became more obvious that ignoring my needs greatly confuses matters for everyone by implying that I am either superhuman, sub-human, or otherwise exempt from the laws of nature.

Denying my needs and desires also:

- Creates unrealistic and entitled expectations in my kids.
- Confuses my partner about his role in our relationship.
- Creates boundary issues with family and friends.
- Cultivates codependency.
- Breeds resentment, disempowerment, and eventual burnout.

Because the fullest expression of our truest selves is no less than a fundamental driving life force, our needs and desires will not go away, no matter how deeply we stuff them. By failing to bring them into the light and examine them for what they are and instead of reacting to the feeling of frustration they generate within us when repressed, we deepen our pain and suffering, behave in ways that are inconsistent with who we truly are, and then feel shame when we are inauthentic. We then blame others for not meeting our needs for us, feel guilty for being reactive, and feel even less worthy of having our needs met!

It is an exhausting, self-perpetuating cycle. Our energy is better spent understanding and communicating our needs rather than resenting others for not anticipating them or reading our minds.

Hiding behind the needs and desires of our children does more than merely distract us—it detaches us from the essence of who we are, compounding our discontentment. Reasoning that we are happiest when others are happy, though noble sounding, is also often evidence of codependency. Depending upon the happiness of others and living in such a way that we assume will ensure this happiness places a disproportionate degree of responsibility on us for their needs and them for ours. This arrangement leads to all kinds of disconnection and, ultimately, dysfunction.

Throughout history, women have been told (and sold) three predominant stories about our needs and desires:

- They can be satiated through the acquisition of material possessions.
- They can be conveniently buried beneath the needs and wants of others so that we don't have to feel them day in and day out.
- We are not worthy of our deepest desires anyway, so we may as well hedge our bets on a gold-paved afterlife.
- The first story is quite clearly the foundation upon which marketers make their millions. The second is a pain management strategy of the disempowered and oppressed; and the third, whatever your take on religious traditions, is a relatively effective way to keep unhappy people hopeful and thus, pacified.
- In addition to the stories we are told, many of us learn to put others' needs and desires ahead of our own because it seems so much easier.
- It is easier to give in when they beg us beyond set boundaries because we want peace, and they will be quieter quicker.
- It is easier to clean the house frantically before guests arrive than it is to feel ashamed of our mess and judged for the way we live.
- It is easier to keep quiet in a room full of people whose opinions we disagree with than it is to be vulnerable and speak our truth.
- It is easier to build even thicker walls around our hurting hearts than it is to face the fear of deconstructing them.

In many ways, we want to believe others' needs are more important than ours because it saves us the pain of having to face how discontent or disconnected from our truths we are. Motherhood is a wonderful hiding place when we can't bear to face the truth of our soul-starvation. Though ignoring our needs may seem to speed up the process of achieving the positive feelings we want, in reality, it slows the process of growth and change necessary for true and lasting inner peace.

Alone time is right up there with sufficient sleep and nourishing food and regular exercise when it comes to needs, I cannot afford to compromise on. If thriving is my goal (and it is), devotion to these needs is essential. Right behind these primary needs are a few that come in a close second. Contemplative conversation, time to create, enlivening my wildness, and time in the woods are needs that I can go a little longer without meeting before I feel their absence, but not much.

Devotion to the tending of my needs makes me a better, more whole-feeling person. It is good for me, and it's good for those around me, which, ultimately, means that it's socially responsible.

What I did not realize early on in my mothering experience is that my family needs me thriving. That deep down, just as much as they want me to take them to the mall or make them dinner, they want to see me happy and centered. Valuing my own needs is a gift not only to myself but also to every family member, friend, and individual I interact with.

5

Seven Steps to Peaceful Parenting

Step One: The Peace Within

I cannot emphasize enough the role of parents. Your role should be as a role model—pun intended. We expect our child to grow up as emotionally stable adults, but their highly impressionable minds are constantly taking silent queues from us, whether we intend for this or not. One of the most attractive and successful traits in any person is emotional intelligence. This means that we should be able to regulate our feelings in the face of distress, anger, fear, and even disappointment.

Think back to the example of implementing a subtle form of meditation in your day when you run short of time. This will be difficult in the beginning, but you can use the motivation from seeing your child thrive in adulthood as a passion for practicing silence and regulation. Commit yourself to the parental "stop, drop, and roll."

Let's say your child is throwing a major tantrum in the supermarket, and your face is turning blood red. Turn your attention to your breathing and listen to the sound of air passing through your respiratory tract. Breathe deeply three times and look around you to identify five objects. What can you see? What can you hear? What can you smell? What can you feel? Finally, what can you taste in your mouth? The last one might not always be possible, but you may have a lingering taste of toothpaste or food.

Use your five senses to bring yourself back to the present before you erupt like Vesuvio. This happens fast and jerks you back to here and now so that your brain can process information and feelings quickly to handle the situation without yelling at the top of your lungs. It prevents us from reacting in a way we regret, and your child is not scorned with a reprimand.

I want to share a fun science fact with you before we move on. Self-control is an innate skill we all have, and certain practices can improve it dramatically (Self-Control, n.d.). Our ability to regulate our impulses reside in our prefrontal cortex, and this is how we solve problems, regulate emotions, and choose our responsive behavior. Activating and training this part of the brain can lead to a volume increase in your gray matter. Yes, we can grow the size of our brains. Emotional regulation is another skill we need to learn, and if we can change the size of our brains, why can't we change the content of it?

Step Two: Familial Connections

Connecting with your child is another topic I have brushed before, but I will expand a little further now. Let me tell you once more that peaceful parenting is not possible if you do not have a bond with your child. It will complicate matters if you simply drop punishment from the table because your child still will not have the motivation required to do the right thing. They will see you as a pushover who has gone soft and take advantage of you every chance they get.

The first thing you do is dedicate 15 minutes a day with each child. This time is for the two of you, and you can do anything. Small children love bedtime stories, and you can create a night-time ritual in which you act out the scenes from their favorite storybook. Spend time doing what they love and keep a close physical bond. Do not forget their goodnight kisses and tuck them in comfortably. Teenagers can be more complicated, but you can get involved in their hobbies and support them.

You can explain what is happening once you have established a considerable bond. Sit them down and speak to them about the changes taking place. Ask them if they have noticed that you yell less now and welcome them on board to the new family plan. Make them feel appreciated and acknowledged by asking them straight out for their cooperation. This might take more than one tries.

Step Three: Limitations

Punishment is off the table, so how do you discipline your child? This will only work if you have created a bond of trust between you. You have had that conversation in which you discussed the new strategy in your home, and there is no need to change the rules. The previous step, combined with compassion, allows you to see your child's point of view now, and that is a good thing. A family is a unity of people who work together, and there is no need for one person to be miserable to make everyone else happy. However, limits are the only way you discipline your child now.

Bedtime is a limit, and you can practice empathy by telling your child, "I know you'd love to play more, but you won't have the energy to play tomorrow if you burn it all up tonight." You have seen and acknowledged their desire to continue playtime before you reminded them of the rule of bedtime. Limits play a huge role in discipline, and if you have followed the steps thus far, your child is more likely to collaborate with you.

Step Four: Reparation

This relates strongly to old habits again because a job will feel unfinished if you let something go that would normally be punished. Another new habit for the collection you have gathered so far is to learn to repair rather than punish. It will also give you closure on a situation and avoid leaving you feeling incomplete. I suppose in those terms, this one is for the parents' benefit.

Give your child the floor to speak before you interrupt them so that they can share all the details with you. Gently point out the consequences of their reaction without applying blame to them. Explain how it hurt their brother's feelings when they yelled at him. Their little brother might fear them now and feel distant. Now comes the important part because you should not tell your child how to repair the damage.

Ask your child how they think it can be repaired. You are not forcing an apology. This responsibility you hand to your child will empower them when they are free to correct things themselves. Talk about a relationship struggle you might have had with a friend and how you repaired it. Try and inspire them to do the right thing without instructing them. They will relish their own make-up with their sibling when they decide how to do it. There can be resistance from your child, and this is when you need to help heal from their pains further. Make sure that you are speaking from an example and seeing things from their viewpoint.

Step Five: Dealing with Emotions

Emotions are inevitable, but you can respond differently. Children are developing automatic responses, and every time a "bad" emotion gets them into hot water, they learn from this and begin suppressing their feelings instead. Accumulating emotions is the worst thing possible because your child will explode when they are provoked at the wrong time. Punishment is the reason kids repress their feelings because they become afraid of showing them.

It will take plenty of connection time to overcome this. Watch a sad movie with your child and never tell them they are not allowed to cry. Allow your tears to flow with theirs. I knew a man who used to tell his son that it was inappropriate to laugh alone. He would refer to "crazy" people who laugh for no reason.

Besides creating an emotionally friendly environment, you can encourage good behavior with appreciation. Tell your child how proud you are that they handled the situation correctly. Explain how it pulled your heartstrings when you saw their reaction to the homeless man. Make your child want to repeat their behavior by giving them recognition and appreciation for it.

Step Six: The Safety Net

Parents are supposed to be the safety net for their child when they go through life's traumas. Adulthood does not make us immune to distress, and even we still need someone to be our shoulder to cry on. I want my child to feel as though they can tell me anything, even when they are 30 years old. There is one trick to this, though, and it goes back to your emotional regulation. You need to react to something your child tells you and remain calm. The moment you respond aggressively or out of disappointment, you break the bond, you have worked so hard to create.

Think of it as walking on thin ice. Our child experiences trauma differently than us, and they might not have the coping mechanisms that we do. They can break down and sink into a hole of depression or anxiety. Continue expressing compassion and wait until your child opens to you. You might be able to see the surface of the scar, but you cannot always see what caused it.

Our child often turns to anger to cope with their fears or insecurities that formed from past wounds. It does not matter how mad they get; you stay tranquil and wait for them to share with you. Anger cries have a healing effect on their own. Haven't you noticed how much better you feel after a good cry? Encourage the flow of tears so that they can release those hurtful emotions inside of them.

6

Mindfulness from a ToT

I've explained how mindfulness can't be described in simple words. The definition of it is vast and complicated. We will tackle the main aspects of the "mindfulness alphabet" because it does not only involve meditation.

Awareness

One method of reaching a new level of this stage is to keep a journal. Whenever something happens that ticks you off, you can jot it down in your journal. You will broaden your awareness relating to an emotional response and can even look at various strategies to correct it. Writing is therapeutic on its own, and when our words touch down on the paper, we can see things clearly. It is similar to taking a moment to breathe before you respond emotionally to something. Our written words bring us to the present time and help us observe their memories while they are fresh in our minds. There is nothing like a silent room with a pen and paper to bring you to a heightened level of self-awareness.

Feeling

I am sure this word is explanatory on its own. The feeling aspect of mindfulness lies within acknowledging your emotions and not avoiding them. You want to feel the emotion because it can be a conduit to something residing in your subconscious mind. I know that some emotions are just painful, but we cannot overcome something when we hide away from it. These feelings are often a precursor or an after effect of something that needs attention. You need to stop suppressing your anxiety and embrace it, however painful it may be in the beginning. There is nothing wrong with having emotions. It is part of being human.

People who become mindful will learn to regulate their emotions rather than shoving them aside. Emotions are a response from thoughts, and sometimes, they can be related to memories. Feelings walk together with the experiences that you've encountered.

Listening

This mindful aspect makes me think of how women are generalized on television. There is always a lady who is fighting with her husband or partner about not listening to them. The partner will simply nod their head in agreement even when the woman speaks of how she is about to key her husband's car. This is a poor generalization because of the difficulty of listening and hear someone else is common among women and men who have not become mindful yet. The entertainment provided by these sitcoms is often hilarious, but they can touch a subject that is only partially true. The only difference is that we all suffer from this.

Listening is difficult because our lives are constantly distracted by noises, emotions, and interruptions. When was the last time you listened to yourself? Your body speaks to you, and so do your thoughts, emotions, and desires. Learn to listen to yourself and then listen clearly to the people around you. Practice your skills until you can hear every word your partner shares with you, and vice versa. It plays a role in communication and is the groundwork for healthy and long-lasting relationships. You want wholesome relationships to become a close-knit family and reach a peaceful and mindful state. Besides, you will uncover secrets in your mind and the minds of your family when you listen to them intently.

Meditation

Meditation is one of the most widespread techniques of reaching and sustaining mindfulness. It is the method of training your mind into the desired format. Meditation gives you access to your inner mind, or subconscious, where ideas are born and raised like children. Your subconscious mind is the conscious level that is most susceptible to suggestions, and becoming a mindful person or family is, in fact, an idea that needs to be reared by your unconscious mind. It is the part of your brain that functions at speeds that our conscious minds are unable to. It is where thoughts, emotions, and responses originate.

There are various kinds of meditation that you can try. The first is called concentration meditation, and this is when you focus on one thing until it becomes the only thing on your mind. Voice-guided meditations help you do this because you focus intently on the voice you hear. It can also involve concentrating on your breathing until your body falls into the ultimate level of comfort. Some people use mantras or the sound of a gong to shift their attention from all the interruptions that love hindering us during our peaceful silence.

The second kind of meditation I would like to mention is mindfulness meditation itself. This form is famous for breaching your awareness and observation. You are also guided into a calm state where the subconscious takes over, and you observe the thoughts that move through your mind like a speeding train. This method can be mastered as your observation increases, allowing you to slow down these thoughts to acknowledge them and see them for what they truly are. There is no involvement or interruption from yourself, and you merely watch them pass by. This technique helps you find a balance when you recognize patterns that should not be present in your mind.

Peace

Our judgment can become clouded when we fail to see the good in situations or people, and this happens because we cannot see the good in ourselves. Peace is a state of ultimate liveliness and should never be confused with unconsciousness. People think they can drink to overcome their emotions but then realize that the emotions did not go anywhere the next day. We cannot sleep our thoughts away either because they'll simply return when we wake up.

There is also the delusion that peace equals happiness. This is not entirely true because happiness can be defined as a temporary state where you get "high" on the circumstances around you. Change comes, and our gleeful attitudes fade away. Peace is a deeper level of contentment, one that lasts for a long time. Peace comes from acceptance and understanding of the everyday disasters that befall us when we learn to cope with them and avoid them overwhelming us. Past experiences and future concerns can often disrupt our peace. We find it once we learn to steer clear of anything that does not belong in the present. Trusting yourself and your ability to remain mindful will help you stay on the path.

Rest

Rest is the next contributor to mindfulness. We live in a world that is constantly moving forward and waits for no one. However, rest for the mind and body is essential to keep our minds and bodies at peak health. Life is challenging, and we commonly enter the rut of burning the candle at both ends. We feel as though we need to finish everything today, and we forget that tomorrow is another day. Yes, I teach you about the present moment, but what is your body telling you at that moment when you feel like you have been running full steam ahead for the past two days?

Our minds and bodies are fragile, and we should listen to them when they tell us it is time for a break. This applies to both mental and physical exhaustion. A mindful person will prevent fatigue from reaching this stage by using practical resting periods to enhance their performance. It does not feel great when you force your mind to work overtime. You can often imagine the smoke coming from your ears, and your focus is below par when you reach this level of exhaustion. Take the time to rest when you need to and spend 10 to 20 minutes a day in a silent retreat of your choosing. This can include meditation, complete silence, locking your phone away, scheduling time for activities, reading a book, and even pursuing a hobby that relaxes you. There are no limits on how much rest you need, but your body will tell you. Keep track of how much time you feel you need to get a sense of your necessary rhythm.

Time

Time is an essence of this universe that we cannot easily manipulate unless we are in the present moment. We have, unfortunately, not invented time travel yet, and the moment you realize that now is all you have is the moment your mind finds peace. The past is an attraction for our mind to visit, and the future is the reason for our anxiety, fear, and any distress. The problem is that we cannot change them. Even if you want to alter your future, the way you do it is by implementing a change now.

Time travel does not exist, and neither do fortune-tellers, in my opinion. No one can predict tomorrow, and life could throw you with lemon after lemon. That lemon will not strike you in the future because the moment it hits you is the present. The world is filled with distractions that are trying hard to remove our mindful state, and life is one of those.

Death is a terrible reminder of how we cannot regain the time we have lost. We know that we can never hug the person again or even speak to them on the phone. Their presence in this world had come to an end when their time ran out. I know this is a grim example, but it is the most eye-opening of them all. The grim reaper comes at any moment, and what happens at this moment is what defines us. There is no peace in guilt, anger, grief, or even sadness when someone leaves this world. Grief itself is the consequence of losing time because the person we lost existed in a time we can never regain.

7

How to Come Up with A Discipline Strategy That Is Ideal for Your Son or Daughter

Educating our children is not easy. So, here are some tips on how to encourage good behavior in children without having to punish and scold every second.

Stimulating good behavior in children is one of the best ways to impose limits, without having to apply punishments constantly. The only problem is how to do that. In most cases, our little ones tested our limits and seemed to do anything not to obey.

Here are ways to stimulate good behavior:

Be the Example

Being an example is the most effective way we have to teach our children anything - both good and bad. When it comes to encouraging good behavior in children, it is no different. Here are a few examples of what you can do for your child to learn.

Catch your child's attention when you split snacks with your husband or when you have to wait in the bank queue, pointing out that adults also have to share and wait too.

Realize the Good Behavior

If you are like any parent in the world when your child is behaving well, you leave him playing alone and take advantage of the time to do anything you may need to. But when your child is behaving badly, you direct all your attention to him to resolve the situation. Your attention is what kids most want, so to get this attention, and sometimes children will behave badly. The best way to encourage good behavior in children is to pay attention when they are behaving well and to take your attention from them when they are behaving badly. This is completely counter-intuitive for us and can be a difficult habit to cultivate. But once you get used to it, it will become easier and easier.

A great way to do this is to play with your child when he is quiet in his corner and praise him when he obeys you the first time you speak.

Understand the Stage of Development

This tip is easy to understand. Each child has a behavior; however, you cannot require a child of three to act as the same as a child who is ten. That is, do not try to go to a three-hour lunch with your little boy hoping he will be quiet for the whole lunch. Do not want a two-year-old child not to put everything in his mouth. Each age has a phase, and it is no use wanting to demand different behavior from a child.

Have Appropriate Expectations

This is a continuation of the above tip. Parents have high expectations. This is not wrong when expectations are possible. For example, do not expect a tired child to behave well, or a one-month-old baby to sleep through the night.

Uses Disciplinary Strategies

Rather than humiliating or beating children, there are positive disciplinary strategies that teach, set boundaries, and encourage good behavior in children. Some of these are: give options, put somewhere to think, talk, give affection, and a system of rewards (reward can be a simple compliment, it does not have to be gifts or food).

Understand That the Bad Behavior Worked So Far

If throwing tantrums and disobeying worked for him to get your attention so far, changing this behavior will take time, he will have to realize and understand that you will no longer pay attention to him when he behaves badly, but when he behaves well.

Instilling good behavior practices in young children is a must for any responsible parent, but sometimes it can also be quite complicated and laborious. However, beginning to instill this type of behavior as early as possible will help build a good foundation for the child's behavior and attitudes in the future. It is necessary to be aware that in the first years of life the children are like "sponges" and results will be better if you begin to show them early and direct them to appropriate behaviors of life in society.

Here are some more ideas to help parents with the task of encouraging good behavior in their children:

Models to Follow

Children tend to mirror the behaviors of parents and those with whom they coexist more closely. Therefore, be careful about your behaviors and language used when the child is around to avoid misunderstanding ideas and misconceptions about how you should behave towards others. This includes talking properly and behaving politely to both your partner and family, as well as to the child. Try to avoid loud, unstructured arguments when the child is around. We do not mean you can't disagree with your spouse, because the child must also be aware that these exist. But try to have the arguments always controlled and civil around children.

Be Firm

Parents should be affectionate, but still adamant about instilling discipline in their children. The child must know how to respect his parents, even when he does not have what he wants. Understanding when to say "no" at the right times is an important step in your education.

Positive Body Language

Your body language has a huge impact when you are trying to instill a particular behavior in children. Given the height of the child, a parent standing while correcting the errors and applying discipline is often viewed as authoritative. It is advisable to place yourself at the same level as the child's eyes. Sit next to the child while talking to them and always maintain eye contact.

Establishing Limits

It is fundamental to establish limits, rules, and consequences for unwanted behavior. Increase limits on children to be able to distinguish right from wrong. They need to know what is not acceptable and clear reasons that make it wrong so that there is no doubt in the child's mind about the behavior to adopt.

You started tracking your child's progress long before he left the warmth of your belly: in the tenth week, the heart began beating; on the 24th week, his hearing developed and listened to your voice; in the 30th week, he began to prepare for childbirth. Now that he or she is in your arms, you're still eager to keep up with all the signs of your little one's development and worries that he might be left behind. Nonsense! Excessive worry will not help at all, so take your foot off the accelerator and enjoy each phase. Your child will realize all the fundamental achievements of maturity. He will learn to walk, talk, potty, and when you least expect it, you will be riding a bicycle alone (and no training wheels!). He will do all only in his time.

Stop taking developmental milestones so seriously. For example, your 7-month-old son will be able to sit alone, and at age three will be able to ride a tricycle. Consider what is expected for each age just for reference. The best thing to do is to set aside the checklist of the abilities your child needs to develop and play together a lot. There is no better way to connect with and develop your child than through playtime.

To help you even further in realizing the goals mentioned above or processes, I would like to mention some tips here that stimulate a child's intellectual, motor, social, and emotional development.

Rainbow

The baby starts noticing colors at around three months of age when the vision is no longer so blurry. That is why, at this age, the idea is to stimulate with strong colors, which can be in toys or mobile in the crib. Babies also love contrast: you can see that stripes are not missing in children's toys. At about a year and a half, your child will begin to notice the difference between one color and another, even if he does not know the color's name. So, start saying: "Let's play with that blue ball" or "take the red tomato from the salad." This way, colors become part of their day to day life.

Books

The role of parents is fundamental for children to learn to love reading and to make books a pleasure, rather than an obligation. According to the latest edition of the Portraits of the Reading survey in Brazil, for 43% of readers, the mother was the main influence for developing the desire for reading. For 17%, the father was the one who played the role. From the third month of your child's life, you can use plastic books in the bath. From the sixth, when the baby can already carry objects to the mouth with his hands, leave cloth books in the cradle—in addition to being able to bite them, he will not be able to rip the pages! At all ages, talk about the cover, the pictures, the colors, and let the child turn the pages.

Memory

Memory is a form of storing knowledge and must be permeated by a context. Start by making your child memorize or familiarize words by showing a represented object. If you are walking or crossing on the street and saw a bicycle, point and say, "Look, son, a bicycle." This is how he will build associations. From the first year, he will say a few words and try to repeat the names of what you show. But it is from the age of 2 that the ability to retain information increases.

Creating

Create characters and a dream of fantastic worlds. All of this is important in developing the creativity of little ones; it also contributes to problem-solving. To make the narrative more exciting, how about testing the improvisational ability of the two of you? Separate figures from objects, landscapes, colors, foods, and animals—they can be drawn or cut from magazines. While one narrates, the other can select images that portray elements that should be included in the narrative. The challenge is to be able to fit them together so that the narrative continues to make sense.

Always Ask

When picking up your child from nursery, you say, "How was your day?" And he says, "ok." It was not exactly what you wanted to hear, right? To avoid generic responses, develop the questions so that the child needs to express what he thinks and justify his response. Ask: "What did you enjoy most today?" or "Is your friend Cody there?" "Did you play together" And he will be forced to develop more elaborate reasoning, requiring him to work linguistic and logical skills. At three years old, he can already relate experiences he went through and say whether those were good or bad. At 4, you can ask for details, descriptions, and names of friends who were with him.

8

How to Come Up with A Discipline Strategy That Is Ideal for Your Son or Daughter

Familiarity Breeds Contentment

Put yourself in your toddler's slipper socks. Every day her world is changing. She's growing bigger, stronger, and able to do more things on her own. One day she can walk, the next she's running. Everything has a word to describe it—so many to learn! Even mealtimes bring wonders anew, with different colors and textures on her plate to explore and taste. Then there's a spoon to master, and eventually a fork, a coat zipper, a tricycle, and more. Your child is discovering, too, that he's his own little person, with likes and dislikes, moods, and a personality all his own. And he's figuring out the many ways he can express that individuality. He's learning that complying achieves one result, crying brings about another. And when all else fails, there's this marvelous tool known as the temper tantrum. All this novelty and power is intoxicating—and often overwhelming. That's where routines help.

A predictable order to the day is one of the greatest gifts a parent can give to a toddler. Routines provide essential, reassuring structure. They're a reliable oasis amid so many new things, a refuge in the storm of emotions that marks a typical day. Daily rituals build trust, too. They help a child relax, knowing his basic needs will be met. Since a toddler can't tell time with a clock, routines also provide a framework by which he can pace out the day. Parents benefit from routines, too.

A better-adjusted, well-regulated child is an easier one to live with. Without a gentle sense of order for the day, life with a mercurial toddler can quickly dissolve into chaos. Regular ways of doing things serve as unspoken rules. Arguments over when a child needs to sleep, for example, are minimized when they're part of a predictable pattern expected by both parent and child. Some parents use a schedule with their babies almost from the start. Others fall into routines gradually as their infants grow hungry and sleepy at the same time every day. Routines are meant to evolve naturally, along with your child. If you haven't initiated regular routines into your family life yet, toddlerhood is a wonderful time to start.

Little Rituals Matter, Too

Routine refers to the general order and pattern of activities throughout the day. You provide the basics of life at the same time and in the same way, more or less, day after day. Your child should have a routine whether he's exclusively cared for at home or attends out-of-home care. For a 1-year-old, this may mean a schedule like the following: Wake up at seven; get dressed; eat breakfast at seven-thirty; play; eat a snack; nap from ten-thirty to eleven-thirty; wake up and eat lunch; run errands with Mom; snack; nap from three-thirty to four-thirty; play inside; eat dinner at six; watch a video; have a bath; read books; go to bed at eight-thirty. A 2-year-old's day is roughly similar, with the exception of the morning nap; instead, he may take an earlier (and longer) afternoon nap. Peppered throughout the day are apt to be many little rituals shared by you and your child.

A ritual is a specific action or activity that's done in a certain way. Toddlers love rituals as much as they need routines. Often of the child's concoction, rituals are a way for a child to exert control over the general helplessness of his life. They're reassuring, too. A ritual might involve choosing a certain placemat for lunch, or the special order in which the child likes the parts of his body to be scrubbed in the tub.

Toddlers often get stuck on rituals that seem peculiar to grown-ups. Because Daddy sat in a certain chair one night, for example, the child insists Daddy must sit there every night, and woe to the visitor who tries to perch there instead. Or a child may insist that you address her a particular way, such as "Mary, Mary, Quite Contrary" rather than merely Mary. Rituals tend to escalate in their elaborateness. One night you're sweetly bidding good night (with a kiss and a hug) to your child's favorite stuffed animal. Before long, he wants you to kiss each and every animal in the room and in a very specific order.

It's best to humor rituals. More than whims for a young child, they are tangible forms of security. That's not to say they should be limitless. Indulge routines within reason. Nobody wants to (or should) spend forty-five minutes kissing every stuffed member in a toddler's menagerie. Instead, tell the child to pick three favorites whom you'll tuck in with him. An underlying need for routine remains throughout childhood. Fortunately, however, the absolutism and redundancies that are so characteristic of toddler routines will begin to wane as your child grows older and more confident.

When Routines Are Disrupted

Inevitably, your daily schedule will require variations when you can't stick to the habits your child expects. Family vacations are a prime example. One parent may need to go on a business trip, a relative may visit, or the holidays bring a burst of parties and late-night events. How will your child weather such changes? Fairly well, if he is prepared. Kids are surprisingly resilient. Let your child know in advance when there will be a deviation from the norm. Tell him what will probably happen instead: "The babysitter will give you a bath and read you three stories just like I do, and then tuck you in bed, and when you wake up in the morning, Daddy and I will be home," or "When Grandma visits, she'll be sleeping on the extra bed in your room. But we will move your crib into Mommy and Daddy's room, and all your pillows and blankets will be there." It's best to keep the basics of the day as close to normal as possible, even on vacation. Provide extra love and attention during times of change. TLC helps buffer the stress of the change.

Whatever you do, don't attempt to reassure your child by making promises that you can't follow through on. It's unfair to tell him that he can have a certain kind of food at a restaurant if you're unsure whether it's served (unless you bring it along). Likewise, saying, "Don't worry, I'll tuck you in at bedtime" when you know you won't be home on time is not something a 2-year-old will soon forget. But neither should you worry that straying from the established pattern of your child's life will cause a long-lasting upset. A routine that's disrupted for a spell can easily be put back into place when the conditions are more suitable. All routines should be flexible.

Household Rhythms

There's one kind of routine that many parents fail to consider at this age —or rather, that they do for their child almost unthinkingly: household chores. Certainly, with a 15-month-old, you're more concerned with keeping her clothes on her body than with teaching her to pitch them in a hamper. But as she approaches 18 to 24 months, she's ready to begin taking part in the household routine. In fact, the sooner you start giving a child responsibilities appropriate to her developmental level, the more she'll come to think of them as normal, no different from eating or sleeping.

Bear in mind, however, that for toddlers, the word chore is to be used only loosely. You can't expect a child this age to do these things regularly, nor should you enforce them as assigned responsibilities yet. That's not a good idea until your child approaches kindergarten or the early elementary-school years. Your toddler is ready to begin to learn about such tasks, nothing more. Toddlers love to imitate adults. In their play, for example, they love to cook at a stove and put babies to bed. They can mimic you in realistic ways as well. When milk spills, don't rush to mop it up yourself. Give your child some paper towels. You'll certainly need to finish the job, but not before you've imparted a lesson in taking responsibility and bestowed a sense of pride and accomplishment. Don't expect your child to execute them perfectly, or even to finish a job.

More things toddlers can do:
- Water a garden or plants.
- Pick up toys.
- Help you use a small broom and dustpan.
- Help to cook (cutting out cookies, adding ingredients to a pot).
- Help feed a dog or cat.
- Dust (unbreakable objects, of course).
- Help empty non-breakable items from the dishwasher.

- Put napkins on the table.
- Wash her hands.
- Begin to feed by himself.
- Begin to dress by herself.

Create Structure and Routine

A child with a structured routine tends to behave better. They already know what to expect and are used to it. A child with a routine feels safe and thus lives more calmly. A child without a routine has a sense of insecurity that will disrupt much in the time to educate and encourage good behavior.

9

Forming the Right Habits for Your Kids with the Use of Technology

There are so many things our kids do that can be regarded as a bad habit, but my focus is mainly on the one that affects modern kids the most, regardless of how he/she was brought up or what country they live in. Yep! You guessed it, their bad habits with technology. Every child today knows how to use a phone, the internet, computers, applications, and whatnot. One moment you are celebrating your child's first steps and words, then you blink, and they already know how to download a video game.

Ever since the inception of technology, parents, or should I say adults, in general, have been worried about how technology would impact their children—socially, academically, physiologically, and psychologically. These are all big words, but the bottom line is that there is a fear about how so much dependence on technology could affect our children's lives negatively.

These days, our kids are doing one thing or the other on the internet. The truth is, the internet is very addictive, and almost anything relevant to the social world these days is happening on the internet or on a screen. The question is, are you going to decide to cut off your kids completely from the use of technology, or look for ways in which we could use it to the advantage of our kids? I would recommend that we opt for the second option.

It may seem tricky and scary at times, but as a parent, you should not worry, because there are always old and new methods that can be applied for the children of today. Perhaps you have a long list of your worries and struggles (especially when it comes to technology and your kid using it), but in the following lines, you will read handy tips and information.

When your child is still young, it is quite easy to keep them under control towards everything, even for the use of technology. Doctors warn and parents worry that extended screen time can seriously affect a child's health (posture, sight, night rest, anxiety, excitement, aggression and so on). Not all screen time is bad, and naturally, your child will want to watch cartoons or play their favorite game. Just bear in mind that screen time can be constructive, passive, or interactive.

Passive screen time is defined as spending time on a device (tablet or cell phone) or in front of a big (TV or computer) screen. Constructive screen time includes actual work and creating something new, such as web development, writing codes, designing websites, creating music (digital), drawing and so on.

Passive time, as the name suggests, means watching a film, TV show, or a video. Interactive screen time involves playing video games, finding or downloading apps, and on-screen activities (sports or fitness).

Parents must be willing to control each type of screen time because too much of anything is not good.

Here are a few tips for your child's screen time:

- Spend time talking to your children about their favorite online programs. Make sure it is not their only source of entertainment. Find a balance between their screen time and physical activities, play dates with their friends, learning, dining, and relaxation, but also creative and strategy games.
- Avoid commands because they usually never work. Pick nice words to encourage your kid to take breaks from their screen time. Once they realize that taking breaks in between watching TV feels nice for their eyes and entire body, they will willingly do it on their own.

Internet Access

The Internet is an upgrade in your child's technology life. The moment they get access to the network, they will realize that only the sky is the limit. No matter how useful and easily things can be found online, the Internet will make everything more challenging. At this point, every parent starts to worry about what their kids watch, read, play, and so on.

Video Games

I know you were probably thinking about it: "Oh yeah, Sandra plays games too much."

So, let me start with the positive aspects of gaming for your kids. Many types of research have been carried out concerning games, and many parents would like for it to be conclusive that all that video games do is make your kids anti-social. The results of the research have been the opposite of that; here are some of the advantages of letting your kids play games.

Better hands and eyes coordination

A lot of games that your kids get to play could involve them having better coordination of their hands and eyes. By playing these sorts of video games, your kids will develop habits that are fundamental to helping them better their coordination as well as their puzzle-solving ability. The overall advantage of this is that they are able to easily solve complex problems when confronted with them in the real world.

Higher Cognitive Function

Usually, it has been found that when something is done repeatedly for a long period of time, the brain works like the supercomputer that it is and finds a new way for it to perform those functions even faster. Basically, what the brain does is create new pathways and structures to help your child solve similar problems faster, and this also spills over to real life, of course.

Health Problems

Too much of anything is indeed detrimental, and this is true for video games too. One of the health issues that has been associated with playing video games is obesity. Due to the long hours spent sitting in one place and not doing any physical activity, your child can become prone to being obese. Another condition is the development of weak bones, weakened muscles, numb fingers, and weakened eyesight. All of these issues are prone to affect your child if he/she spends too many hours playing video games.

Social Isolation

Video games are mostly played indoors, and if your kid turns out to be a hermit in the first place or has a personality that makes him enjoy isolation instead of social mingling, playing video games might just be the right excuse that he or she needs to stay all day and all week indoors. The truth is that even without video games, a shy kid would still not prefer to interact with the outside world, but at least they can be more easily persuaded to go out and have some fun. However, with video games made available to them, trust me: there is no getting that kid out of the new Razer gaming chair you just bought for him/her.

Declining Academic Results

Anything fun has a way of making itself seem more appealing than listening in class, doing homework, or studying for a test. Even just doing an activity like skipping the rope after school can be more interesting, than the impending doom of a test that your kid has to study for.

Moral Issues

Most of the games out there are geared towards teenagers and adolescents. This is because it is believed that at least a teenager can distinguish between what is right and wrong. However, kids who are still in their preadolescent ages might find it hard to distinguish between what is okay to do in a video game and what is not okay to do in the real world. This is where the choice of the kind of video games parents allows their kids to play matters.

Tips for Growing Children with Mobile Devices

As your child grows, he or she will ask for a phone of their own. Everyone else has it, so they must have it too; you already know that story. This isn't bad per se; you would feel safer knowing that you could call them and ask where they are or if they need something. We are talking about the age when they are old enough to go to school alone, visit friends, have sleepovers, prepare simpler meals—you get the picture.

Part of today's kids' socializing is using social media.

So once your child (no matter if he or she is an adolescent) creates an account on social media, it is your responsibility to check what is going on there. Forbidding it will not work, but, again, limiting the time spent on their phones can ease things up. If you see that they spend too much time using their social media and chatting with friends, you can easily pick an internet policy with limited mobile data.

10

The Top 10 Challenges of Being a Parent in the Digital Age

Every stage is challenging and surprising in its way. Although you will enjoy periods of relative calm and ease with parenting, you can't become too complacent. Another set of challenges awaits you at the next turn.

It's these challenges that test our resolve as parents who value a mindful approach to child-rearing. Committing to mindful parenting is one thing—acting on it is quite another, especially when you're in the trenches and trying to craft a response to your screaming banshee that doesn't involve chugging whiskey straight from the bottle and setting yourself on fire.

Over the last few decades, parenting styles and the relationship between parents and children have changed profoundly. Although parents now spend more time with their children and have closer bonds with them in adulthood, they also deal with more anxieties, guilt, and conflicting advice than their predecessors.

The clear and authoritative guidelines set by parenting experts in earlier decades (like Dr. Benjamin Spock) have given way to inconsistent messages about how much to involve yourself in your child's activities and academic endeavors. You're unsure whether or not to provide less structure with more free time for your child to explore the world.

If this sounds like a depressing characterization of life for today's parents, that's not our intention. We don't mean to paint an alarming picture of your experience raising your kids. But you do have to contend with some issues unique to parenting trends over the past few decades, cultural changes related to marriage and work, and easy access to technology in virtually every corner of our lives.

Just so you're completely clear about what you're up against, let's review the top ten challenges parents face in this complex Information Age.

Challenge 1: Lack of Time

Most moms and dads today work full-time jobs with dual incomes. As a result, parenting has become a juggling act in which you're struggling to balance conflicting demands on your time and energy.

Parents don't have enough time for self-care because when they are home, they feel they should spend every minute engaged with their children. This lack of time leaves parents feeling guilty, exhausted, stressed out, and worried they aren't doing anything well. Maybe you can relate.

Challenge 2: Emotional Demands

Whether they are infants, teenagers, or any age in between, your children will frequently exert their emotional needs and make emotional demands on you that feel overwhelming.

Some of these emotional reactions relate to cultural changes children face today with ever-present digital devices, little free time or time spent outdoors, and increasing pressure to perform at school and with extracurricular activities.

Behaviors like temper tantrums, whining, arguing, back-talking, and insults will test you to your limits. As hard as you try to stay calm and composed when your child has an emotional outburst, you will often feel at a loss for how to best respond.

Sometimes your child's emotional demands will trigger strong emotions in you that you can't control. You may lose your temper, say things you regret or inflict knee-jerk punishments that aren't well-considered. All of this adds to the emotional turmoil in your home.

Challenge 3: Aggression

When your child gets emotionally flooded, his or her feelings may come out in aggressive behaviors, especially if he or she regularly witnesses aggression in others.

Hitting you or other children, being destructive, kicking, exhibiting intense anger, and picking fights are behaviors that can trigger your own fight-or-flight responses if you don't know how to handle your child's intensity.

Challenge 4: Judgment from Others

Family members, friends, and parenting experts all have opinions about the "right" way to raise your kids. You may have people in your life who believe they're helping you by telling you what you're doing wrong and how you need to change.

Comments like, "Why aren't you breastfeeding?" or "In my day, we'd let the baby cry it out," can make you feel defensive and doubt your own judgment.

In addition, social media can be another guilt- or shame-inducing forum when you see other parents (and their "superstar" children) who feel the need to share their parenting doctrines and why they are more successful than all of the other loser parents out there.

Feelings of judgment and peer pressure can cause you to feel insecure about your parenting, and may even compel you to send mixed messages to your children—something they will pick up on and use to their advantage.

Challenge 5: Seeking Perfection

Judgment from others on your parenting is bad enough. Still, self-judgment can erode your confidence and undermine the joy of being a mom or dad.

You may have a vision of what it means to be a "perfect" parent, and when you fall short of that vision, you feel like a failure—like you've failed your child.

Previous generations of parents didn't feel as responsible for their children's success, self-esteem, and happiness. But you want to protect your kids from pain, failure, disappointment, and heartache.

As a result, today's children don't often encounter the natural consequences, challenges, and setbacks that are an important part of learning and becoming a self-sufficient adult.

Challenge 6: Technology and Screen Time

Constant connectivity through computers, television, electronic games, and cell phones is creating a generation of children who can't disconnect from the digital world.

As a parent, you're torn between the convenience of these modern-day, child entertainment (and babysitting) devices and the knowledge that too much time on them can cause a host of issues, including attention deficit disorder, learning problems, anxiety and depression, and speech or language delays, according to research.

There's so much pressure from peers, television, and social media, that trying to manage your child's digital time feels like an uphill battle.

Challenge 7: Over-Scheduling

Today's parents feel less comfortable than previous generations of parents allowing their children the untethered freedom to play outside and roam short distances away from home on their bikes. There are too many real and imagined dangers to allow that kind of autonomy.

Parents are also more performance-focused and worry that their child won't survive in our competitive economy if Mom and Dad don't intervene early and often.

As a result, parents invest more and more time (and money) into arranged playdates, enrichment classes, and extracurricular activities to ensure their children have every advantage.

But this overscheduling creates more stress and pressure for both parents and children and doesn't allow kids just to be kids. Many high-achieving young adults are suffering from anxiety, depression, and other mental illnesses in an effort to rise to parental and self-expectations.

Challenge 8: Not Listening

One of the most common complaints you hear from parents is that their children don't listen. Getting your kids to pay attention and follow instructions feels like herding fleas.

Often, you repeat the same request a dozen times before it sinks in (or it's acknowledged), and your child takes action. You resort to nagging or yelling to get his or her attention, but then you feel guilty and bad about yourself for losing your temper.

The old rule, "I'm just going to say this once…" no longer applies. Your child is too distracted or doesn't fear the consequences, and therefore tunes you out. You feel conflicted and out of control.

Challenge 9: Letting Go

As your child gets older, it's natural that he or she will gain more and more independence and accept more personal responsibility. You want to trust your kids, but you also know all the ways they can screw up and jeopardize their own paths to success.

You want to protect your children from harm, poor decisions, and mistakes, but if you want them to learn valuable life lessons, you must let go and allow them to "fail forward" if necessary.

Many parents find this process the most challenging of all, as they have invested so much time and energy into their children that it's hard to bear the thought of their children squandering their efforts with one bad decision.

There is an epidemic of young adult children who "fail to launch," still living at home or depending on parents emotionally and financially long after they should be self-sufficient and managing adult responsibilities.

You may not be worried about this challenge now, when your child hasn't even reached their teen years, but it's wise to recognize this problem is real. It's never too early to teach your kids the practical skills they need to become independent adults—beginning with natural consequences, personal responsibility, and saving money.

As a result of creating child-centered environments at home or protecting their kids from consequences, parents can find themselves in the untenable position of pushing their child out of the nest rather than watching them fly away with ease.

Because we remove obstacles from our children's lives and do backflips to ensure their happiness during childhood, young adults often don't have the coping skills to face real-world challenges. As they flounder, you are left wondering, "What did I do wrong? I gave them everything!"

11

20 Rules for Parenting with Gentle and Love

Many unwanted behaviors are caused by primary needs that only need to be met so that the child can move on to what he or she needs or wants to do. Before you complain about a child being whiny or irritable, pause and think. Is the child hungry? Thirsty? Too hot? Too cold? Sleepy? Tired? Did the child skip a nap? Is the child overwhelmed by noise or too many strangers in his face? Is her coat itchy or her leggings too tight? Is the child in need of attention?

Make Sure That Your Needs Are Met

We get grumpy and angry much, much faster when we are in some kind of physical discomfort. This can mean that you need a bite to eat, a bathroom break, a massage, a nap, or a quick shower. Whatever it is, make sure you get it. You'll be a better, calmer parent after.

Create a Child-Friendly Environment

Too often, children get blamed for things that were not primarily their fault. That vase would not have broken if you had kept it on a high shelf. Tiny champers would not have ruined that book if you had saved it for when the child is older. The dog wouldn't be neglected if you had made sure that Robert understood the concept of responsibility before you bought it for him.

Acknowledge Their Feelings

"That must have been embarrassing." "That must have come as quite a shock." "You're angry at Conrad." Even when a child's reaction seems illogical, her feelings are real to her. Show empathy by giving your child's feeling a name. This shows the child that you are on her side while also teaching her how to identify and acknowledge her own emotions.

Validate Their Feelings

Children are only just beginning to experience and understand their own emotions. Help them understand that their feelings are valid and that they won't (or shouldn't) be judged for showing any kind of emotion by saying things like "that made me sad too when I was little" or "I still get scared of the dark sometimes."

Breathe.

Try to Decipher the Underlying Cause

If you merely act on the outward behavior, the underlying unmet need will continue to surface until it is finally met. Think about the cause of the child's behavior instead of just responding to the behavior itself. Try asking questions such as "Are you mad because I got home late and we didn't get to play together? Do you think we can do it after dinner?" or "Are you sad because your sister is at camp? Do you think we should go to the park so you can play with your friends instead?"

Give Yourself Time

Count to ten (slowly, silently) before you respond. This is especially helpful for parents who have a tendency to react immediately and forcefully. It also helps to say something like, "Give me a minute. I need to think this over."

Give the Children Time

Another good way to teach children autonomy is to give them a little space and grace to figure out what they should do and whether or not they are ready to cooperate. Statements such as "Let me know when you're ready to share" or "I'll be waiting here until you're ready for a story" give children a sense of control while avoiding confrontation. Take care not to say these in a sarcastic or exasperated tone. Of course, these won't always be appropriate (particularly when you're in a hurry to get somewhere) but when you can, use them.

Find a Win-Win Solution

If you can calm yourself enough to think a situation through, you will often realize that there are ways to get out of it where both parties get what they want. This usually means reaching a compromise and learning how to communicate in a non-violent manner.

Take a Break

It's okay to step out of a situation that has become too intense instead of trying to muddle your way through it right then and there. Don't wait for the situation to escalate. Say something like, "Let's take a break. We can deal with this later."

Reassure Them

Misbehaving is often just a child's way of expressing his need for love and attention. It's not a sensible way of going about it, of course, but that is what many children can manage. If they knew how to express their needs in a more mature way, they would. But in the meantime, they don't. So make sure that your child knows that he is loved, that you are there for him when he needs you, and that you appreciate him for who he is.

Offer Choices

This is essential to raising children who will grow up to be independent, and able adults are letting them feel that they have a voice.

Sometimes, even the choices that don't seem all that significant ("How do you want your eggs today?") help children feel that they have a say in what goes on around them. This is particularly beneficial for children who have recently undergone major life changes such as a move, parents divorcing, or the birth of a sibling.

Whisper

We are so used to a loud, noisy world where everyone and everything from the TV to our various gadgets are trying to get our attention by trying to out-shrill the next thing. In a sound-filled world such as ours, you'd be surprised to find out just how effective and refreshing a simple thing such as whispering can be. Whispering gets the child's attention (and what a nice break from the usual that would be for him) and calms the parent.

Go Outside

A change of scenery is often the very thing that both parent and child needs. Step out and have a picnic in the yard, play in the park, take a hike or a stroll, and visit friends. Even a short time out of the home can make a real difference.

Remember that Children Think in Pictures

Make specific instead of abstract requests: "Climb down slowly" instead of "Be careful!" "Stop jumping!" doesn't work because the action word "jumping" tends to drown out the word "stop." "Slow down!" will get through more easily.

Have a Sense of Humor

You wake up to Sophia pouring an entire box of cereal and an entire jug of milk into the dog's bowl. The image is so incredulous and frustrating and funny, and you're torn between laughing and yelling at her. Stop.

12

Montessori Discipline

For your little one to know how to be self-discipline, another element that's only as essential since the right collection of substances to your youngster is the fact that the youngster has to be directed to achieve liberty. Montessori considered the youngster has to receive the chance to operate well with the surroundings. It is essential as kids learn through the usage of these senses; therefore, they will need to govern matters. The youngster isn't going to learn whatever. For this reason, parents must pick out their toys to the kiddies precisely, together with all the targets of mastering expertise at heart.

Still, another variable is the youngster has to be helped to build up the will. The youngster could be permitted to select which task he wants to do the job with. As he's plumped for the task, he is going to possess the attention to focus on it, and ergo finishes the entire endeavor. This may aid in the creation of his self-discipline since Montessori considered that every child includes an all organic inner impulse that'll guide him purposeful pursuits like replicating the actions as a way to correct the art learned. This replicated action can aid the kid to add control within himself and also the environmental surroundings. He is learning how to make their or her conclusions about things such as, for instance, precisely what he wants. It enables him to accept responsibility due to his actions merely. The game which he undertakes may allow him to know that the constraints of actuality, therefore causing him into self-knowledge, self-possession along with self-discipline. Self-discipline is just a rather crucial feature for your kid to accomplish, so to allow him personally to produce elements like the strength of concentration and attention and also the liberty to execute imagination and work while to ease finding out.

For your little one to become helped in acquiring self-discipline, he should be supplied work. It's thus the educator's or so the most critical care giver's occupation to choose the clues by the little one regarding what experts have to get improved and exactly what activities may appeal to him at that time. The youngster must perhaps not be exhibited with numerous functions as to confound his intellect and interrupt his or her development. Ergo, it's necessary for your educator along with your physician to know the youngster and also be in a position to reply professionally. While the youngster enjoys to govern matters and also learns very best through drama, the task posed needs to be enjoyment and also attractive to the kid. Just this manner, would the little one be in a position to come up with his self-discipline because he knowingly calls himself into his preferred section of the job.

Kiddies are likewise proficient manipulators, and until this period since the anticipations have turned into part of the everyday regular, they are going to decide to try to observe just how they can drive and transform the guidelines to match themselves. It's for that particular reason why the rules and expectations have to get made evident first in the college season.

Frequently we get cheated and wind upward, ignoring the youngster's feelings and predominant him for an activity he wants to carry out. We might believe that we're serving when the truth is the youngster feels that we're "overpowering." this will probably cause some tantrums, once we aren't letting him be himself.

Bear in mind that every kid differs, and ergo you have to find out what works better for your kid. By observing, we will know whether your son or daughter needs assistance or maybe not, of course, when yet to precisely what level. This calls for patience (a great deal of it), a careful eye, and also an ability to confine ourselves out of needing to do everything to your kid.

Authentic misbehavior occurs when a kid chooses to misbehave. Before you do it, think about these tips regarding the subject:
1. Is your little one doing something amiss?
2. Can there be a genuine problem, or are you tired and outside of patience?
3. When there isn't any real trouble, discharge your stress away from your kid.

4. When there's an issue, go into the following question.
5. Consider a minute about if your youngster is capable of doing precisely what you expect.
6. If you aren't realistic, then re-evaluate your expectations.
7. If your expectations are honest, then go into the following question.
8. Did your youngster understand during that time they were doing something wrong?

If your son or daughter didn't realize that they were doing something very wrong, help them know what you expect to complete and how they can try this. Give to assist.

If your youngster knew what they were doing was wrong and blatantly dismissed sensible anticipation, they misbehaved.

If the behavior was a collision, such as wetting their trousers while sleeping, then it wasn't misbehavior. If the response wasn't a collision, ask your child to let you know that their reasons to do what they did.

If a kid is old enough, then ask how they may fix the issue or fix the circumstance. Kiddies grow by believing a subject and developing potential solutions.

Answering Misbehaviors

Listed below are five approaches parents and other health professionals may utilize to respond to child misbehavior. Rules need to be fully clarified and known before misconduct does occur. Whenever you can, involve kids in creating the rules to your relatives or the classroom.

Logical Consequences

All these are ordered effects that follow particular misbehaviors. The little one ought to have the ability to realize the way the behavior and the outcome are directly associated with it.

Fix-Up

If kids harm something, they want to help mend clean or it up it. Should they induce somebody distress, then they ought to be alleviate.

By way of example, "since you just made your brother shout, please come back and allow me to soothe him."

Re-Direction

This approach could work once you discover a kid, not after the rules and getting stubborn. Instantly get your kid's attention and still present another activity.

By way of instance," tom, please allow me to send the flowers today. You've been riding the bike for quite a very long period now it's Lena's turn."

13

Be a Montessori Parent: Be Present, Be Kind. Be A Gentle Leader

Positive Discipline from Positive and Conscious Parents

There are two types of education: the formal and the informal. Informal education is self-taught, without any help or guidance from a proper educator. The person gathers knowledge and information from their surroundings, making their self-education a priority.

Formal education comes through established institutes and teachers. These institutes cater to the children according to their ages. Kindergarten, primary or elementary school, high school, college, and universities are examples of such institutes. The roles of parents and teachers work parallel to each other.

Montessori Parents

When it comes to education, there are two ways to get educated that are formal and informal. In informal education, the person gets self-educated without any help or guideline from a proper educationist. He gathers knowledge and information from his surroundings, makes self-studies his priority. While on the other hand, formal education comes by means of proper institutes and teachers. These institutes cater to the children according to their ages. Kindergarten, primary, elementary, high school, college, and universities are examples of educational institutes where a person gets educated. The role of parents and teachers goes parallel. Parent-teacher and the child are connected in a triangle. All three interlinked with each other. Both teachers and parents have some responsibilities they have to fulfill according to the needs of the child.

A Parent as a Directress

A parent has the toughest responsibility of raising a child. They are responsible for bringing the toddler into this world and addressing their needs before and after birth. Even so, a parent should acknowledge the fact that they are their child's caretaker, not their sovereign. It's their responsibility to provide a child with a safe and well-prepared environment for their potential growth.

The parent is the first formal educator in a child's life. From infancy, and throughout their lives, a parent will stand by their child's side, offering guidance as to the child's needs. Of course, we're talking about the parent as a guide, not an adult who forces their views on the child. Restraining, pressuring, and controlling the child will never yield positive results for a child or parent.

A parent should realize the difference between guided instructions and forced behavior. They should give the child enough freedom and independence to develop the confidence needed to survive in society. Letting the child make their own choices will enhance their decision-making skills in the future. They also are the judges of whether their choices were right or wrong, and will eventually learn to make sensible decisions.

Parents should build a strong connection with their children so that they can learn how to build trust in others. A parent should also address their child's individual needs or wants. If the child is hyperactive, for instance, special care and a sensible approach are needed to enable them to learn better.

For this purpose, parents have to learn to become keen observers so that they can sense the needs of their children and act accordingly. They must also learn to control their temper since outbursts of anger can harm their child. If a parent displays a positive attitude, their child is sure to pick up on this and live a happier life because of it.

Your relationship with your child is just like every other relationship. For it to thrive, healthy communication is crucial. In simple terms, communication is when you send and receive information to and from another person. This information can be visual, auditory, or some other kind.

The Montessori Directress

Dr. Montessori referred to educators using her method as "directress" rather than "teacher." This is because "teacher" is a common term given to a person who teaches their students. But because within a Montessori environment, the child is learning through guided instructions, not by the traditional method of learning, the educator in charge is only offering the child guidance.

A directress is in charge of preparing a safe environment with lots of physical and mental activities for the child to explore and learn. A directress should let her presence be felt and offer instructions to the children, but never interfere or make restrictions. As mentioned before, Dr. Montessori believed that the restrictive attitude of adults could shatter a child's self-confidence.

Dr. Montessori proposed two significant roles for a directress. One is preparing the environment for the child, and the other one is the preparation of the adult as an observer and guide who knows how to prepare and take care of the child. A directress should guide children and make them spiritually strong. To accomplish this, they need to understand the child's needs.

According to Dr. Montessori, a directress is a scientist who connects with the child in a way that enables the child to explore the world around them. Instead of knowing how to teach, a directress should know how they can become a better guide and exploit the child's full potential. Also, she should be a refined observer, be fully aware of their spiritual and scientific approach, and above all, their ultimate goal: to serve children and to help them to discover their hidden qualities.

Communication with the Child

Communication builds trust, and as such, you must get it right, especially in the early stages of your child's development. If your child feels like you understand them, it will be easier for them to relate to you and form better relationships in the future.

Healthy, open, and expressive communication with your toddler will benefit them for the rest of their lives. Everybody loves to be understood, appreciated and respected. Toddlers and children are no different. When you communicate with them often, it makes them feel you value and respect them, which boosts their self-esteem.

Parents and educators who communicate openly will often have more obedient children. When you can communicate effectively with your toddlers, they are more willing to do the things you tell them to do. They see reason in what you are telling them to do, they understand you, and do these things not only because you asked them to, but because they want to. Remember, they are independent.

Communication with toddlers can be very tricky, though. You have to know just the right things to say in the right situations and what to avoid so as not to hurt their feelings. Here are a few tips on how to tread this slippery road.

- Ask and wait for a response. A child's mind is always wandering. They could be completely absorbed in an activity one moment then run off to play the next. This is due to their need to explore anything and everything around them, so when you ask a question or give an instruction, wait for a response. When they wander off or begin to talk about something else, draw their attention back to the subject and, nicely but firmly, ask for a response.
- Children have spats with one another; it doesn't necessarily mean anyone involved is a troublemaker. Human beings and conflict are inextricable from one another. However, what you do in these situations goes a long way in the development of your child. If your child has a disagreement with another child, instead of settling the issue, guide them in resolving their problem. This instils social intelligence in everyone involved, teaching them that disagreements and misunderstandings can and should be solved by dialogue.
- It's frustrating when children refuse to share. It causes a

ruckus and it seems like there is no just way to settle it. So, Lisa wants to play with Chloe's doll, but Chloe doesn't want to share. Lisa gets hurt and begins to wail, but Chloe is set on her decision: it is her doll, after all, and she is not sharing. Instead of taking the doll from Chloe and handing it to Lisa, ask Chloe to share. If she refuses, let her be. Children are wired to think of themselves first but can be given when they want to. Find something else for Lisa to play with, then when Chloe is done, she can have the doll.

- Let your child know that you understand them when they're sad, instead of just assuming to know why to ask them about it. Prompt them to talk and listen without judging. Ask them why the situation is making them sad, then ask them what they want to do about it.

- Always ask questions. At this point, you probably already know the importance of asking your child questions instead of jumping to your conclusions. You might think you have a handle on what the problem is, but hearing them talk about it will give you a fresh perspective. It also allows them to vent and express themselves. This step will also make them feel like they can talk to you about anything, no matter how big or small it is.

- Never turn a blind eye to the feelings of your child. When you have hurt them, whether you think they deserved it or not, acknowledge it and apologize. Explain why you did it and call a truce. Children are human beings with real feelings, and they are infinitely more sensitive than the average adult so that the smallest things can get to them.

- Try not to lie to your child. The truth is children are very observant of what goes on around them and even though it may not seem like it, they know when you lie to them. The child may not call you out on your lie or contradict, but they still know.

- Use the proper words for objects. Avoid slangs as much as possible; we don't want our toddlers picking up on wrong words, right?

14

A Montessori Children Home

Many parents feel overwhelmed when it comes to creating a Montessori home environment. There is a lot to take in. However, as we mentioned earlier in the guide, you are learning along with your child, and it isn't necessary to incorporate everything all at once. It's better not to do that because both you and your child may feel overwhelmed. If you have a newborn child, it will be easier to start introducing Montessori right away than if your child is a little older. Nevertheless, no matter the age of your child, they will be a great benefit and adjust quickly.

One of the many wonderful things about Montessori is that it can be applied to most settings. Even if you have a small space, you can still create Montessori at home because it's about making the most of what you have, not what you don't have. This is a perfect opportunity to get creative. Here are four ways you can implement Montessori at home regardless of how much space you have:

1. **Less is more**. When you look at other Montessori home environments on blog posts, social media, etc., you will notice that there aren't a lot of materials and the items they have are few, high quality, creative, and colorful or stimulating. This is the Montessori way. Any activities that are on display should be the ones your child is currently working with. They should be age-appropriate. Remember, the younger your child is, the fewer items or toys they will need. You will need to provide some more resources once your child grows, and their skills and abilities develop—but it doesn't have to be a lot more.

Since children are looking for order at this stage, it's much better for them if there is no clutter and tiny materials around. That way, things are organized, and it's clear to them where things are so that they have easier access to what they want or need. This is how they will develop independence. A chaotic environment will likely result in a chaotic child.

If you have a small shelf in a room that's just for your child, then that's fine. If you have no space to dedicate a whole room to a Montessori environment, then that's fine too.

2. If things don't look aesthetically pleasing to you, likely, they won't to your child either. Just remember to present materials in a way that looks appealing and will interest your child. It's a good idea to make sure that your child has their own space, but it should be a part of the family setting and not completely separate. When they go off to play, they shouldn't be cut off from the rest of the family.

3. Use pretty, naturally woven baskets to help you organize materials and activities. A basket or even something else that's made from wood or natural materials will help you to store the child's activities neatly, especially if they are being kept in the common area of the home along with other household items. You can easily find these at a thrift store. Your storage boxes, baskets, or trays don't have to match either. It may be pleasing to your child's eye to have them not match.

4. Focus on practical life activities.

Suiting Materials & Activities to Meet Needs

Many parents get overwhelmed with the feeling they need to have both the right amount of space and the right materials. Many people believe that if they don't have all the equipment, materials, and resources, they won't be able to apply the Montessori Methods properly. That's not the case. The purpose of Montessori at home is to involve the child in everyday activities and encourage them to feel like a valued family member who is contributing to the home. A simple way to do this is to get them involved in practical life activities. For instance, if you have a small water bottle and a cloth, you can have your child help you wash the windows. You can even sing songs at the same time. If you are folding freshly washed laundry, why not have your child see if they can match up the socks for you? It can be as simple as that.

It's important not to force your child to do practical life activities. For instance, it's not necessary to tell your child they have to stop whatever activity they are doing to help you with the dishes. Instead, if you naturally make the practical life activities fun and exercise patience as they are learning, eventually they will want to help. Remember, children have a desire to be useful, and helping out gives them a sense of achievement. Many activities can be started before the child can even walk. For instance, they can sit down and sort laundry by color. Every child's learning needs are different. If you have more than one child, you will likely understand this as well. You know your child well and will be able to determine if an activity or certain materials are suitable for him or her.

In the beginning, you may or may not have an idea of what materials and activities your child wants or needs. However, this is where your "scientific research" will come in handy. You will quickly develop an understanding of what they require, the more you observe them. Then it will be easier to provide some of those materials.

Changing & Adapting

You will find that as your child grows, their needs, desires, preferences, and behaviors will change. This means you will be changing too. What works amazingly well in your Montessori home when the child is a newborn will need to be adjusted by the time your child grows to an infant and toddler. You must anticipate change and are open to it. Otherwise, it will hinder your child's ability to progress in daily life and develop as a person. Since children at this early age are looking for routine and order, there is bound to be discomfort for a short period when changes are made around the home. It's best to make any changes that are needed as gently as possible, taking into account how it will impact your child. Children can become very attached to certain items such as toys. However, if you can see that the toy is starting to look a little worse for wear, or is broken and cannot be fixed, then it needs to go into the trash. Of course, the child may become upset. Just be as understanding as possible rather than getting upset with them for crying or having a tantrum. You could also use this experience to help your child learn about releasing things and emotions.

You may find that your child suddenly gets bored with an activity or hates it in the first place. That's fine. Don't try to force them to do this activity if they don't like it. This goes against the Montessori approach. They may let you know verbally or nonverbally what their interests are. Remember, we want to guide children with their choices of activity. Any activities or equipment that are no longer in use can be taken out of the home. It's important to do this; otherwise, you risk your home becoming cluttered.

1 2   M o n t h s

- They can utilize their feet to push themselves along on ride-on toys.
- They show interest in balls and playing with them.
  - At this age, throwing or tossing the ball to your child is the key for some motor development. Begin by rolling a soft, small ball back and forth between you and your toddler, ensuring that you are gradually moving farther away. In time, they will eventually have the desire to throw it.
  - When teaching them to kick a ball, show them to use their feet instead of their hands.
  - To catch a ball, have them roll it up an incline to catch on the way down.

1 5   M o n t h s

- They can walk without your help, but with the assistance of walking with their feet spread apart and their arms to contribute to proper balance.
- They can get themselves up from the sitting to standing positions by utilizing their hands to push themselves up and sit down with the use of their hands.
- They can bend down to pick things up themselves.
  - In time, this action will turn into being able to squat. To assist your toddler in developing this motor skill, when they start to bend over an object, show them how to bend their knees.
  - Practice makes perfect, of course. Line up some toys and have them pick them up. This will also help in the mental

development of when clean-up time is as well.

1 8   M o n t h s

- They can drink from a cup without assistance.
- They can draw/scribble/write on paper using a variety of utensils.
- They are capable of climbing onto low furniture.
    - Toddlers are inevitably going to attempt to climb whatever they think they can get on, blatantly because of the mere fact it is there.
    - Climbing is a vital physical development. So do not prohibit them from climbing, but rather create safe opportunities for them to do so. Throw sofa cushions on the floor and create a padded-playground for them to enjoy.
    - Ensure that heavy furniture and other objects in your household, such as bookcases and televisions, are properly anchored down so that your child will not knock them over on themselves.
- They can build a tower out of block-like toys.
- They can now pick up small objects since they have practiced the pincer grip.
- They are able to push wheeled toys in front of them.
    - Once your child becomes more confident in their walking abilities, they will have the desire for pushing and pulling around toys and other objects. Ensure that during this stage, you offer them push or pull toys to play with.

2   Y e a r s

- They have the ability to push buttons and turn knobs.
- Most can walk down the stairs by holding onto the railing and placing both feet onto a step.
- They can easily run in one direction and stop when they need to.
- They are able to walk backwards.
- They are capable of running.
    - Each child is different, but some toddlers may go from crawling to being able to sprint at rapid rates in what seems

like a matter of seconds. Some children take risks faster than others.

- Encourage your toddler to play tag on softer areas, such as sand or grass.
- Chase your child around, encouraging them to run from you. Then have them chase you around.
- They are capable of getting themselves off the floor without using their hands.
- They can take off articles of clothing.

2 ½ Years

- They can undress.
- They are learning ways to pick out clothes and dress properly.
- They can throw a large ball in the direction they intend.
- They can walk up the stairs.
- They can kick a large ball, even though it usually does not go in the direction they intend to.
- They can feed themselves with the utilization of a spoon.
- They can drink from a regular cup.
- They are capable of getting on and off playground equipment.
- They are able to run smoothly (and with speed).

3 Years

- They can feed by themselves using both a spoon and a fork.
- They have begun the potty-training process.
  - This is the milestone that parents look forward to maybe the most because this means no more diapers. The age at which your toddler is ready to undergo the process of properly going to the bathroom can vary greatly. Here are signs that your toddler may be ready to start the process of potty-training:
    - Looks down at diapers, and grabs and pulls them off when soiled.
    - Crosses their legs or squats when they need to go.
    - Shows interest in potty-related things, such as discussing

pee or poo or wants to watch you go to the bathroom.

- They are capable of throwing and catching a ball if they utilize two hands.
- They can kick a ball with more force.
- They can jump.
  - Toddlers during this stage will begin to jump off the ground or off low objects. Jumping requires bilateral coordination skills as well as the ability to utilize both sides of the body.
    - Encourage "curb hopping." Hold your toddler's hand and stand next to a curb or step and say, "One, two, three... jump!" then jump down with them.
    - Teach them to leapfrog. Demonstrate how to get down into a half-squatting position and to throw their arms up in the air while hopping.
- They can balance themselves and can walk on tippy-toes.
- They can walk both up and down the stairs without the parent's help.
- They can begin to play with ride-on toys like bicycles.

The toddler stage is quite a unique one during the course of human development in the fact that toddlers are no longer consider babies by they are not considered to be preschoolers yet either. There are a lot of crucial developmental components that occur during this time frame, which is why as parents should always be encouraging growth and watching for signs that our young child may be falling behind developmentally. Of course, all children learn and grow at different paces.

Gross Motor Development

Gross motor skills are physical capabilities that utilize large bodily movements that require the entire body. During the time your child is a toddler, they stop toddling and look so particularly awkward when they walk. They begin to walk and are able to do so more smoothly. They are able to run and at much faster rates, as well as hop and jump. They have the capability to actively participate in throwing and catching a ball and can push themselves around by themselves or while upon a riding toy.

Fine Motor Development

Fine motor movements are vastly different than gross motor skills because they require the ability to utilize precise movements to perform adequately. During the toddler stage, children can begin to create things they imagine with their own hands. They can build towers out of toy blocks, mold clay into recognizable shapes, and are more than capable of scribbling on paper with crayons or pens. They quite enjoy toys that allow them to insert specific shapes into one another. This is also the time parents will start to notice which hand their child prefers to use over the other, as they begin to become either right-handed or left-handed.

The Need for Continued Learning

You are going to find that unexpected things will come up in daily life, and you may not be sure of the best course of action. This is natural and happens with all parents. As a conscious Montessori parent, you may question your actions and choices at times, and that's fine. Please know it's important that you permit yourself to keep studying the Montessori approach because there's a lot of information to absorb.

Popular Blogs

There are many popular blogs out there that are dedicated to the topic of Montessori at home. Many of these blogs are run by parents like you, who are dedicated to raising the best human beings possible with the resources that are available to them. Many parents have made what they may call "mistakes" along the way, and they share their experiences on their blogs. You will find blogs that relate to specific concepts of the Montessori Method as well as those that discuss all of the areas.

Over time, you may even decide to set up a blog yourself so that you can share your experiences with other parents and caregivers to help you on this journey further.

Ideas and Inspiration on Instagram and Pinterest

If you ever need some inspiration on how to create your environment, then Instagram and Pinterest are ideal places to visit. Many Montessori parents like to post images or create pinboards that show how their home environment is set up when the child is a newborn, infant, and toddler. As you browse through the countless photos, you'll notice that many differ from each other, which should reassure you that there is no right or wrong way to create your own Montessori environment.

There are a lot of ideas for DIY projects and activities, so if you're concerned about your budget or space, don't be. Start a pinboard on Pinterest and save your favorite pins on Montessori ideas so you can easily refer to them. You will never be short on ideas and inspiration. If anything, this is what can overwhelm parents. However, I would like to remind you again that it's a good idea to keep it simple. If you find yourself spending hours at a time looking through Instagram posts or Pinterest boards, it may be time to look away so that you don't feel stuck. There are many beautiful home environments that others have created, and seeing them can leave you feeling doubtful of what you can create. The key is not to allow yourself to get too caught up in other people's ideas that you don't believe in your own. Also, it can be very easy for many new Montessori parents to feel inadequate or disheartened because they compare themselves to what other parents are doing. The purpose of using social media is to uplift you and open you up to a wide range of possibilities for your child. It should inspire. If you find yourself feeling discouraged, then step away for a while. You will also find articles, videos, and blog posts on how to deal with feeling overwhelmed or uncertain when it comes to setting up a Montessori environment at home.

15

How to Introduce and Set Up an Activity?

A child's mind is very absorbent; hence things impressed in mind at this stage stay with one for a lifetime. This period of education and development is referred to as a sensitive period—it is as if the child picks things, patterns, sensory and motor stimuli very effortlessly from the environment; hence this is the best phase for:

- Language acquisition; this happens effortlessly between 0 to about 6 years when the child learn sound and words so easily.
- Motor skills
- Interest in objects, based on color, shape, or size; between 18 months to 3 years of age. The child is building attention; both top to bottom attention (that is attention based on their inner decision and choice to focus on a particular detail in the environment, for example, looking for yellow color as a result of their decision to find all objects of that color) and bottom to top attention (that is interest in things in the environment that catches their attention, for example, a child's eye is caught by a yellow colored object in the environment because of how catchy the color yellow is).

Language Acquisition Activities

Books. This cuts across all ages, but the teachers tailor the books based on the life the child is living, their interests and of course what they ought to know at the particular age—remember the objective for this kind of education is to get the child to explore and learn himself and the world through his senses and not through the eyes of the teacher. Book activities could include;

- One colorful picture per page for infants, so that the child can begin to take note of specific forms and begin to appreciate pictures.
- One picture per page with one word
- One picture per page with a sentence.
- Then build to making simple stories per picture.
- As you make progress, we begin to build in more complex stories.
- Get the children to arrange books in an accessible way either in a basket, or on a shelf—with this, they also learn respect for books and to order.
- For a start, a book made of the board is just fine, for handling purposes, then move on to hardcovers and then paperback books.

Rhythmic Language and Poems. This activity boosts the child's language acquisition as they begin to say words rhythmically and also, mentally match words together that seem to sound alike but have different meanings. This helps them develop a stronger grip on the language.

- Very short poems, songs, rhyming ditties; they should also be simple and be relatable for the children at their age—if they are too long, they may become very overwhelming for the children, so a few sentences or lines can do.
- Make these poems, rhymes and songs to go with certain body movements, could be the fingers, feet, or torso—it might not be an outright dance step, you understand what I mean?
- Make these songs real and let them not be void of some emotion.

Create Activities for Self-Expression. Create avenues where the child can share something with the teacher or other children, teachers in the Montessori education system take this seriously—those moments of interaction and self-expression.

- For non-verbal children, let them make sounds and body gestures, while the teacher pays attention to understand what they are trying to communicate as well as showing emotional responses that he or she is paying attention to what the child is saying—this may demand you just restating what the child just said in your own words, repeat the sound he or she just made or just say out loud "Really!" "Wow!" "Oh My!" "Are you kidding me?" "Don't say,"

"You do not mean it."

- For verbal children encourage them to use words, then phrases and sentences, of course show empathy and mirror the child's emotions—do not "over-do it," making all those weird faces when what the child is saying is not that serious; children know when you are not mirroring their emotions.
- Teach the child to maintain eye contact where it is culturally acceptable, by coming down to the child's eye level and maintaining eye contact.
- A bag that contains 4 to 9 related items like cooking implements, children sized cookie cutter, spreader, bamboo whisk, spatula etc. A kimono bag filled with Japanese items, another bag filled with garden tools, hair grooming tools etc.; this would help the child learn to group things. From 2 and half years, you can start putting related things and one or two unrelated things and tell the child to spot the odd one out—apart from learning how to group things the child's register and vocabulary will expand.
- Thinking and conversation exercise; here, the goal is to get the child to think and make conversations as naturally as you can— helping the child make coherent and sensible conversations, this is for children above the age of two. You can start the conversation with "Do you remember when we planted the bean seed?" "What did we plant it with?" "Can you remember what the seed needs to grow?" "Tell me what we did as we planted the seed." This is to help the child make directed and coherent conversations with given registers as naturally as possible.

Matching Cards with Identical Objects. This helps reinforce language in the child, their ability to identify objects in the environment and what they are called is adding to their language—the child has to do well in a world of things (objective reality) and meaning (subjective reality); therefore his ability to merge words or pictures in a card and the actual object, in reality, is building a deep seated balance in their interaction with the world around them.

- Classifying sets of objects that match in a card or picture.
- Taking pictures of furniture or equipment that are in the right place (for example, all of these are found in the living room except _____, the child may spot that a refrigerator is not supposed to be in the living room and should be in the kitchen etc.)

- Matching identical sizes, colors and positioning.

Vocabulary Cards. Depending on the infant's age, this may come as games, wherein a child is given a picture of an object to tell its name, spelling, its uses, the application is vast, or any other form of matching such as color, size, shape, and texture.

- Set classified cards that relates to the child's everyday life and activities.
- Simple classifications where the child will talk about pictures that appear on the flashcard, this small talk can be based on anything the child knows about the picture. Of course, you will be generous with the appreciation.

Letters, Word Pronunciations and Phonetics. Cards with individual letters, two letter words, three letter words and so on as the child makes progress. From there, the child can learn those words, and other words that sound alike, spotting their differences in spellings, meaning and usage—all of these depend on the child's age and level of development.

- Flashcards with letters.
- Plastic letters in their three-dimensional form.
- Combining letters to form words.
- Identifying numbers.
- Building pre-reading skills.

Telling the Time. This is effective for children from three years and above, it helps them to appreciate better and tell the time. Provide a calendar where the child can change the day and month and also the weather; with guidance from the teacher, he can be able to communicate the date and probably the weather of the day—more details can be added later as the child grows up.

Motor Skill Activities

These are skills that help children develop muscle coordination, smooth response of the muscles when triggered by the brain, balance, poise, and grace in movement—all depending on their age and stage of development.

Music, Dance, and Movement. This helps the child make rhythmic motions, stretches calisthenics and, at the same, time enjoy music.

- Play music out loud, by that I mean it should not merely be a background song so that the children can sing and dance along.
- Videos of music and dance and the children can dance and sing along.
- Infants that cannot walk and talk yet can be placed in front of a mirror to watch their own body movements as they sway to the sound of music.

Grasping and Interlocking Materials. This helps improve their eye-hand coordination and also works on their reaching and grasping abilities.

- As the baby grows, he begins to reach out and grasp interesting materials in the environment.
- Objects placed in the child's hand can be grasped with a firm grip with a reflex grasp, but, as the child grows, he or she begins to make intentional grips.
- Ability to reach for an object, by rolling over to it, crawling towards it, or walking towards them, this can be done by placing an object of importance to the baby a little distance away from him or her, allowing them to make efforts to reach out to it.
- Toys and dolls: depending on the age of the child, he or she can use them to play, create a drama, or just bang them on the floor; all these are training motor skills.
- Place plastic or wooden interlocked rings which are able to give off sounds if rattled: children depending on their age can manipulate, mouth or throw them about.
- Hand them over bowls and scoops to scoop water or sand into a container: a distance can be created from the point of scooping to the place where they offload, to make the activity a little bit more challenging; more examples include: putting plastic balls in a basket and counting them probably to know which child picked more.

Climbing Stairs with Rails. Children can be encouraged to climb platforms to perform: climb small stirs, or climb ladders to playing equipment—this helps improve their gross motor skills and their body coordination. Make stairs broad but not high, and let them be fitted with rails.

Sporting Activities. This can include: running, jumping, dancing, or a combination of all to improve their motor skill and balance. These activities may or may not be competitive.

- Running down tracks with arrows for direction and filling a basket with balls: the child with the most balls wins. This helps them run, squat, reach, grasp, and throw in the right basket.
- Jumping over a flat line on the floor: once you can achieve getting a child to jump with both feet, you can now introduce elevations little by little and, of course, with a soft landing. In addition, the child can jump across slight distances.
- Riding: for about 3 years, you can introduce riding with pedals and balance wheels behind.
- Swinging: get swings that are low from where the children's feet can touch the ground so that they can swing themselves with their feet and also get on and off the swing.
- Crawling through tunnels: straight tunnels, Y shaped tunnels, caves et cetera, with time they may start moving and finding their way through labyrinth boxes.
- Ball swinging: throwing balls through distances, as they make progress, you can introduce targets.
- Gardening and composting: this can serve as a recreational activity for the children.

16

It Is All About Observing. The Montessori Schemas from 0 Till 12 Months

Good Parenting

- Each baby is different.
- They need your attention.
- They need your love and care.
- Good parenting does not mean providing your child with perfect things.
- Good parenting is about giving attention and lots of love.
- Good parenting is about being nice to your child.
- It also means bringing up your child in a happy environment.
- How to monitor the growth of your baby?
- It is a good practice to keep a notebook/diary for your baby.
- A diary, is like a quick reference.
- You can note step by step growth of your baby.
- You can also maintain the vaccination schedules in the same diary.
- Carry the diary whenever you visit the health center for regular check-ups.

How to Communicate With Babies?

- Talk to your baby from its birth as it will start recognizing your (mother's) voice.
- Talk about what you're doing as if it is understanding.
- Sing songs and rhymes.
- Read books and tell stories to your baby from birth.

- Listen to your baby's first efforts at babbling and then respond.
- Name the toys and objects around it.

Understanding Development

Physical activities

Around 3 months	3-6 months	6-9 months	9-12 months
The baby tries to lift his head.	The baby tries to roll over.	The baby tries to sit & play or crawl around.	The baby tries to get up with support and try to walk.
Baby tries to lift its head to see you, tries to smile while looking at you.	Place some toys around for the baby to reach out to them.	Give the baby safe toys to play, he or she will learn to hold and play with them.	Be watchful and alert at all times as your baby tries to crawl or stand up and explore.

- As your baby advances, its sleep pattern will be more defined. Between each nap there will be more gaps, note them and try to follow a pattern in feeding.
- Take out time to play with it; each member of the family can contribute to its growth and development.

Social and Emotional bonding

Around 3 months	3-6 months	6-9 months	9-12 months
The baby develops trust in you.	The baby will show its feelings.	The baby reacts to familiar surroundings.	The baby enjoys playing with you.
Comfort your baby if it cries, so that he can trust you	Babies can express love and fondness just like you.	Babies hesitate to go to strangers, don't force.	Play with your kid, and they love your bonding.

- Babies develop a bond with their mother, father, and siblings.
- Babies develop a bond with their surroundings as it grows.
- Babies feel safe and secured among familiar people.
- Babies may fear new faces, crowded places & new surroundings.
- Hence, talk to your baby in a soothing tone while introducing it to new people and new places.

Baby's responses

Around 3 months	3-6 months	6-9 months	9-12 months
Your baby will respond positively to your touch.	The baby tries to hold things.	The baby tries to play and learn.	The baby moves around and is inquisitive.

The baby can see objects within 13 inches from it and show excitement.	The baby learns and familiarizes with different objects with feel & touch.	Play with your baby by building blocks. Try to teach colors and shapes of the objects.	Watch her closely, as she is moving all over the place. Baby understands you tone and expression when it hears your voice.

Talk to your baby, show eye contact and encourage it to make sounds, so that he gets familiar to everyone's voices. Baby will gradually learn to look around even when it hears a voice from a distance.

Baby knows best

Around 3 months	3-6 months	6-9 months	9-12 months
The baby knows your touch and feel.	The baby knows it's routine, hence follow one.	The baby knows to comfort itself.	The baby knows your simple commands.
Sing a song, or play some rhyme while you hold your baby close.	Feed your baby, give him a bath and put the baby to sleep at the same hour	Babies can comfort themselves by holding a toy, a blanket, or by	The baby can respond to you simple "NO" and "DO NOT

	everyday.	sucking thumb.	TOUCH" commands.

- If your child is crying hard, it's because this is the only way she can tell you that something is wrong.
- Maybe s/he's cold, hungry, have pooped or peed or can be in pain.
- Don't ignore your baby when she's crying as they are too small to sort it by themselves yet.

17

It Is All About Observing. The Montessori Schemas From 12 Till 24 Months

Montessori materials are an integral part of the so-called pedagogical "preparatory environment," which encourages the child to show the possibilities of his own development through initiative, corresponding to his personality.

Montessori materials in terms of clarity, structure, and logical sequence correspond to the periods of greatest susceptibility to the development of the child. These periods, which are favorable for teaching certain types of activities, identifying talents, developing self-mastery, and forming attitudes towards the world, can be optimally used with the help of developing materials.

Materials and their functions should be considered in conjunction with the vision of the child accepted by Maria Montessori, namely with his anthropology. She saw in the emerging child powerful internal creative forces that carry out the work of developing and building his personality. At the same time, the materials significantly help to streamline the child's comprehension of the world. The teacher is focused on the child with his individual and socio-emotional needs, while materials play a supporting didactic role.

For a child, Montessori materials are the key to the world around him, thanks to which he organizes and learns to realize his chaotic and raw impressions of the world. With their help, the child grows into a culture and modern civilization. From his own experience, he learns to understand nature and navigate it. In the "preparatory environment" created according to Montessori, the child can exercise all physical and spiritual functions, shape his spiritual integrity and comprehensively develop. By organizing the preparatory environment, he learns to bring his previous experience into the system.

Sensory Development

Frames with clasps—training in specific skills needed when dressing. Children are offered frames with buttons, buttons, zippers, buckles, laces, hooks, pins, and bows.

Brown Staircase—represents the differences between the two dimensions and introduces the concepts: thin, thinner, the thinnest, thick, thicker, thickest.

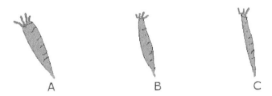

Pink Tower—represents differences in magnitude in three dimensions and helps the child in differentiating the concepts of large, larger, largest, small, smaller, smallest.

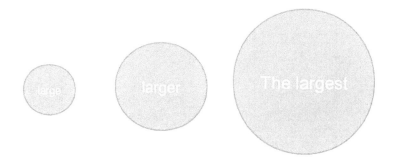

Red bars—represents differences in size in one dimension (length) and introduce concepts: short, shorter, the shortest; long, longer, the longest.

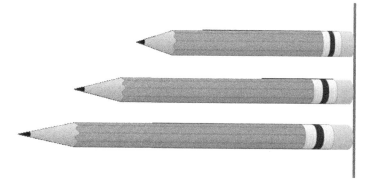

Cylinder blocks—are four sets with nine cylinders in each. The first set consists of cylinders of various heights; the second—cylinders of various diameters; the other two include cylinders of different heights and diameters. Selecting a cylinder for the corresponding hole helps in distinguishing the size and developing the fine musculature of the hands necessary when writing. Color cylinders—each set corresponds to the size parameters of one of the sets of cylinder blocks. Noise cylinders—this set consists of two wooden boxes, each of which contains six cylinders. Each pair of cylinders has its own sound, i.e., for each sound of the red cylinders, the corresponding sound of the blue cylinders is selected.

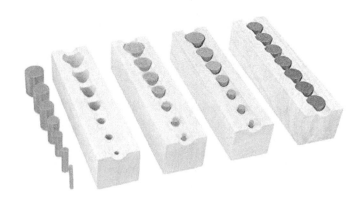

Speech Development

Letters cut out of sandpaper allow the child to recognize the outline of each letter by touch and associate the sound of the letter with its outline.

Metal tabs—ten mathematical tabs of different geometric shapes. The tabs have a small handle for holding and moving. Tracking the outline of a tab helps prepare your hand and eye for writing.

Mathematical Development

Red-blue rods are a set of 10 rods of the same size as the red rods, but each bar is divided into red-blue parts. These exercises teach the basic principles of counting and can be used to add subtraction, multiplication, and division easily.

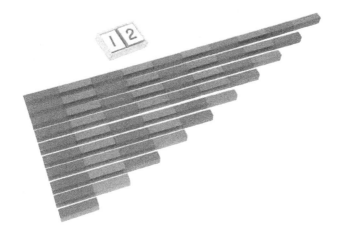

Box with spindles—two boxes with sections from 0 to 9 are used to teach counting and the concept of quantity. The child places a certain number of spindles in the appropriate section.

Golden beads—these materials provide an introduction to the concept of counting, quantity and basic mathematical functions.

Geometric bodies—teach visual and tactile differentiation of geometric shapes. The set consists of a cube, ball, cylinder, quadrangular pyramid, rectangular prism, ellipsoid, ovoid, cone and triangular prism.

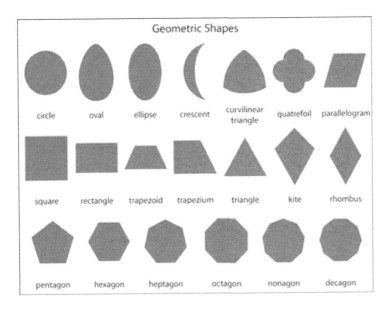

Geometric Shapes

circle	oval	ellipse	crescent	curvilinear triangle	quatrefoil	parallelogram
square	rectangle	trapezoid	trapezium	triangle	kite	rhombus
pentagon	hexagon	heptagon	octagon	nonagon	decagon	

Before Buying Montessori Toys, There Are Things That You Need to Know

You want your child to become a smart, trustworthy student. But to do this, you must carefully plan the operation. No pain, no benefit, as the saying goes. You must ensure that his muscle motor is established in a healthy and uninhibited environment. You will inspire him to take on the tasks you have created. He feels safe. The learning process should be imaginative, enjoyable, and realistic in this regard.

It's important to know how children develop Montessori Toys. This is because you can awaken his interest through these inputs, improve his cognitive capacity, and help him perceive fundamental similarities and differences. These works are instructional aids. Hold these things in mind before you buy the supports and inputs.

1. Must Suit His Age Range

Some of the Montessori toys that help children to distinguish objects by weight may not be suited to the needs of your one-year-old kid. He's not going to understand its purpose. So, find him the ones that suit his age and interest.

2. Check the Quality

As has already been saying, playthings serve as teaching aids for learning, so that they comply with the safety parameters. But at the end of the day, you should be twice as sure as otherwise. Check the quality of the material. See how powerful it is. If screws are found, attaching one part to the other, see if they are loose, or if the color is worn out, with repeated use and application.

3. Should Encourage Creativity

Find out how it relates to your sensory experiences and experience before purchasing the content. Kids love to color, variety, and creativity, so the inputs they choose should appeal to their imagination and insight.

4. Must Make the Child Active

The chosen play should develop the child physically and psychically. While you can give him perspectives to sit and play at a corner, you also need to find things that help him understand by getting him that run, drive and leap.

5. Should Be Changeable

You will do some homework to find the correct selection of playing things that can also be used as your child matures and grows up. Find those that are modifiable and can, therefore, be used later in the next step of its growth.

Example: Doing some easy household chores like keeping his/her toys.

6. Should Motivate Learning

See whether your kid can use the product to solve a job or problem before you purchase the item. Many of the playthings like textile swats, silent games, and simple tablets help kids think critically. Find out how this piece can help your child learn and develop skills.

How Can Montessori Toys Devolve Your Children Activities?

Schooling is an important part of the life of a child in which a child establishes his personality that helps him in his life. In addition to schools, teachers, and the environment, materials, and educational equipment are also necessary. The activities and toys used help build the intelligence and power of the child. The most positive thing for children is when these toys and games are mixed.

Some of the many ways to help children learn toys and games are given here.

Better Learning Experience

Toys for education are effective in developing a child's learning experience. In addition, making children play with literature and words, many forms of educational and interactive toys are available on the market that helps them learn something new every day. Various types of fun and enticing toys help the kids concentrate on them during their activities.

Toys like alphabets, matching colors, different types of puzzles, and medleys are used to enable children to learn language fundamentals as well as math. These Montessori toys have magical powers that help them increase not only their grasping strength but also provide basics of education for various activities using toys.

Entertaining and Engaging

The available education toys are very colorful and have a quite enticing look that allows the children to be entertained. Montessori toys are magically capable of entertaining not only the children while helping them to learn, but they can also remain involved for longer periods. This helps to increase their focus and eventually boost their efficiency.

There is, therefore, a wide range of toys suitable for infants and children, in stores like Kid Advance Montessori. There are various activity toys with which the kids can take great interest and stay active for longer periods, in addition to their schooling.

Sharing and Caring

Most toys are intended for group play. It improves children's cooperation and love. Group toys help children perform the activities in a group that makes them comfortable in their company and enable them to learn the quality of time and space sharing with each other.

Simple toys are suitable for babies and children with educational programs. Such instructional and interactive toys support the child's brain. Several options such as activities, games, puzzles, lacing, and sorting toys are ideal for building a foundation for children's skills in learning, interactivity and social competencies.

18

It Is All About Observing the Montessori Schemas From 24 Till 36 Months

I f your toddler doesn't fit the general description of the typical accomplishments, you may want to talk to your doctor, or you may want to simply back up in the book and work on the exercises for 24-month-olds. We want to make sure that your child is ready to be cared for in the particular ways that we describe. Your child's communication has likely exploded. They can be thoughtful, funny, and curious. They are trying on the varying shapes and sizes of independence in a thousand little ways every day. Don't be fooled. They are not adults. They do not have the same neurological capacities for logic, temper management, impulse control, and self-soothing that you do. You are still their primary source of calm, routine, and wisdom. Don't expect too little, but definitely don't expect too much. Their combustibility is a normal part of their development. Patience is your primary parenting tool right now.

Muscles

This kid moves at a surprising clip, and no obstacle gets in their way. Am I right? At two years old, your child has far better motor control than even a few short months ago. They can climb, run, jump, stand on one foot, and kick you in the shin. Their fine motor skills allow them to manipulate utensils and other small objects, scribble colorful pictures, and hold a cup in one hand. Their confidence and mastery in this area are but a reflection of the proficiency they feel in other areas as well.

Language and Communication

The dramatic increase of your toddler's language is exhibiting has allowed them to make meaning of other people's conversations finally, structure sentences with subjects and verbs, and sometimes hilariously, insert themselves into social relationships and communities. The gap between their expressive and receptive language is beginning to narrow. They are using language to interpret and create meaning and express their inner world. When they can't verbalize things, frustrations abound. The wonder of it all can be startling.

Social and Emotional

As new skills develop, so does the desire to exercise them. Your child's remarkable physical growth and communication prowess can cause conflict between them and their caregivers. They desire autonomy but still need limits to help them feel safe and manage the mass amount of information they take in every second. Their brains are growing quickly, and it is exhausting. Their abilities and skills have changed, and two-year-old overgeneralize this growth in all areas. They feel limitless—and the fact that they are not limitless can be a harsh reality for them.

Intelligence

Your child is entering a whole new world of play and imagination. They use their new motor skills to manipulate objects (such as trucks and dolls), tell stories, and make sense of their world. They can imitate the adults around them and mimic their routines. They are learning to interpret other people's emotions and create new ideas. Their thoughts are both practical and symbolic.

Wellness

Encouragement is a powerful tool for the development of self-esteem, but the way it is done matters quite a bit. When done well, praise is a powerful cure for hopelessness and failure. When it's done poorly, it can create feelings of helplessness in the face of challenge and reduce persistence. Since we want our children to be as resilient as possible, it is good to be intentional about the types of praise that we introduce.

Compliments have two distinct variations, each of which has very different long-term implications. I want to help you build your skills in the praise process.

Proper nutrition and good sleep hygiene are important for your child. There are plenty of online resources and, from your pediatrician, to help you determine the proper parameters for these things. We will focus on social-emotional wellness by building your skills of encouragement and praise.

Learning

This is a year full of wonderful leaps and bounds in development. Your toddler is experiencing drastic growth in their expressive language, their imagination, and their abilities to problem-solve and build relationships. Learning at this stage requires patience. A two-year-old kid needs calm and present caregivers to help them name and manage their growing internal world of feelings, thoughts, and impulses.

Reading together with your toddler at any age is always a good choice. At two years old, it's transformative. Reading together at this age builds language and vocabulary, creates meaningful conversations, nurtures their critical thinking, and supports their powers of problem-solving, attention, and determination. It also provides moments for a warmth, nurturing touch. When you read with a toddler, you create opportunities outside meltdowns to discuss fantasies, fears, and challenges. You create hospitality toward emotions and demonstrate empathic atonements.

Learning Skills at This Stage

Although, social-emotional competencies are very important. I also want to provide you a checklist of skills and activities for practice during your child's second year that will round out their thinking skills and get them school-ready—even if academics aren't necessarily a priority, getting your child ready to succeed in the educational environment matters.

As you go through this list, place a checkmark beside the things that you already do regularly. Look back at the end and celebrate what a great job you are already doing.

- Encourage your toddler to scribble with markers and crayons.
- Talk with your toddler about their day at dinnertime or bedtime.
- Regularly plan opportunities for your child to interact with others their age.
- Encourage your child to use logic by seeing how they make connections. For example, "I am hungry. What should we do next?" or "It is cold outside. I wonder what we should wear"
- Use a kitchen timer to help your child learn to wait.
- Read together.
- Follow your child's line of vision and notice the things that they are seeing.
- Ask questions even if they can't answer. Wonder together about cause and effect.
- Talk with your toddler about things you are doing, especially during food preparation, driving, playing, or doing chores.
- Acknowledge and label feelings while setting limits. "I know this is your favorite toy. Still, we are not allowed to grab it from our friends. I know it is frustrating. How can I help?"
- Avoid yes or no questions. Instead, be open-ended. "Tell me about..." or "What don't you like about...?"
- Don't be afraid of tantrums. They happen. The less you react, the more quickly they can recover. Count to 10 or practice a calming technique.
- Label your child's feelings. Validation always has to come before redirection or assistance coping. A child won't accept your wisdom until they feel your care.
- Use "Pretend" play to help your child handle new or challenging situations. If you ran into a problem yesterday, act it out with dolls today and wonder about better solutions.
- Let your child lead the play.
- Encourage your child's problem-solving skills with puzzles.
- Your toddler is asking questions. Ask them what they think before you answer. Be encouraging.
- Use big challenging words around your kids. They won't always get them, but new words will create curiosity and conversation.

As your toddler becomes increasingly aware of their individuality and their growing powers of movement, thought, and language, are driven to assert themselves. If your child isn't occasionally expressing their likes and dislikes in demanding, angry, or rude ways—then Houston, you have a problem. These things signal healthy neurological growth, happening in the context of a healthy parent-child relationship. Further, their "upstairs brain" is at the very beginning stages of development. This means that their capacity for self-control, logic, coping, and waiting is still very small.

Families that know how to stay calm, give choices, validate feelings, and set appropriate limits have the basic skills to intervene when the children are agitated. They can prevent further upset, create a loving environment, and avoid overly frequent explosions of temper.

People often want to know what to do when their child has a tantrum. We will cover those things, too, but I always start with prevention. "I hear your family is struggling through the tyrannical demands of your toddler, but first, let's see if we can reduce the frequency of outbursts." Not only do these skills curtail the number of tantrums, but they also make de-escalation much more comfortable to accomplish.

Discipline

I know you're eager to dive into discipline. Your child can feel like a brutal jerk sometimes, and you want action. I get it. We will tackle about discipline. For toddlers, the skills that I have reviewed are the foundation for all effective control.

- Understanding their limits.
- Holding your limits.
- Expressing empathy and offering validation.
- Thoughtfully considering their behavior and trying to create solutions that teach, comfort, and prevent further escalation.

Luckily, I've been working on these things. In addition to these, your discipline at this age, which is to say your caring behavior management and teaching, should also include an ample dose of two additional things:

- Ignoring inconsequential, unwelcome behaviors.
- Selectively praising all no problematic, value-affirming behaviors.

I want to leave you with one gentler reminder:

You are the anchor in the storm. You are a teacher. You can offer natural consequences, but be prepared to comfort their big emotions. Your first job is as a comforter and a teacher. Your role is not punishment. Discipline is not punishment, and you should never, ever, under any circumstances, spank or hit your child.

19

Boredom and Screen Time Gadgets and TV

It's no news that kids nowadays are born with in-built manuals for electronic devices and gadgets in their brains. Toddlers are attracted to anything that has a screen, but these screens, however, according to research, although they have their benefits, have been found to do more harm than good. Therefore, parents are warned to put a limit on the amount of time their kids spend on screens (TVs, video games, iPads or tabs, phones, and every other thing that has a screen). Babies in the age range of 0-18 months, advisably, are not allowed, in any form, to see the screen (except, maybe it's as important as videos chatting with family and friends-which helps in enhancing good communication skills). As they grow, they are allowed to use screens, bigger toddlers are allowed more time than more little ones, but the general maximum amount of screen time allowed for a toddler is One hour. Some parents need some space sometimes from their kids, like when they want to cook in peace or a little chat with their partner or some other important talk, so they just buy themselves some time by giving their kids the chance to use a screened device and do not care if the standard limit has been exceeded, it is okay to allow yourself at sometime to assign your toddlers adult chores but do not make it as a habbit, you can make this as your bonding but do not exceed on the limitations, instead, wait for your toddlers to be ready.

Screen Time for Toddlers

- 0 - 18 months: no screen time (except for video chatting).
- 18 - 24 months: some screen time with parental guidance.
- 2 - 3 years: a maximum of one hour a day (also with some parental guidance).

The Disadvantage of Screen Time

As much entertainment and enjoyment kids derive from these devices, spending too much time with them can cause some problems in the development of kids. When kids spend too much time on screens, they have no time for some real-life developmental activities in the sense that, they have lesser time to practice walking, they have lesser time for interactions which is supposed to build their communication skills and abilities. Too much time on screens can cause for a sedentary lifestyle, which in turn increases chances for obesity.

Therefore, the two major disadvantages of excessive screen time are:

- Setbacks in kid's development.
- Sedentary lifestyle that eventually causes obesity.

Tips on Handling Toddlers' Gadgets and TV

Set a daily schedule: A daily schedule has to be set a limit the screen time of your toddlers, a daily schedule that has a lot of non-screen time. Be sure to fix in other exciting, entertaining, and of course, occupying activities to keep them busy and stop them from believing that screens are the only option available in whiling away the time.

Give explanations: Use your words to let your kids know that too much time on screens can cause harm to their health, give them reasons why they can't watch the TV, or play their videos games, or watch Netflix.

Parental guidance: Your presence at screen time is very important, be with your kids at screen time so that you can guide them through what they are watching (or playing). This also creates a chance for interactions, thereby building their communication skills.

Only recommendable apps and games: In the case of apps and games, be sure that the apps you get for them are tested, trusted and recommended ones, that not only entertains but also educates. In other words, make their time spent in front of the TV or any app worthwhile.

Parental control: Be sure to make use of the parental control systems that are provided in TVs, phones, and other gadgets, in case of any form of absence.

When we think "toddlers," what comes after is "play," especially when we are busy, maybe doing some house chore or the other, we never believe our toddlers can be of help. Parents need to learn to understand their kids (even though it's easier to say than to execute); we also need to understand that toddlers, too, apart from tantrums and other displays of anger, can be severe at times. When they see us doing some things, they also want to try, but parents always think otherwise. Sometimes, when we even recognize their willingness to help, we simply refuse and tell them, "no, you'll get to help when you're bigger." We also just prefer to do these things by ourselves just because, if we allow them to do it, they end up messing it up, it is true toddlers aren't yet perfect at doing these things, but stopping them from trying doesn't help either. Allowing kids to help in house chores aids in their growth and development into adults.

Benefits

Below are some good returns of allowing toddlers to help with tasks.

Sense of belonging: When kids get involved in doing the household chores, they get the feeling that they, too, are recognized as an important part of the family.

Confidence builder: Being allowed to a part in the house chores make them know that you have trust in their abilities (no matter how tiny it might seem); this, therefore, gives them a level of confidence, which eventually becomes part and parcel of their personality.

Enhances their cooperation with others: Working together with your toddlers in doing house chores helps build their collaboration and cooperation skills. Working with other people won't be hard for them since it's what they've been doing since toddler-age.

Promotes appreciative spirit: When kids get appreciated for helping, they grow to become appreciative beings, since you are their role model.

Builds self-discipline: Self-discipline and responsibility-taking are also portrayed by kids who are involved in carrying out house chores.

However, with all these being listed, it's not all kids that want to help at all time, and getting them involved when they are not interested initially can be exhausting. Still, they can be left alone because toddlers need to be taught to help with house chores for their personality's sake, so some tips have been developed to get them to help.

Tips for Getting Toddlers to Help

Not by force: As I have always said, kids, like adults, never like being bossed around or dictated to, there is no room for dictatorship if you want to get them to help out with house chores or other things, let them decide they want to, when they are forced, there is a very high tendency for refusal.

Encourage collaborative work: Do not make tasks like clothes folding personal, instead of asking them to fold their own clothes while you fold yours, you can just allow them to fold anyone.

Expect and allow the mess. Help from toddlers can indeed make things a little slower, sloppier and messy. Still, you have to learn to allow for the mess to happen, although you will take care of it, it shouldn't be immediately, so as not to give your kid the wrong impression.

No task is too small: Be sure to expose your kid to every possible chore, give a wide range of tasks from helping while sweeping, to helping out in the garden, to helping with laundry and dishes. Do not limit their exploration, try and make them redirect their energy usage from throwing things, hitting, and all that show of power, into using it for useful work for the family.

Sense of contribution: The chores you let them do, of course, can't be "big," but be sure that the tiny ones they do are significantly important that it gives them the impression that they are truly contributing.

Kids also develop gross and fine motor skills when they carry out specific tasks (with parents' help, of course), involvement in chores also help sharpen kids' brain, which helps improve their problem-solving skills.

20

Nutrition and Sleeping Routine

One other thing to be taken care of in front of the babies or toddlers are that the parents must eat healthier too. If you keep on binging on fast foods and sweets, the babies will eventually want to imitate. If not given, they will throw tantrums and reject any other nutritious meal delivered to them. Children can be stubborn. However, if when start weaning your child you will do it with an open mind and expose them to all fruits, vegetables and protein sources one at the time, you will stimulate and train their palate, getting them used to most tastes and even learn what food they really do not like and the ones they actually love. Do not surround general misconceptions; Many little ones are fond of broccoli. Influence on them so extra care must be taken to avoid the risk of them going on little adventures of their own behind your backs just out of curiosity.

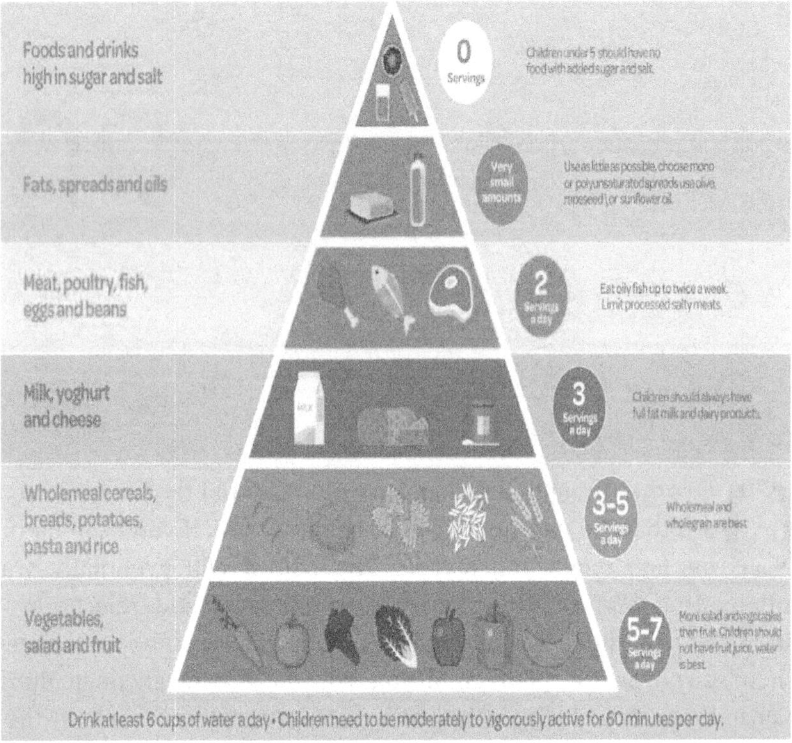

Foods and drinks high in sugar and salt
0
Servings
Children under 5 should have no food with added sugar and salt.
Fats, spreads and oils
Very small amounts
Use as little as possible, choose mono
Meat, poultry, fish, eggs and beans
2
Servings a day
Eat oily fish up to twice a week.
Limit processed salty meats.
Milk, yoghurt and cheese
3
Servings a day
Children should always have full fat milk and dairy products.
Wholemeal cereals, breads, potatoes, pasta and rice
3-5
Servings a day
Wholemeal and wholegrain are best
Vegetables, salad and fruit
5-7
Servings a day
then fruit. Children should not have fruit juice, water is best.
Drink at least 6 cups of water a day • Children need to be moderately to vigorously active for 60 minutes per day.

If, in the early years of life, your child becomes colic, often, it is nothing to worry about. Water with fennel seeds is a great remedy. Just take about a cup of hot water and boil fennel seeds in them, drain the water and give it to your baby by spoon. It helps with the pain. Other than that, gripe water can also be given.

Carbohydrates are an important source of energy for the child. Bananas, apples, strawberries, vegetables, oats, brown rice, quinoa, chia seeds, pumpkin seeds, lentils, kidney beans, peas, potatoes, hazelnuts, walnuts, peanuts, and many sweets things are rich in carbohydrates. They supply about 4 calories/g, and the main storage form of carbohydrates in the body as glycogen, which is broken down into glucose to be supplied as an instant form of energy. The regional daily allowance of carbohydrates is 130g/day.

Lipids and fatty acids, on the other hand, are also very important for a child's growth. Essential fatty acids such as Omega3 and Omega6 are very important for a child's brain and heart growth. These are also the primary source of energy used in the pumping of the heart. It has about 9 calories/g double to that of carbohydrates.

Lipid containing foods are nuts, chia seeds, fatty fish, eggs, cheese, avocadoes, and butter. The regional daily allowance of fats for children is 25g/day. Trans fatty acids like margarine used to increase the shelf life of food are very dangerous to health as they increase the quantity of low-density lipids and decrease healthy high-density lipids causing heart problems.

Proteins, on the other hand, are a good source of energy and help in the development of muscles. Foods containing proteins are meats, eggs, and dairy products. The regional daily allowance of proteins is 13g/day for children of 1 to 3 years. Some diseases due to deficiency in proteins are prevalent all around the world, which includes kwashiorkor syndrome. This occurs due to low protein intake. The growth is retarded with a protruding abdomen and many more problems. Another disease commonly caused by low-calorie intake is marasmus which is characterized by severe retardation with the facial appearance of an old man, a shrunken belly, weak and atrophic muscles with bodyweight less than 60% of normal. Hence, normal protein intake is very important in growing children as they need it for growing muscles.

Vitamins contain an adequate amount of minerals, which are essential for the baby's growth and development. The fact that these are included in a balanced diet is a good way to cover their daily needs. If your child does not like to eat certain foods containing vitamins and minerals, you must find an alternate source of it as they are widespread.

On the other hand, you must be clever with how to feed your child with certain foods. Some children hate vegetables, so cook things they like and add healthy foods in small portions so that they do not notice it. If they don't want to eat something, don't force that onto it as it will only worsen the situation. Try being a little flexible rather than forcing them to eat. They will eventually eat it when they feel hungry. Just try not to resolve the issue by feeding them snacks, particularly unhealthy ones. Otherwise, they will soon learn the strategy of avoiding meals to get the snacks. Another option is to try and get them used to smoothies where you can easily hide fruits, important nutrients like nuts, seeds, all vegetables, including avocados and broccoli.

While feeding, make sure your child is not talking a lot and sitting upright to prevent any danger of choking. If your child manages to choke himself with food, what you must do is come behind him and wrap your arm just around their diaphragm below the ribs and squeeze to push the food out in a gently way. First, you can try and pat their back and if that does not help, the above-mentioned technique is always there.

Make easy food for your children and pleasant tasting. Foods can be semi-solid or even fried for an older child as they tend to enjoy such things more. Snacks are important in a child's diet as they provide the energy and some calories in between the main diets.

Coke is a big no. Fresh juices are the way to go, but processed juices and foods should be avoided as they do more harm than they can do good. You must give your child occasional access to things they like, like ice cream and chocolates but not in excess as it will lead to dental cavities and obesity-related problems.

One other problem that the kids face is that they are forced to eat a lot, and when they start to get overweight, they already become habitual of eating more than required. The parents that restrict them from eating, which only adds on to the problems, they feel like they are not full and they still experience hunger pangs.

They get irritated and will eventually affect their day to day life leading to problems at school and home too. So, care must be taken in what you feed your child and by in much quantity. Excess of everything is bad.

Please take note that by applying a Montessori Method does not advice the sleep training or things like 'cry out.' However, by organizing activities, meals and naps and by following similar patterns every day avoiding overloading and overstimulation, toddlers should fall asleep more or less at the same time every night.

21

Writing, Reading, Music and Arithmetic, Movement, Arts and Crafts, Language

Structured play is often referred to as "play with a purpose." This approach employs entertaining quiz sports, games, as well as other activities to show a learning objective as well as helping young participants develop particular abilities or know certain theories. These preschool games and also different kinds of drama are directed by instructors (or by parents, at a house setting), that help the kids meet their targets or further comprehend the training aim. Structured play isn't necessarily formal or exceptionally coordinated; tasks within this category could consist of puzzles, games, music classes, organized sports, and on occasion, maybe folding clothes.

Although you may presume that the only thing about pre-school games is having fun, organized play may foster ample chances for the child to learn and build up their abilities and their personality.

Physical Development

Through play, your child will probably grow their fine motor skills and coordination. Preschool swimming lessons, football, or maybe a form of the grab can aid your child to become better organized and produce a historical love to get physical fitness center.

Agree with Skills: Preschool games such as "Simon Says," Duck, Duck, Goose," and "Follow the Leader" can foster coordination and fine motor abilities. They are also able to help your youngster develop their listening skills. By learning that after guidelines let them fare better at the match, your child should arrive to join this doctrine to the regions of your lifetime.

Social Interaction: In a conventional classroom setting, kids may not necessarily have the chance to create individual bonds together with their educators and sometimes even other students. Structured playlets for social interaction from the name of they are learning. By boosting the significance of communicating and personalized expression in early stages, your kid will appreciate these connections all through your lifetime.

Self-confidence

Your child will understand the importance of playing with being more independent and more self-assured. That's because organized play boosts the resolution of a creative problem and critical thinking. By mastering the aims put forth with the way of a specified activity or match, your little one will come to feel a sense of achievement they can execute to other areas. On the lookout for a fantastic preschool could be dangerous, when it might be challenging to find a quiz that provides both an academic-based program and ordered play. But your child will continue to learn and grow through such varied tasks in a variety of approaches.

Practical Exercises

Parental involvement is vital to some of the 1-year-old's development. Really, "parents interacting with them, teaching them matters, and exposing them into age-appropriate experiences and challenges" promotes interaction and exploration, says Dr. Myers.

But there's no need to pull a mountain of toys. All the whistles and bells; simple tasks also work. "I will sit with a young child with one particular block and also develop 100 distinct tasks as it's exactly about being lively and getting together using them," explains Roni Cohen Lederman, Ph.D., dean of the Mailman Segal Centre for Human Development in Nova South-eastern University, along with co-author of both Let us Play and Learn Collectively.

Not sure how to begin? We piled several interesting Learning actions for 1-year-olds in your home.

1. Create Music

Make audio utilizing percussion tools enjoy rattles, spoons, pans and pots, bells, cymbals, and drums. "Find interesting songs to play which possess a rousing be at," suggests Dr. Myers. "Perform together with her well as inviting her to play with herself."

Skills discovered: Listening skills, Coordination, and musical quest.

2. Play-house

Produce a fort out of a cardboard box, drama with the tube, or playhouse. Include an entry and an outlet, and invite your kid to move in and outside. You could have to reveal him first. Boost the entertainment variable with some play, such as rapping on the door or ringing the doorbell and asking if anyone's living, Dr. Myers suggests.

Skills learned: Social abilities, gross motor abilities, and investigating their environment.

3. Call a Friend

Hand a telephone for your kid and maintain you for yourself. Pretend to create forecasts and hold conversations with each other or fanciful men and women. Utilize funny voices, and make absurd characters on the opposite line. Some drama phones also permit one to capture your child's perceptions and play them straight back, which can improve the fun.

Skills discovered: Language and Social growth.

4. Utilize Water and Sand

Once your child reaches 18 weeks, fill a large bathtub with sand or water, and offer him free rein to dig, scoop, and much more. "If you are having fun with them, sing and talk together," says Dr. Myers. "Invite them to replicate everything you do, then try to replicate exactly everything they are doing." Never leave your child unattended around water. This enjoyable activity for a 1-year-old kid is especially beneficial for its creation of motor skills.

Skills heard: Creative drama, Fine motor skills, tactile stimulation, and societal development.

5. Talk Throughout a Tube

Talk via a cardboard tubing, and watch just how your baby reacts to this change from your regular voice. Let her choose a twist to find out what sounds she will create. "Children of this age want to play with speech, also this task gives them the chance to rehearse novel and new noises," Dr. Leiderman states. "Language is actually about copying sounds. Babbling turns in to real words, which turns out into a sense of humor."

Skills discovered: Auditory Discrimination, flip taking.

6. Fetch Objects

Send your kid on various "errands" around your home, requesting him to receive his shoes brings you the chunk or find his cup. Aside from practicing receptive language skills by adhering to guidelines, this learning task for 1-year-olds creates an awareness of liberty and achievement.

Skills discovered: Recognizing Instructions, memory skills.

7. Walk Contact Paper

Were they searching to get sensory activities for 12 months old? Cut a piece of contact at least 2 feet. Remove the tape and backing the touch paper, sticky side to ground, or carpet. Then make your child enjoy running, jumping, and dancing, or merely looking at the newspaper while wiggling their feet on the tacky surface. "That is a brand-new way of learning bodies," Dr. Leiderman explains. "Quite frequently, individuals as parents think we all now have to own rules for matches and do things in order. Sticky paper is only an enjoyable free for all." Parents may also put modest toys on the tacky surface and also let toddlers make an effort to pick them up.

Skills discovered: Sensory Awareness, muscle strength, human body awareness.

8 . Change Her Reflection

Put a dab of red lipstick onto your own toddler's face and distract her for a few minutes before placing her in front of a mirror. If your child responds to her image by touching her nose trying to wash off the mark, then it means she realizes there is something from the standard in her expression. "Tiny kids have no feeling of ego, however in that age, it's evident for those they truly are once they try the mirror," Dr. Leiderman states. But do not worry when she does not react yet—she will soon.

Skills discovered: Self-awareness and individuality.

9 . Count Fingers and Toes

Toddlers want to rely on their hands and feet, so reveal your baby just how to get each digit only once since you count out loudly. Do not worry if a kid stands outside of sequence, Dr. Leiderman states. "Children counting so isn't very important," she states. "Much like you are giving new words, amounts are a part of a lifetime. Use the context to rely on objects or feet. Therefore, they can learn the concepts of numbers finally."

For distinct variants of the learning activities for 1-year-olds, count on the staircase as you move down and up, add as you are waiting for your light to turn green, and then rely on the bubbles drifting in the atmosphere.

Skills discovered: Basic number Skills, one-of-a-kind correspondence abilities.

10 . Write on Crumbs

Spread rice or crumbled crackers in a cookie sheet, and then reveal your 1-year-old how to "write" from the grinds along with his palms. "This provides kids the opportunity to mimic the adults and older sisters in their own lives, and it can be a leading purposeful activity of early youth," states Rachel Coley, occupational therapist, writer of Simple Play

Skills discovered: Historical Handwriting capabilities, understanding cause, and effect.

22

Mechanisms to Follow the Montessori Style in the Outside Area

The mechanisms are as follows:

1. Creation of Outdoor Playhouses

The creation of an outdoor playhouse is a very splendid way to boost Montessori principles in the minds of the kids. When they are at the house, you have interior spaces designed for them, but when they are out, they need a similar attached house for their Montessori upbringing. The outdoor playhouses can be positioned at every corner of the lawn, and the children can get more and more about the level of Montessori in them. Finding a house for them, they can keep their environment for themselves, and they will feel liberated from daily chores in a respective manner. Thus, the creation of outdoor playhouses can boost more and more productivity in the kids and over time, they can evolve into good kids.

2. Designing a Play Area for the Kids in the Lawn

Swings, creative landslides, jumping rods, hanging rods and many other things can give more creativity to the kids in the lawn. With time, the kids can come up with an incredible amount of pleasure for the people. The kids need to learn all the prospects of a healthy regime, and they will do a lot for the people and children if they can play with the kids in the lawn. However, there might be a small issue in the making of the lawn because children are less assured of it, and they want to have fun within their Montessori ideas. But still, if you can make the Montessori in a lawn, then your kids can have all the entertainment for it, in no time.

3. Embankment Slide with the Door

The embankment slide is a jolly idea that is complacent with the Montessori slide. You are taking a ride outside the door, and your toddler sees this slide as a fun game to slide and come to the ground. The embankment slide can be made with every piece of intellect and intend to raise the kids in a good way, and the parents must not feel agitated while they are making it. The embankment needs to be assured in all possible ways with the help of other principles mandatory for the upbringing of the children.

4. Montessori Outdoor Exploration

The Montessori philosophy advocates that the child always pursues greatness and adventures. You have to create some anticipated adventurous moments for the kids that they want to travel in that specific area. Traveling is always food for health and nourishment, and it yields many productive modes of Montessori for the kids. You can design an adventurous outlook for a child, and over time, s/he will get to know more about the insight of himself. Also, he will be attracted to such a place, and in time, he will learn a lot for the home and from you. Therefore, create a Montessori outdoor exploration for the kids, and you will see magnificent results for the project.

5. Sequencing with the Plants

The children can learn a lot when they see the discipline shape of plants. Nature has an interesting way of providing education to the children, and the children will come across many habitual and productive ways to learn with nature. This is a Montessori activity for the kids, who want to learn Montessori outside. They will sequence with the plants, and hence, they will be learning the significance of preservation of plants for the kids. Therefore, sequencing with the plants is a healthy activity for the children to learn, and it needs to be done for the children by all means necessary.

6. The Journey of a Grain of Sand

A grain of sand travels a lot when it is nurturing, and the kids can learn the prospects of love and affiliation through it. The journey of a grain of sand can tell the children more about the respect of nature. The prospects of evolution and precision can be integrative for the child's conscience, and they can apply the journey of a grain of sand for their betterment. Therefore, the journey of sand must be taught to the children in all ways necessary.

7. Sand Tray Variation

A sand tray variation is a healthy exercise for the kids to know the prospect of art and love and education. For instance, if the kids are not able to learn letters of the language, then use a sand tray to teach them. In a sand tray, make the letters appear for the kids and teach them to emulate them. The children will learn many letters of any language through it, and since it is outside, they will have more and more fun while they do it. So, the sand tray variation is an outdoor Montessori space for the kids, who want to be independent.

8. Just One thing activity

If you want the kids to learn the art of story-making, then apply a story behind every piece of nature. Nature has many elements like trees and plants, and their stories can boost Montessori creativity in the minds of the children. Just one thing means that one story is applicable for one day and on a daily basis, the children can harness more and more skills while they are doing it. In this way, the just one thing activity will create more and more aesthetics for the child's brain, and over time, the children will learn more assertion in no time.

9. Story of a Tree

The story of a tree has many prospects and emblems for the child to understand. The journey of a tree started when a seed was sowed in the soil, and with proper making from the outsiders, the seed was able to be transformed into a tree. The tree has many components like the branches, seeds, fruits and branches, and later it can be very helpful for the child to understand the process of evolution. The child will also bear in mind that how did the tree prolong its growth pace and how it was able to survive the dark times of life. Thus, the story of a tree is a clever Montessori philosophy for the kids to understand.

10. Playing Games with Stones and Mud

Children learn a lot of Montessori when they are given stones and mud to play with. Clay is a basic ingredient used for the creation of men by the holy deity, and there is a special connection between clay and human. The soft-touch, the encompassing particles and the inducted creativity can teach the young child a lot about art and fashion. It is a healthy exercise for the brain, and the toddler will come up with greater evolutionary Montessori Methods. Plus, the clay will keep the child busy and avert him from any obscene and maleficent attributes by all means necessary. Therefore, playing games with stones is a source of time utilization and proper mental development for the toddlers. Parents must have use of it in all ways possible.

11. Learning About the Ecosystem

A child can learn about the ecosystem in a greater phase more than learning in the class. The teacher is not able to teach pupils more if they are able to teach them in the class and not let them get close to their natural instincts. The ecosystem is everything that the child needs to learn in the habitat of his house. Being a parent, you can teach him the processes of photosynthesis, the natural flow of sunlight and the presence of chemicals in the atmosphere. All such understandings can be given to the children in a greater phase, and people can learn more about the ecosystem in a faster phase.

Therefore, these are the activities that can be helpful for a better understanding of the Montessori philosophy outside the house.

23

Skills Essential in Child's Learning

There are different skills essential to our everyday living that we need to continue developing. The ability to think, visualize, and focus on something is basic to us humans that developing them is crucial to what you will be and where you will be in the future. These skills somehow determine your ability to decide and solve the problems you encounter.

Even children need these skills in their learning processes. To help your children develop these skills, you have to understand each of these skills to be able to guide your child in their learning development.

Critical Thinking

Critical thinking is a clear and reasonable reflective thinking focused on deciding what to do or believe in. It involves asking the 4 Ws (what, why, when, and where) and how questions to arrive at a certain decision. It involves many challenging assumptions instead of merely accepting someone else's idea.

If you want your child to excel in their learning, they must learn how to think. Although teaching them to read and write in addition to memorization and fluency in languages may help, they are not enough.

But how can we encourage our children to think critically when they are still too young?

Encouraging your children to be inquisitive—e.g. is to ask the question—in a field where they are experts; you will help develop this much-needed skill of critical thinking.

Even when you're too busy with something, do not discourage your children from asking questions. If you don't have the time or the focus to answer them, encourage them to explore for the answer but never make them feel they are neglected. Furthermore, encourage your children to report what they had learned from school and from there, ask them questions that go beyond the "what" like "why" and "how" to develop their inquisitiveness in school.

By asking children how they came to know the answer, they will learn to justify it, which requires them to reflect on their answer to support it. Also, make your child aware that how they see things could be different than how other people see it. For example, when your child talks to you about animal poaching, ask them why people are poaching and how it can affect nature and people in general.

Finally, you can ask them how to solve the problem. You will be surprised at how children will answer your question. Children learn faster than adults because their prefrontal cortex, where working memory is stored, is developed more quickly at this point. In adults, they begin to develop functional fixedness where adults see everything exactly as they are. Let's say, an adult can see a broomstick as it is, while from a child's viewpoint, they can see it like a javelin stick. This is due to the creativity produced by their prefrontal cortex, giving them the ability to be inventive and flexible.

It is likewise fascinating to know that children can be very creative and constantly discover new things.

Therefore, by encouraging your children to be inquisitive, it would be a great way to help them develop their skills and talents while still very young.

Critical thinking is not just for children. This is applicable even for adults. We can also improve our critical thinking skills by asking a few questions each day.

Here are some examples of how to improve your child's critical thinking:

- Guessing the toy will enhance your kid's critical thinking because they will have to make some guesses that will develop their way of thinking.
- Making a new menu with your child will enhance their critical thinking because they will come up with new meal ideas that will develop your child's love for food.
- Food Tasting will enhance your child's critical thinking because you can ask them the foods that they like and dislike. This will help because they will be introduced to new foods.
- Browsing at the Family Photo Albums will enhance their level of thinking because it leads to a deeper level of learning.

Analytical Thinking

To solve problems, we often break them down into smaller chunks so it will be easier for us to deal with them piece by piece. We call this analytical thinking. It allows children to solve complex issues by filtering through relevant information and identifying patterns and trends. It is a significant skill that everyone needs to achieve success in school, at work, and throughout life.

How to Develop Analytical Thinking Skills?

Let Them Solve Math Problems

Solving problems is a common and easy way to improve analytical skills. Math depends on logic, and mathematical problems are structured in ways that children are given a certain amount of information. The problem must be solved using only the provided facts. You may correlate everyday life with math problems and allow your children to solve them.

Provide Them with Learning Opportunities

Children learn through exploration and discovery. Providing them with more tools and resources will help them get a better understanding of the world, and this understanding will help them solve problems. Resources could be in the form of books, newspapers, videos, science magazines, or community classes. There is a vast range of information that one can easily reach via the internet, but make sure that you are properly guiding your children when using these unlimited resources of information.

Visualization

Visualization is a technique to help your child create images, diagrams, or animation to relay a message. Using visualization through images, visuals, and graphics has been an effective way to communicate concrete and abstract ideas.

In learning, visualization is a cognitive tool that accesses imagination to realize all aspects of action, object, or result.

Often, we find children who have vision problems and cannot visualize or create images in their heads. However, once corrected, there can be a significant improvement in reading.

Here is the best method to help your child learn the skill of visualization. Show them a picture and allow them to examine it for about 5 minutes. After the allotted time, ask your child to draw what they have seen.

Focus/Concentration

Some children are struggling to pay attention in class and having a hard time completing homework and class activity due to lack of focus and concentration. Issues like these can have a big impact on a child's performance at school.

There can be many reasons why a child finds it hard to focus—it could be from organization problems or comprehension. What is important is that it is possible to help your child improve their focus and concentration.

- Let your child have a complete sleep.

- Ask your child to play some memory games like crossword puzzles, jigsaw puzzles etc.

- Always serve your toddlers some dark chocolate and nuts for it has powerful anti-oxidant properties that enhance focus.

Tell Them to Do One Thing at a Time

For children with issues on focus and concentration, multitasking is a problem. Jumping between activities causes them to lose momentum. To avoid this, train your child to do one thing at a time instead of working on many things at once. This will teach them to focus only on what is before them rather than thinking of many other things which only leads them to accomplish nothing.

Break Things into Smaller Pieces

Some tasks become unmanageable for children, so teach them to break big tasks into smaller ones to improve their focus as things become manageable for them.

Learning How to Deal with Distractions

Distractions can be everywhere, and you can't completely safeguard your child from all distractions.

However, you can train your child to avoid them. Mindfulness techniques, which are a form of meditation, is one of the best ways to teach your child to gain focus.

- Always take away distractions like toys when your child is trying to focus

- Always explain the challenges your child is experiencing in a positive way to make them more motivated

- Allow your child to take some frequent breaks for them to relax.

24

Mistakes Parents Make When Listening to their Kids

Sometimes, instead of listening to your child, parents make the mistake of talking too much. This happens mostly when a child has made certain mistakes and you want to discipline them. Talking too much will have an impact on how your child listens to you. Also, your child will know that you rarely listen to them. So, the best way of responding to you is by shutting you off.

It is crucial that you embrace the idea of listening more and talking less. This provides you with an opportunity to understand what your child is going through. Maybe some of the mistakes they are making stems from anger. As such, by listening to them, you can help them find a solution for dealing with their emotions. Ultimately, this prevents similar incidents from occurring.

The prefrontal cortex (logical section of the brain) only develops completely once one is aged 25. This means that the emotional brain and the limbic system are the parts of the brain that children use to make decisions. Unfortunately, parents fail to realize that their kids cannot reason or think as logically as adults. They expect much more of them than is developmentally available. Keeping this in mind, a one-year-old child will comply with instructions only 40-50% of the time. On the other hand, a four-year-old child will comply with instructions about 80% of the time.

This shows that parents need to realize that their kids are still in their development stages. Hence, there is no need to yell at them when they are not listening to you. In fact, as an adult, you should be there to listen to them and guide them appropriately.

For parents with more than one child, there are times when kids can just frustrate you beyond limits. For instance, consider a scenario where you are preparing dinner while doing your best to make sure that your little angel doesn't cry that she is hungry. On the other side of the kitchen, your son is busy trying to open the refrigerator. As you juggle with all of these things, you can easily lose patience with your child and shout at them. Sorry to say this, but this is a terrible mistake.

Responding to havoc with havoc doesn't teach a good lesson about listening. It is no wonder that your kids will also want to respond to you by yelling or screaming at you. They learned this from you.

There are other times when parents shout at their kids to stop their tantrums. This is especially true for kids who are less than five years old. The truth is that you do not understand how your child is developing and how they cope with emotions. Tantrums are just part of a healthy way to express themselves. With the help of these tantrums, children can understand their social boundaries. Given time, they will realize that this is not the best way to get your attention. So, while they are still young, please listen to them and help their brains develop the right emotional regulation tactics.

Before you can give instructions to your children, you must get their attention first. Many times, parents shout at the top of their voices without first finding out if their children are listening. The best way of teaching your kids to listen is by ensuring that you have their attention before saying anything. Just to remind you, you should make eye contact and use appropriate body language to get their attention.

Tips to Consider When Listening to Your Kids

The fact that you want your kids to listen to you should be a convincing reason for you to listen to them. Listening to your child increases the likelihood of being listened to. The following are considerations you should have in mind.

Another effective strategy of listening to your kids is by listening to yourself before saying anything. Stop to think for a moment about how you plan to respond. Doing this will prevent you from making rushed decisions that will affect the good relationship you have with your kids. It is worth noting that your emotions can easily get the best of you, especially when you are frustrated or angered. Sure, you might not mean the bitter words that you will be saying to your child but rest assured that your child will never forget.

Your child will be hurt emotionally. So, instead of making harsh statements like "You dumb fool" or "You stupid idiot" or "Now is not the time to bother me," take a deep breath and listen to yourself.

Taking a pause will give you a few moments to consider whether your actions and statements will have a negative impact on your child's self-esteem. Take note that if you constantly criticize your child, they will think that they are not worthy of attention. As such, you will be psychologically affecting them. Eventually, this will have an impact in all areas of their social lives.

Also, there are other times when your children might misbehave, and you don't know how to approach the situation. Often, parents will choose to lecture their kids about the bad behavior that they exhibited. This strategy never works as kids will only think that their parents talk too much. This will lead to them shutting you off and waiting for you to complete your lecture before they can do whatever they were doing.

The mere fact that you will be doing your best to listen to your kids more doesn't mean that you should be pushy. Don't ask your child about how they are feeling and be pushy about it. If they respond with one syllable answer, relax. Give them time. They might not be ready to open up. You should make it clear to them that they can talk to you whenever they feel like and that you are always there to listen to them.

The space you give to your kids helps them to reflect on how they are feeling and try to manage their emotions on their own. With time, they will open up as you had made a promise to listen to them.

Certainly, your children will not connect with what is important in their lives. This is because you are constantly reminding them of what they should not do. Why don't you change this by engaging in inspiring conversations with them? This way, they will begin to see and relate to important things that could change their lives for the better.

Taking everything into account, there is a lot that should be considered when listening to your kids. Your aim should not be to lecture your kids around without first understanding their feelings. Parents should realize that children expect them to listen and help them manage their emotions. Therefore, they should not expect a lot from their kids since they are still growing. Before talking to your child, you should pause for a moment and think about what you are about to say. Will your statements hurt your child? It is crucial that you think over your responses before saying anything. This guarantees that you don't end up hurting your child out of anger. Generally, parents should develop an understanding attitude toward their young ones.

25

When Your Child Needs Special Help

There are certain situations in life when you need to pay special attention to your kid. It is not necessary that your kid needs special attention only when he is with some special needs. A normal kid in his life needs some special attention to meet up the regular challenges. The core concept to understand is the need for such help in the normal routine as well.

Unable to Focus

If your kid is unable to focus on anything, whether it is a practical demonstration or learning, then you should get an idea of something happening wrong. Maybe the kid is not interested in the activity or exposed to some confusion or fears. You can help the kid in understanding the activity and help him to focus on the situation without getting worried about anything else.

Example:
- You can help a kid focus on something by doing one task at a time and always bring in planned breaks that would help the kid relax.
- Always set a reasonable time for doing a task, manage your child's time well.

Having Sleep Issues

One of the core issues that kids have is in bedtime. Sometimes they are feared of darkness, isolation or nightmares as well. In such a situation, forcing the kid to sleep is not a good idea. You need to make him deal with the situation and fight back all the ideas and fears in his mind.

Example:

- Read Meditation stories that will help the child relax and fight his/her fears.
- Create a good sleeping routine before going to bed; you can also give your child a warm bath to help him/her relax.

Health is Not on a Good Note

When the kids are not feeling well, they are in a vulnerable situation. They can react to different things all the time. Mood swings, anger, sadness all of these feelings can come up together or on an interval basis. You need to understand the situation and help our child to overcome the fear or feeling of not being so well in that specific time.

Examples:

- Always give your child the freedom to play indoors/outdoors or with you.
- A child must feel the love, support and understanding from their parents.

Unable to express

Some kids are not good with expression. They do not have any idea about the selection of words or expressions to say what they feel. When there is a situation of unrest, you need to help the kid by understanding behaviors. At this time, you can rescue the kid by helping him in feeling comfortable telling you what is cooking insides his mind.

Mixed feelings of anger, excitement and sorrow

One of the critical situations with a child is when he is unable to identify the real feeling. At this time, he behaves differently due to the mixed emotions toward a happening or person. You need to help the kid about knowing that is happening to him and why. Moreover, you should help the kids to deal with such conditions efficiently.

Examples:

- Always talk to your child what issues/problem is making him/her worry.
- Teach some breathing exercises that would help your child to relax.

Growing as a Family: Finding Support, Resources, and Sanity

Positive discipline is not about letting your kid learn all the things independently. It is not a kind of high school training where your kid needs to learn everything on his own. It is about a family, a home and all the peers together. If you want your kids to be healthy in body and mind as well, you need to grow as a family.

Family is not just about having food together, living in a house, going on vacations and all the good things. Family is there for anyone in the hard times and bad things as well. To encourage positive discipline in your kids it is necessary to make them understand the need and importance of the family.

A person craves for three things from his family, support, resources and sanity. All these three things have integral importance in the overall learning of kids and their growth as well. The most important thing is to consider that without these three elements, a family cannot have a healthy future.

Hit the Help Resources

Finding the resources to help your kids and family is another important thing that makes a family. If there is something that happened wrong, there is a fault line in your kids or a deficiency; you need to hit the right resources to help. These resources can be of personal, individual, family-based and outsourced as well. You need to identify the appropriate resource as per the need.

Medical Attention

Feeling unwell is one of the common problems faced by the kids. Anything new happens to them makes them feel sick. It is not about the real medical problem all the time but sometimes a change in hormone, conditions and brain activities. Sometimes, kids can be serious too. Medical changes are a kind of complex issue that can hit the kids badly. In such matters other than family support and condolence, medical attention and professional help are necessary. Make sure to be with your kid all the time, as it is necessary for him to have someone he can trust and rely on. It can help the kid in not to panic.

Additional Attention

Sometimes kids need additional or special attention when going through a feeling or phase. Mostly it happens in case of any loss, trauma or bad health. You need to use your attention as a resource and give the maximum attention and time to the kid. It will help him to get close to you and open to the issues and problems. The close relation can help to make things even better between the families and keep the unit connected.

Discussion and Debate

Sometimes the perceptions about the problem are not good enough. You need to discuss and debate the issue with the kids. At this moment, the kids can express what they feel and the real problems they have regarding a specific issue. This can actually help in making a real difference in the overall situation. As a family, it is important to discuss issues, conflicts and problems with each other in a healthy environment.

Educational Grooming

Sometimes there are behavioral issues that kids have shown in certain situations. It is because they do not have any education about dealing with the situation. You need to invest time and look into the educational grooming of the child. It is about solving the problem he is having inside the mind and make things even for the rest.

Getting Study Kits

If the child is unable to study well, then you can get him the study kits. These resources help a child to know things better. Using simple and easy themes, these kits can breakdown the complex terms easily and let the kid know better and more. You need to select these kits carefully to get the right results.

Understand the Variation

It is not necessary that all the kids are of the same nature and have the same needs, behaviors and reactions to the things. If your kid is behaving differently than others, it is necessary for you to know that everyone is different from each other. This variation is the beauty of humankind. This difference makes a person capable of doing something different from the other do. To grow as a family, you need to understand this concept of variation and take further steps for improvement.

Explore the Options

Other than support, resources and understanding, there are multiple options you have to make your family stronger and kids table. Remember, it is not necessary that if you have a challenging, kid only then you need to pay extra attention. For every kid, there is a need to look around for the best options and get the right things in the box. Every single kid is different, and you need to explore the options for all your kids differently. You cannot match all your three kids – if there are – with each other and expect them to behave the same way.

Here are some other practical things that you are supposed to consider and work on:

Match Interests

Being a parent, you need to be the closest friends to your kids. It is only possible when you are sharing the same interests with them. It is not possible that the whole family will have the same interests, but they can grow. As parents, you can set up some of the common habits for all the kids so everyone can have a good time together. On the other hand, do not restrict any new interest of your kids. In fact, you can participate in other activities with them so they can rely on you. It will help you kids, so share what they feel and how they perceive the other things around. Moreover, you can help them grow better by knowing things better.

Examples:
- Be your child's best friend, support him with his likes and hobbies
- Develop bonding and activities that you can enjoy with your child

Participate in Making it Rational

If your kids are differently doing something because they are unable to do it the way others do, then it's fine. You do not have to be worried, instead of getting them out of their comfort zone, you are supposed to make their zone comfort for themselves. As far as your kid is trying hard to be something, so you are supposed to help in with that. Your participation in the task can make this unique style rational, and it will not make your kid feel awkward about it. Something with participation can make your kid learn the right or rational way to do something. All you need is to observe, participate, and anticipate the problem.

Examples:
- Participate in the activities your child likes to do to show your support and guidance
- Let your toddler enjoy what he likes; let him discover new things.

Boost Your Kid's Confidence

If your kid is doing something different, that is not as per the specific gender or social roles for him. You are supposed to support him in every manner. It is important to boost his confidence with the best arguments and tools. You can make the kid feel normal about his diversity and do not make him answerable for the diversity in him. The actions of support can help him to be better with everything exclusive he holds in himself.

Examples:
- Always remember to appreciate your child's effort no matter what

they do. Win or lose, show your support.

- Always let them figure out their problems themselves (but with your guidance, of course) and let them act their age.

26

Why Montessori style Spaces Are Important?

The following are one of the many reasons why Montessori style spaces are important.

1. Creativity

Montessori style of spaces are important in a manner that they give creativity to the mind of the toddles, and by all means, they are able to get more and more about their intellectual level. You will notice that in a Montessori style of space, the kids are able to see more bright colors and formations on the wall. They see more cartoons and depictions on it with time. They are able to garner more knowledge and ideas about things that hit the minds of the toddlers. They can receive an equal amount of courage and stamina for watching the Montessori depiction, and they will finally come in contact with the purpose of excellence for the kids. Thus, the edifice of creativity is very acceptable for the kids, and they are able to get to the most required amount of acceptance that they want from a Montessori Principle. This is the reason why you are able to induce creativity in the minds of the public due to which you are all fine and great in the coming matter. Therefore, creativity is given to your child through a Montessori style space.

2. Playing With Toys Encourages Stamina and Love for Others

Often, in a Montessori style of teaching, the toddlers play with the toys so that he can learn the art of passion and compassion for others. The toys of the children are the tactics and techniques that the child can learn more and more about life.

3. Using the Style for Activities

In the Montessori style, the places are utilized for many activities. Activities like painting, music and art play are important for the kids to learn, and they develop great skills in the kids so that people can learn more and more about it. The style is simple that the children be allowed to do whatever they want to do, and with time, they can reach the zenith of life and space. The activities are positioned at every corner of the room, and the parents are allowed to teach the child more and more about the working of the room. The first and foremost impediment to this activity can be in the form of painting and coloring. The painting and coloring can help make the kids more productive and get all the possible accessible versions of it. There is enough room in the mind of the public, and the kids can also qualify for the benefit of themselves.

The style of activities is pertinent for the kids to learn at all means necessary, and you can come up with any possible discretion to get to the best of your kids. So, the best use of these activities is to give your child a possible way to groom and evolve.

4. Montessori Style Teaches the Importance of Reflection

In a Montessori style of decoration, the child is blessed with a plethora of mirrors that are placed at many angles. They are placed at many angles so that the child can see his-self and can get to know himself coherently. The idea is that the child is not able to recognize his eyes, ears and hair or any body part by the name of them, and as a child, it takes time for them to recognize it. However, when you have a toddler toddling on the floor, and at the moment, he reaches on the floor and looks himself in the mirror, he sees a different yet disparate himself that is apparent. He sees a different version of himself in the mirrors and he gets himself by all means. He is able to see his eyes, ears and hair and all of a sudden, he has a new friend to get acquainted with.

146

Therefore, the child is able to get all his ills and whims efficiently. The whims are that he sees himself and the ills are that there are wrong modes in his brain that need some change. Thus, the importance of reflection is harnessed when the Montessori style spacing is implemented at the earliest.

27

Montessori Activities

List of Montessori Activities for the Toddlers

Following are the list of the Montessori Activities that are exhibited in Montessori Schools that you can replicate at home.

Music and Dance

In this activity, the students or toddlers are taught to dance and respond to the audio messages positively. The parent is also allowed in this class, and the students are taught to dance while a parent is holding his hand and having fun while doing it. The child also listens to a beautiful and soft music tone that gives child momentum to move his limbs. The child is allowed to murmur beautiful songs and audible tones that reflect the inner artist of the child, and he feels very happy while he is doing it.

Reading Books

These are not big and illustrative books but are designed in a unique way to let the child understand the picture with full sheer responsibility. There is a book that has multiple pages in it, and each page has one picture in it that the child understands carefully. The picture can be of any content intended to explain the child of the nature of the content. For example, at infancy, the child is not able to understand the shape of a car, and he must be illustrated with an example. The car is a perfect example, and he can easily understand the idea of a car while looking at the picture. The same is for any other thing.

Music Box

This activity is essential for the development of the child. Still, it should be said that this activity is for the nurturing of the soul, and it allows the students to learn things more quickly. It is a hanging box, and to activate it, children need to pull the string attached to it. This box plays a classical tone of the music of children, and the children are able to enjoy more music out of it by all means necessary. It is also used as an instrument for nap changing. The students can take napes while they pull the string and take a nap while the music is being played.

The Interlocking Circles

This activity is designed to infiltrate the mind of the child with mathematical quotations and mathematical expressions. Two graphical circles are given to the children, and they are taught hypothetically how to join them. At first, they are given the understanding of circles that are circles and then they are allowed to join the circles by giving them to shapes. These two shapes are interlocked with one another, and then they are attached using the grips. The older babies are allowed to transfer the load with the circles; hence, the children are able to get the bigger picture of the pictures acceptably.

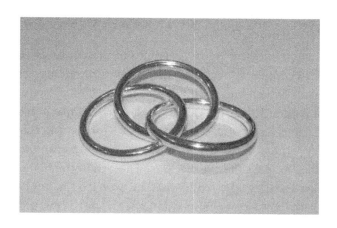

Making Stylish Papers

This activity is yet another activity that is designed to increase the visual development of the students. The toddlers are given a pack of papers, and they are shown first the art of making a figure, and they are explained how to make them. For a horse, the teachers will first teach them the art of making a horse by making them cut various specimens of the paper. Then the paper will be attached so that the horse will be made and then used for proper productivity. Fishes, pinwheels and dancers are of the many examples that can be harnessed in this regard.

Making Wooden Figures

This activity creates more creativity in the minds of children. There are wooden chopped figures, and then there are pictures that are put in front of them. The children are advised to make the wooden shapes with the help of parents, and they can learn the possibilities of more inclusivity through it. There is an attractive color that is present in them in terms of more variety and vitality. Hence, the wooden figures can be used in many more designs as possible by the kids. The activity enhances the further evolutionary escapes in a child that he governs in himself with time. Therefore, this activity is more fundamental in terms of progress and productivity.

Using a Rubber Ball With Protrusions

A rubber ball gives a lot of knowledge to a young toddler, who has to learn a lot. There is a rubber ball, which is placed in the hands of the toddles, and they are allowed to do a lot of learning through it. The ball has many protrusions on it, and the child can suck on it and learn to grasp it. When the ball comes to an older toddler, the child will learn to grasp it and try to play with it. In this way, the toddler will be able to hold the ball and play it in all the possible manner and tactic. Therefore, the rubber ball has many learning aspects for the toddler and the infant; thus, the activity of using a rubber ball has many benefits for the people.

Toying With Little Balls

This activity is another mode for teaching the infants the mode of grasping other things and maneuvering them for their good. Some balls are placed in front of the toddlers, and they are advised to play with them. Once they play, they fall and with every fall, they learn their lesson. Hence, the activity is a very inspirational mode of learning for the toddlers, and they become very bright and active while they toy with little balls.

Grasping Beads

This activity is very interesting for young toddlers to learn and they can great skills while they do so. They have to grasp the beads, and they have to make the arrangement of it strictly and cohesively. They have to identify which of the loop will come first and how they can relate it with the other character. Therefore, the grasping beads need to be arranged so that the maintainers can get the uttermost benefit of it.

Ringing a Bell on a Ribbon

The bell, which is on the ribbon, can ring many times and the children who ring them, can develop many auditory and visual developments in them. The ribbon is provided to them and they are told to ring the bell, which is attached to the ribbon at a distance. They can learn the music tone of it. Children can also come in the cognition of placement of ribbons, and they learn an important value of the bell that it is very fundamental in coming to everyone's house. Also, the ribbon is present in many colors, and those colors are used to induce a good sense of imagination in the children. Hence, this visual Montessori Activity is very crucial for the children to accept.

Interlocking Rings

Another Montessori activity designed for the child's visual development. This development enhances the grasping abilities of the child, and he can learn to hold things effectively. There are two or three rings that are of three colors like red, blue and green, and they can be used also to give visual development to the children. Therefore, the interlocking of rings is another Montessori activity for the individuals.

Home Objects

This activity is essential for children to bear the manipulation in the children's mind, and these are some small home objects that can be accessible by the children. These objects include honey dipper, dolly clothes, spoon, belt buckle, bangles and keys. Children are given these materials, and they are taught to hold them in their hands, through which they can learn more and more about the grouping of home materials.

Bamboo Cylinder Rattle

This is an audible educational activity that vouches to induce sounding in a child. Through it, the child can learn more and more about the voices of the bamboo, and this bamboo is used for the students to make the grounds of him more effective. The rattle is made of tinny pebbles and chains that can be sewed together and can be used for the child to learn the art of the bamboo cylinder.

Cylinder Rattle With Bells

This is a cylinder rattle with bells that is designed for the student to learn the music of the tone. This is a sanded smooth that is attached to some bells, and it is a given in the hands of a child so that he can learn the art of music from it. Some sharp bits can be used to trigger some noises in the baby, and the baby can learn a lot of new tactics through it.

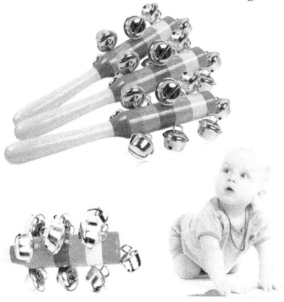

Cube With Well

The cube with the well is given to the children, so that they increase their volitional development. The development is composed of the thesis that it deals with the ability to check the motor skills and the grasping abilities of children. Also, with the cube and a ringing well in it, the children can get closer to noises and voices. These noises eventually can give more sounds to the children, and children can get more attachment to it just because they get more acquainted with it.

Bells on Leather Strap

The attached leather can help the child to bolster their holding abilities. With the Montessori philosophy in mind, they can renovate the mentality of children in a sound manner. The bells, again, give a voice development to the children to learn more about voice concerns in it.

Toying With a Suction Cup Base

For eye-hand coordination, the suction cup base is the best toy to play with. The idea behind it is very simple that the infant needs to put the toys on the suction base, and he needs to be very managerial while doing it. There are child bats, reaches and attempts that can give kids more efficacy in it and they should be able to get more perception-based approach by all means necessary. Therefore, the clever toying can help children more affectively, and they can easily reach the acme of their childish nature.

28

The Commandments of Toddler Discipline

Disciplining an elementary school kid is very different from when you try to do the same for a toddler. The older kid understands language, and they know the rules. They know that mummy or daddy said we should not touch the TV because it may fall and break, and that means we shall have nowhere to watch cartoons. A toddler wonders why they cannot touch that beautiful screen and probably thinks that you are mean—or that they are being kept from the fun stuff.

Does it mean that you let them off the hook probably because you think that they are too young to understand rules and consequences? Not! You want to bring up a good world citizen and a member of your family, don't you? Then do not spare that toddler; teach them to do right.

However:

Discipline for a toddler is quite a touchy issue, and every parent who has succeeded in raising well-mannered and intelligent children has had to learn the following commandments—mostly the hard way. In the practical ways to deal with behavior and emotional challenges, you will notice that the solutions to these issues rely on the commandments below. Observe them as you discipline your child, and you are likely to have an easy time and successfully achieved the desired results.

Statements Must Be Short and Sweet

Their little minds cannot comprehend long sentences. For this reason, you find that they only understand short statements. For instance, they will understand "come here," "no biting," "stop," "no," "no touching."

However, if you go for "Liam, you know it's not good to bite your friends" or "Mandy, you need to stop pulling on the cable." Trust me; you will lose Liam right after "you know" and Mandy at "you need." Just say "Liam, no biting," or "Mandy, stop pulling."

Please, No Yelling

The loudest voice you can use may stop your child from doing whatever—or not, especially when it becomes a habit. However, it signals that you are losing control—of yourself and the situation, and your lovely child may get scared of your voice, but they are not going to respect.

All of us yell at times, but you realize that at those moments, you are not feeling in control—and that little one notices it too. Do not be surprised when they assume your instruction when you yell.

Do not yell. What you do is change your voice. Understand that it's not the volume, but the tone of your voice that communicates and gets the points across. Remember how that soft-spoken teacher was the most respected—and most strict? You probably had a funny name for the yelling one you never listened to—you do not want to be this one.

Therefore, you may want to focus more on tone and keep your volume normal when instructing a toddler.

Act Immediately—on the Spot

They do not have a long-term memory to remember what they did and also, they do not have the mental capacity to connect previous action and present consequences.

If your child is doing something wrong, you should never postpone serving the consequences. If they need to be disciplined, it has to be done right on the spot of action. Do not wait because five minutes later, s/he will be onto something else, and they won't remember what wrong they did to deserve punishment.

Do not Make Promises as 'Pay' for Good Behavior

"If you eat your food, I'll buy you chocolate," "if you are nice to your friends, I'll get you that toy you want" it works, doesn't? They will do what you want to get that reward—no arguments or rebellion. Phew!

It's easy and that's why it's very tempting. Do not do it. It's true you will get them to behave, especially when you offer something they love. However, what you will have succeeded in doing is to bring up a two or three-year-old who knows that any good behavior has a price tag. You do not want your child to turn out manipulative or corrupt, do you?

Choose What Battles Are Worth Fighting

You do not want to fight with your child every time over every little thing they do. They will assume that you are always fighting or saying "no" and won't pay attention to your correction. For instance, if you say "don't touch" 25 times a day, eventually, it will lose its effectiveness—and they will touch.

Therefore, pick your battles. Have behaviors you cannot condone and those that are too insignificant to bother with.

For instance, if they scream every time you pick a call, just ignore them. Eventually, they will know that they will not get a reaction out of you and drop the behavior.

Condemn the Behavior, Not the Child

You love your child, don't you? You want to raise a child who knows that their parent loves them. However, we sometimes jeopardize this when we start to condemn our children when they behave badly, instead of focusing only on the behavior.

162

Always tell them that a particular behavior s bad; never tell them that they are bad. Tell them that what they did was something foolish, but do not tell them that they are fool. This is the best way to communicate, "I love you, but I do not love the way you are acting right now" or "you are smart, but what you are doing isn't that smart."

Correct, Redirect, Repeat

When with a toddler around the house, you'll probably do this all day. You will catch them doing something they shouldn't, tell them "no," and attempt to distract them with a different activity. Chances are, they will try to go back to the previous "wrong activity," which they find to be entertaining for some reason and see if they can get away with it.

It can be frustrating, but if you want to etch the "I should not do this" memory in their little brain, you should not give up. Correct, redirect and repeat even if they have returned to that activity for the tenth time.

There Shall Be Consequences for Actions

Teach your child that there are outcomes for their behavior. They need to understand that actions come with consequences—a lesson that will be of great help in their adult life.

Some consequences include missing out on activities they love, the time-out corner and so on. For instance, if they bite or hit their friends while playing, they ought to know that it will automatically earn them some time in the time-out corner, alone and with no one to play.

Note: missing out on your love should never be a consequence. Do not push them away or refuse to cuddle, comfort or be there for them when they genuinely need you as punishment.

You Shall Not Back Down or Compromise to Avoid Conflict

Sometimes it's tempting to let them have their way, especially when they roll, scream and kick in a public place, and everyone is giving you the "give them what they want so they can shut up" look.

If you want to reinforce or discourage certain behavior, you will need to be consistent in the direction you give your child. There shouldn't be times you allow them to do something you do not want them doing just to prevent a meltdown. For instance, if you said they cannot have candy, stick to your guns even when in a supermarket, and they are standing right in front of it screaming their lungs out.

You see, the message you want to send them is, "you cannot have candy," not "you cannot have candy, but you can grab all you want if you scream loud enough." Remember, toddlers are experts at studying your game, and they will know what drives you to give in—they will do it all the time.

Always Give Them Choices

Make your child feel important and in control by giving them a chance to choose. You do not want to raise a child, who knows only to be dominated, never being able to make their choices, do you?

However, there shouldn't be many options to choose from, as this may confuse the child. Also, they should include the things you want to accomplish. For instance say, "It's your choice: You can put on that dress or this one."

Be a Reflection of What You Want to See With Your Child

Kids do not do what they are instructed to do. They are most likely to learn their behavior and communication skills from their environment. You are their first contact with the world, and therefore, they will learn from you. That kid you think to be too little to see and understand is observing your every move. They are learning how to handle situations and how to talk by watching you

.

Therefore, you have to model the values you want your child to adopt. If you do not want them to talk back, don't talk back to other adults or them, if you don't want them to complain, stop complaining about the weather or the electricity. Do not tell them what you want them to do or become, show them.

29

If Gentle Discipline Isn't Working

Try Not to View Discipline as Punishment

Take a gander at control as a method for effectively captivating with children to help shape their moral character.

With an order, "We are showing our kids discretion and limitation. Discipline is an immediate, pointed punishment or lost benefit that fills in as requital."

Control is unmistakably more compelling than discipline yet requires somewhat more work.

Discover Open Doors for Applause

Pay regard for what your youngster is doing. "Attempt to see when your youngster is effectively occupied with being great, and compliment that person on the excellent conduct.

"Set aside the effort to listen completely to what they need to state, and concur when suitable. When we dissent, we say as much—once more, setting aside the effort to tell them why."

Guardians who are accessible to, and show sympathy toward, their youngsters are filling in as incredibly good examples.

Make Set Points of Confinement and Keep Them

Set aside the effort to tell youths and young people the proper practices you anticipate from them.

"We set these points of confinement; at that point, we finish them. "If your youngster wavers, the individual in question should realize that there will be a steady, anticipated result. There are no curveballs, no new dealings, and no withdrawals."

Try Not to Compromise or Detonate

"Cautioning youngsters, 'You should be great,' is excessively expansive and general a message.

Accepting a youngster should comprehend what we need, not being clear about what we expect ahead of time, and setting ridiculous points of confinement will prompt dissatisfaction.

That invites responding in outrage or an excessively passionate manner.

Be a Parent, Not a Friend

Children need you as a parent, not as a companion, to instruct them as they develop. Restraining your kid and setting cutoff points will ingrain certainty as they figure out how to explore through life.

"With control, we're not inactive spectators; we're effectively included as instructors.

Redressing Behavior in a Child Who Won't Listen

Getting a hesitant tyke to tune in to his parent can be a genuine preliminary for guardians, and particularly fathers. Fathers frequently will, in general, observe listening practices regarding regard; "If my tyke won't tune in and pay consideration, but instead appears to be occupied constantly, it is an indication of discourtesy."

In all honesty, it isn't always about regard. It is likewise a phase a kid experiences as they attempt to deal with their reality and as parental impact winds down through their developing years. So it might feel like disregard. However, it is most likely more about their social advancement than about whatever else.

Indeed, even with that viewpoint, it very well may frighten when the TV, the earphones, or computer games become more significant than mother and father's meaningful interchanges.

Think about the Timing of Your Communications

Fathers frequently need to talk and be tuned in to when we think all is good and well, yet it very well may be useful to ensure that you are picking when the youngster is prepared to tune in. Directly amidst a game or another discussion probably won't be as viable a period as somewhat later. Have a go at something like, "I can see you are occupied at present; will there be a break shortly when we can talk?"

Get Them to Do Some Repeating

One thing an effective dad can do when the children are diverted during a discussion is requesting that they rehash what we said so we realize that the message was gotten. Repeating back is a piece of a procedure called undivided attention where an individual's news is significant enough to be strengthened by redundancy. So, when you do have your correspondence time, request that they disclose to you what they heard. Advising has returned to you will likewise make the message simpler for the tyke to recollect.

Attempt a Gentle Physical Touch

Coming into space to converse with a tyke can be improved if you put an arm around them or delicately press their shoulder. Youngsters will, in general, learn in various ways. When we utilize both verbal messages and fitting touch, we can stand out enough to be noticed somewhat better. Physical contact that isn't as delicate can be a genuine negative when attempting to impart, so ensure that your contacting procedure is tricky, thoroughly considered, and conveys love and regard.

Regard Their Need to Communicate

Demonstrating significant family correspondences examples and undivided attention can complete a few things to urge your youngster to tune in. In the first place, you show them regard when you set aside a few minutes to tune in to their worries, and it is simpler for them to show respect back when they feel regarded. Second, kids gain more from what they see than from what they hear, and they will show your listening practices as they get familiar with relational interchanges. Set aside the effort to talk when they are prepared, and they will be bound to react to you when you need them to tune in.

Family correspondence can be one of the hardest issues guardians need to manage. It tends to be made a lot simpler when we help our youngsters figure out how to tune in and when we model our exceptional relational abilities in our associations with them.

Conclusion

Thank you for making it to the end. By now, you should have gained a good understanding of the Montessori approach and how it can be implemented in the home. Unlike the traditional classroom and parenting style, where the adult tells the child what to learn, do, be, and when, the Montessori approach is a ground-breaking way that encourages independence from an early age. The adult doesn't dictate to the child about what they need to know, nor do they punish the child for not learning or for not being interested in what is taught. The traditional style of learning is quite conflicting. For instance, children are expected to start talking, walking, and moving about by the time they are toddlers. Yet, when they start to do those things, they are reprimanded for it. They are told to "be quiet" and "keep still."

This book combines the Montessori Method for children with a mindful and positive discipline approach for parents. Always take note that reflecting on your parenting journey and acknowledging your successes and failures can promote more closeness, connection, and compassion with your children. Being open to learning and growing as a parent is a mindfulness practice in and of itself. Always remember that one of the tips in positive parenting is setting boundaries and avoiding shaming.

Very few people question this way of bringing up children. However, over the century, there have been some people who have questioned it and then gone on to create something innovative. Dr. Maria Montessori is one of those people. She created the Montessori Method, which has become increasingly popular in recent years thanks to well-known public figures like Amazon founder Jeff Bezos and Google founder Larry Page, both of whom received Montessori educations. Many other people are in the public eye and have gone on to achieve great things. They have also been public about how Montessori school greatly helped them.

The Montessori Method educates children to be self-directive by allowing them to participate in hands-on activities that are fun, stimulating, and collaborative. The activities a child undertakes are designed to engage their five senses of touch, taste, smell, sound, and sight. Dr. Montessori found that when these senses are stimulated through activities, it increases a child's intellectual development. She carried out a large amount of research on how children learn and behave. She found that up to the age of six, a child is very susceptible to their environment. This is an important time because whatever they learn at this point will impact how they show up in the world as adults. If they are nurtured, encouraged, supported, and raised in a safe environment, they are highly likely to grow up as confident, balanced adults. The Montessori Method will help a child to:

- Become independent from an early age.
- Receive an education that is focused on child-centered learning.
- Be creative and imaginative.
- Develop self-control and self-discipline.
- Develop a high level of emotional and intellectual intelligence.
- Become socially confident.

As your child gets older, you are sure to discover more benefits. However, you may even notice them in your new-born.

Adults often forget that children are intelligent beings, so they address them as if they know very little and need talking down. However, by choosing to read this guide, you have started your journey on a different and amazing path. Your role as a Montessori parent is to be a guide to your child as they decide what they would like to learn. Their preferences for activities will change as they get older, and you will need to alter the Montessori home to reflect this. Children have a natural tendency to want to learn, and they also have a desire to contribute to their household or the community at large. They just need to be encouraged to do these things. If you introduce them to practical life skills from an early age, they will want to contribute towards activities that are considered "boring" or "chores" to the non-Montessori child.

In this guide, you have learned about the guiding principles of the Montessori Method, which include:

- The child is free to explore his/her environment.
- The child is a master of his/her learning.
- The child learns through his/her senses.
- The child needs a safe and nurturing environment.

At the start of this guide, you may have had a lot of questions about how you, as a parent, could start to incorporate the Montessori principles into your child's life. This guide intends to leave you feeling more confident as you embark on your journey as a Montessori parent.

You now have the knowledge and the resources at your fingertips to be an empowering Montessori parent.

One of the biggest takeaways from this book is that the child should be free to explore their environment, and you must ensure the environment is safe for them to do so. For instance, your room/s should be childproof. If it means getting down on your hands and knees so that you can perceive things from your child's height, then please do so.

Another major message of this book is that you don't need to feel overwhelmed or stressed out about creating a Montessori home. Many parents are worried that because they have limited space or a tight budget, they aren't going to be able to design an ideal Montessori home or that they won't be able to get it "right."

There is no such thing as the "right" Montessori home because what will work for one parent and their child won't work for someone else. Also, you can create a stunning Montessori home without having a lot of space. There are a lot of parents who have created videos, blog posts, Instagram images and Pinterest boards where they have highlighted how they have made good use of confined space. Even if it's having a shelf in the corner of the living room, what matters is that your child finds it interesting.

It would be great for you to reach out and connect with other parents who believe in the Montessori movement. This will deepen your understanding of Montessori because you will be able to share insights, ask questions, and meet up for playdates.

The first six years of a child's life have them dipping in and out of sensitive periods. Sensitive periods are when children are even more impressionable with their environment. They take everything in like a sponge, so patience and consistency are needed at these times. But those investments will be worth it. You now have ideas for various activities that your child can do to develop through each sensitive period, which includes small objects, movement, order, senses, expressive language, and music. Each of these is very important and has significant benefits for the child.

If you are creative or on a budget, you can always make furniture, toys, etc. to suit your child's needs. Many of the blogs on Montessori parenting give tips and advice on how to make your resources and materials. I hoped to leave you with practical steps you can take to set up your Montessori home, and now you can go and start implementing what you have learned. Please do not feel like you have to integrate everything. It would not be practical or beneficial for you or your child. He should ideally have an environment that is clutter-free, organized, stimulating, and calm. They strongly desire order at this stage in their development because they are looking to understand the world and discover their identities. If your home is chaotic, it will be stressful for them. If you offer them too many activities at any given time, they will feel overwhelmed and will not be able to focus properly.

Your child will thrive with a few high-quality toys and activities that can always be rotated. The Montessori equipment and materials were designed for a reason—they support the Montessori approach. The floor bed, weaning table and chair, child-size utensils and furniture, etc., all allow the child to become independent and be more in control of their daily lives with you as their guide. However, you can substitute, so please don't worry about the cost of all this or where you will fit them in your home.

This is a lot of information to digest. Most of all, please take a moment to congratulate yourself for the effort you are putting into being the best parent to your child. Your choice today to bring Montessori into the home is going to serve your child well as he/she continues to journey through life, and while he/she develops into an independent, strong thinker. Your child will ultimately have you to thank for setting him/her off on that journey. Best of luck to you!

We're here
because of you

If you have found any value in this material, please consider leaving a review and joining the Author's Mission to give the most resourceful start to all children around the world

By scanning the QR-Code below ♥

★ ★ ★ ★ ★

BOOK 2

TODDLERS' DISCIPLINE

A SURVIVAL GUIDE TO TOT(S)' GROWTH SPURTS. GUILT-FREE MINDFUL PARENTING METHODS TO TAME TANTRUMS, ESTABLISH RESPECT AND HAVE TODDLERS THAT LISTEN IN A POSITIVE NO DRAMA HOME

Preface

This book is part of a series of manuscripts from the Mindful Parent Academy. This growing collection contains books that tackle various aspects of the lives of modern parents with its inevitable challenges and unfathomable joys.

All our books are driven by a compassionate, non-judgmental, and positive approach that aims to support parents in their journey into parenthood. Our mission is to build a world that gives back to family its core role as the foundational institution that sustains society and that provides wellbeing for all its members. Our revolution starts here and now. And it starts with You. It starts by wanting to, and being capable of, empathically looking after our thriving little people that constitute the future of our human society. This starts by equipping parents with the right knowledge and activities when it comes to strategically thinking about your toddler's development. At the heart of the Mindful Parent Academy there is a mission that is to shift the current trend that sees parents either feeling guilty and worried for spending too much time with their children to the detriment of their career or personal development. Or vice versa, a world where parents cannot spend enough time with their kids because of the strains put on them by their adult life and their job commitments.

At the Mindful Parent Academy, we believe that any parent around the world should be put in favourable conditions in order to enjoy the right to be fully involved in this wonderful period of their child's life while being supported by the larger society. It is not a coincidence that in any given culture, in any part of the world, family (whoever this includes) is what drives people's actions, interests and passions. Stressed by the demands of modern life, sleep deprived and physically exhausted, modern parents can find it very difficult and challenging to deal with normal toddler's developmental growth spurts. In fact, it is quite normal and should be expected that in order to grow, toddlers will go through cycles of sleep disturbance, irritability, stubbornness, misbehaviour, tantrums and even meltdowns. Unprepared and unequipped with the right tools, parents can feel adrift and end up over-reacting, raising their voices or even misusing their words with their little people.

This inevitably starts a cycle of guilt and despair that will inevitably spiral down with time. Your child and your mental health and your whole family's welfare are at stake here. However, at the Mindful Parent Academy we believe that everyone can build a no drama home full of giggles, loud laughter and singing kids. A place where a sense of harmony and stability reigns, no matter what. With this intention in mind, you need to embark on a personal mission to reach and maintain a mindful balance. We believe that there cannot be a flourishing tree without sturdy roots and that 'you cannot pour from an empty cup'. Therefore, whatever are your circumstances, No Matter What, we support the idea that you must first look after your own mental, physical, and spiritual well-being. And without guilt. We want you to first reflect on the experiences that you had as child and as a parent so far. We want you to consider some of the major aspects that are affecting your understanding and practice of parenthood. What are those stories that you are telling yourself about your kids' behaviours and the reasons behind the way you answer them?

This is important because toddlerhood is increasingly recognised as a delicate stage where parents can really instil the basics for strong, resilient, and confident children. It is during such critical time that you want to work on your communication style and empathy to lay down the foundations for a healthy life long relationship with your children based on common values, cooperation, boundaries and respect for each other. So, how do we build a solid life-long relationship with our children based on nurturing common values and virtues? In this book you will find plenty of ideas and practices that will inspire and support you in your parenting journey. It is never too late to start and if you are here you are looking for inspirational ideas to implement in your daily life. Yet, before you can implement new ideas it is useful to stop and understand your own parenting approach and the generational patterns that are most natural to you. Self-understanding your mental models can help you recognise the triggers of your children's behaviours, take control of the way your deal with the interactions with your kids and find other ways if those ones are inefficient or waning. In this book you will find useful information on how to track and trace back your parenting model and how to move forward from it.

This also includes the tools and strategies to implement effective tactics to discipline today's toddlers to let them thrive and reach their full potential despite all the digital temptations and distractions. We would like to introduce you to ways of keeping yourself mindful and positive with your children even when seriously sleep deprived, emotionally drained and juggling between the many demands of life. Keep yourself sane by finding time to look after yourself whatever that means by revealing the self-help tools that you can apply daily. At the Mindful Parent Academy, we have your and your family's well-being at our heart. You must try every possible way to keep yourself peaceful, happy, connected, and sane while the demands on you as carer and provider are never ending and your energy and patience are fluctuating. Enjoy your reading.

Introduction

The struggle is real: disciplining toddlers is so damn hard. They are so innocent in their mischievousness that they make it ever so difficult to enforce any rule. Toddlers are so adorable that they could get away with all sorts of misdeeds and they will still be loved and cherished. They can still make you smile while they turn you, and everything else around you, into a wreck. Toddlers are blissful creatures that come with no instructions but with plenty of vivacity, expectations and demands. And so, it should be. They are literally life in its full potential.

Parenting a toddler, or more than one simultaneously, can be exhilarating and astonishing at times. No matter how much you have been wishing and preparing to become a parent, by the time your bundle of joy has turned into a toddler at about 12 months of age, you have been developing several unimaginable super powers that you were totally unaware of. Just to name a few: you have never been so sleep-deprived and still functioning so well. You have never felt this exhausted but you still carrying on doing your duties and with added efficiency. You can be so attentive on following what s/he is doing that you can even see what s/he is doing from the back of your head. You have been anticipated many life-threatening incidents and saved his/ her lives on countless occasions. You have never felt so desperate for some peace and calmness that you have found a robotic silence inside yourself. No point stopping the chaos outside anyway. Toddlers can make you realize how much you can be strained and stretched and still bounce back with more profound love and fond enthusiasm. Toddlers are wonder-full and magnificent. They can gift you with glimpses of childhood and even heal the wounds of your inner child if you let them. So why we should discipline them and what is so difficult about it? What are the major struggles that most modern parents encounter?

At the Mindful Parent Academy, we believe that many new parents tend to have quite a 'romanticized' idea about raising a child and little information about what it is actually coming their way. Then again, as an old saying states: 'it takes a village to raise a child.' Well, where has everybody gone? In today's modern world, more often than not, people tend to live away from immediate family members and old friends. Not everybody is surrounded by supportive communities with free baby groups or parks and play centers.

You will definitely agree that raising children, particularly a toddler (or more than one simultaneously), can be, at times, a very draining physical, emotional and psychological experience. However, most of the time, it is still the greatest and most fulfilling experience of your life. Toddlers are amusing. They are pure fun. But only if they are in the right mood and in 'favorable' conditions. There are so many factors that could affect a toddler's mood and therefore the mood of the day and night: hunger obviously, tiredness of course, thirst, change of routine, overstimulation, under-stimulation, teething, 'terrible twos' (for some of them 'terrible threes'), losing a pacifier or a favorite toy, sleep regressions, growth spurts, being teased by a little friend, missed a nap, too long a nap, catching a cold, lack of some key nutrients, push for independency, separation anxiety, a major change in family composition, a new house, starting kindergarten and so on and so forth. The list of factors that can affect you toddler's mood can actually be endless. And only you, and other relevant carers, can try to figure out the source of distress.

Any unmet need or desire of a toddler can trigger every parent's worst nightmare: A Tantrum. A tantrum is an uncontrolled outburst of anger and frustration. However, while a tantrum can last from under a minute up to ten minutes, a more serious incidence is a meltdown. This is a type of tantrum, in which emotions takes over the child and there is a total loss of control. While with a regular tantrum, a child can regain control of his/herself, a child having a meltdown needs someone to recognize their behavior, and needs someone to help them regain control of themselves. Both of these can happen to any child of any family. It should be expected.

181

However, not all parents are equipped with the right knowledge and understanding to tackle these moments and, while in it, actually reinforcing that lovingly and reassuring relationship that every child is so in need of. And this is what this book is about.

All of this is to say that all children will be naughty at some point and even lose control of themselves sometimes. And this is a fact, so let's face it and accept it. It does not define you as parent, it does not mean you are not good enough, that you are a failure for not having children 100% happy at all times. Or for not being able to anticipate a trigger for her misbehavior. Particularly during toddlerhood, you need to stay strong because while you are extremely proud of your kid/s growing up strongly and happily, their brain is still developing and they can get trapped into very big emotions. However, what you want to avoid is to try disciplining your child during a tantrum, or worse, during a meltdown. Simply you are going to fail. Your child will simply be unavailable, unreceptive. You must allow their big emotions to flow out and to be released. To let them go. This though, does not mean you should accept bad behavior. You can allow all emotions within warm boundaries, but not all behaviors. This is because those behaviors can be dangerous for your child and others around them. This book is here to help you gain that knowledge and understand these delicate skills: to anticipate any potential trigger for misbehavior and give you the tools to help them navigate and master those big emotions. We believe that it is possible to meet our young children right there when they are at their worse and be at our best. We can intervene while they are losing themselves and help them ride their emotional roller-coaster back to their calm self.

On the other hand, to discipline a toddler is an all-embracing and ongoing practice that comes before any tantrum occurs. In this book, you will be first guided to reflect on some aspects of your parenthood approach that you have probably overlooked. You will gain a much clearer picture of your most important values useful to guide your daily practices with your children and your family life. You will be invited to take some actions in your daily life that will make you become that parent you aspire to be at all the time. You will learn the tricks to apply effective discipline strategies to tame those tantrums but also to establish respect for your family's core values in a peaceful and mindful way. Your child needs to trust you, to feel loved and appreciated by you, to express their emotions, and learn how to master these big emotions and misbehaviors. However, s/he also needs to know who is in charge and or what consequences follow a dangerous behavior, for instance, crossing the road on their own, handling sharp objects in the kitchen, biting and pushing others and so on. This book will enforce the idea that Balance is the key. Do not intervene all the time. Choose your battles. Be an observer, but make sure your child trusts your judgment about safety for his/her self and others. So how do you reach that so sought-after balance in a mindfully positive way?

What do you need to know to raise respectful and responsible little people based on your knowledge, experience, location and in the face of adversities? What is the basis for a long-lasting relationship with your children grounded on respect and mutual understanding? What are the core ideas of effective but toddler appropriate discipline?

This book will look at cornerstone topics such as:

- Mindfulness Tactics for Parental Stress Managemen **Error! Bookmark not defined.**
- Communication style,
- Respect of values,
- Trust and Love,
- Sibling rivalry,
- Tools for more cooperative toddlers **Error! Bookmark not defined.**,
- Listening to each other.

What this book mostly suggests is that if you can adopt a mindful approach in yourself in order to foster a positive parenting discipline, you will most likely set the basis for a healthy life long relationship with your child and your partner. And ideally, a mindful child later on in his/her life. But how do we achieve and maintain these long-term goals?

The book will explain the importance of being mindful as a precondition for a positive parenting approach. What does it actually mean to be (or aspire to be) a Positive and Mindful parent in the current world and how it can be linked to a guilt-free approach?

The book will point at ways to try and reach a No Drama No Yelling home by establishing clear and solid boundaries while creating an emotional connection and warmth within them. It also suggests to have a completely alternative approach toward toys, playroom, play dates, sports, activities, and so on to avoid overwhelming your child and trigger misbehaviors.

The book will explore ways to communicate and connect with your toddler/s, the tools to redirect their actions, the tricks to recognize the triggers of a tantrum and avoid them, but also how to teach your children how to be responsible, respectful and cooperative. The main aim of this work is to equip all parents with the tools to manage their parenthood journey, knowing what to expect so that they can handle most situations in a calm and constructive way, avoiding yelling, establishing respect, managing tantrums while remaining deeply connected with their children and build that 'wonder-full' lifelong relationship that you will be so proud of. Let's begin!

1

A New Born Mother and Father

When a baby is born, so is a mother and a father. Even if you have already had your first child, you are born as a parent of two, three, and so on. It is always different. It will always be a different chapter of your lives with new challenges and adjustments to be made.

Parenthood in modern times is stressful. The demands on parents are too high and too many. Often new parents tend to have a quite 'romanticized' idea of pregnancy, birth, and parenthood. And find themselves struggling when confronted with the reality of raising egocentric little people.

As a parent, you may find it especially daunting to be present, intentional, and attentive. You're pulled in dozens of different directions by the many demands on your time and energy. And your children instinctively know how to push every reactive button you possess.

They can sniff out when your emotional bandwidth is low and choose that moment to present their less-than-adorable selves. It's no wonder you see red-faced parents losing it when their children have public meltdowns or getting rankled when their preschoolers sulk at the dinner table.

It's hard not to react (or overreact) to your child's shenanigans, especially when you're stressed and overwhelmed. But even at your best, you'll find it challenging to know what to do and how to respond in irritating, emotionally charged, or embarrassing situations with your kids.

Before we carry on our journey though, we would like you to stop for a moment and take some notes, even just mentally if you can't write at the moment. Whatever you are doing stop for a moment and: Deep deep breath IN and... breath Out.. Focus on you. It is important to start reflecting on some very important areas of your life that might have been completely overlooked by you but that maybe are unconsciously directing and affecting your parenthood experience so far.

Have you ever reflected on your parenting style? Who are the parenting examples that you might want to follow? Or that you definitely do not want to follow? Such as your siblings, best friend, cousins? Think about it for a moment. Now focus on you again. Who are the figures or the traits that you would aspire to develop as a parent? Who do You want to be as parent? What are you going to do today in order to be that parent? What are your core values and are they Universal or particularistic?

Now, focus on your experience as child. Were your parents highly critical? Punitive? Strict? Uncommunicative? Often unreasonable? Offensive? Overly permissive or intrusive? Have you been neglected or abused? Have there been any tragic events in your family life? Do any of the above resonate with you? And are they influencing in any way your parenthood approach? In terms of your values, the way your deal with your children's misbehaviors and so on? Although, we appreciate that all parents have tried their very best considering their historical period, upbringing, knowledge and livelihood, it is also true that certain parenting traits can even go from one generation to another unchecked and have an impact in the way we deal with our children. Have a think about it.

What is your experience of Parenthood so far? What are the aspects you are particularly proud of? And the ones you feel guilty or not so proud of?

What are your feelings about yourself? Your post-partum body or your partner's post-partum body (if applicable). Your life in terms of being a carer and a provider? Friendship and family relations, including the relationship with your partner at the moment?

Please reflect on all of the above aspects because these can really affect your mindset, and as a consequence your daily life and your attitude towards others including, and most importantly, your little children.

Parenting your children and building a secure and happy home life for them is the most important job you'll ever undertake. If you enter it —or continue it— without any forethought or preparation, you're allowing in-the-moment circumstances and emotions to determine how you want to respond and make decisions.

Creating this blueprint is a mindfulness activity that ensures you have plans and tools available when you need them in high-stress moments. It also helps you shape your decisions about how you create boundaries for your children, how you choose to nurture and guide them, and how you spend your time as a family.

One of the best ways to discern your parenting values and guiding principles is through self-questioning.

Your answers to the questions we provide here will help you determine the actions you intend to take, both preemptively and in real-time, to support your mindful parenting commitment.

After you answer these questions and define actions, your next step will be to review the values and actions on a weekly or bi-monthly basis to ensure you're staying on track and making any necessary course corrections.

Your family and parenting values may shift over time as your children grow, and your lives change, so revisit them yearly to ensure they are still relevant and aligned with your principles for your family.

We suggest you and your spouse review the following questions and write your answers in a journal. Share your answers with each other and devise one value statement that reflects both answers or a compromise you decide on together. Then brainstorm specific actions you will take to support your value statements.

For example, for question one, "What is the general atmosphere you want in your home?" your value statement might be:

We want our home to be a place of calm and peace in which we prioritize quality time together, encourage healthy self-expression, and spend time talking, sharing, enjoying fun activities, and giving ourselves the time and space to recharge and find emotional balance.

Types of Parents

Researchers have stated that there are four types of parents: Authoritative, Permissive, Authoritarian, and Uninvolved. Authoritative is being perceived as the most reasonable and balanced of all other types, as they either have one problem or the other. In the cases of authoritarian and permissive, these two types are the extremes; the permissive is extremely lenient while the authoritarian is extremely controlling. However, the worst and most damaging type is the uninvolved. I will give a short explanation on each and how they can be exercised below.

The authoritative parent. This is the best method or type of parenting, the reason being that parents with this method are not overly harsh; neither are they extremely lenient. This is a mix of rules and freedom in which the kids are not subjected to only the will of the parents and at the same time know that there is a limit to how free they are. In this method, there are consequences for every wrong action, and there are rewards for, not all, but some positivity, your kid doesn't get a reward for eating, but you can sometimes reward your kid for some kind of display of obedience or any other thing you deem fit to be called a good deed, at least for a toddler, so as to make them keep the good deed up.

Authoritative parents:
- Let their kids know what they expect from them, morally, academically.
- Set rules and regulations that have consequences if dishonored; well-planned daily schedule for important and basic things that have to be followed duly, although not when extremely uncomfortable, and backed with reasons and explanations.
- Create a chance for good and regular communication, which promotes a strong parent-child relationship.
- Are not afraid to implement consequences for kids' wrongdoings.
- Make sure to keep promises made to kids.

This kind of parenting is the one that helps build kids' personalities; this mostly bears the fruit of self-confidence, self-belief, and high self-esteem.

The permissive parent. These are parents that allow "too much freedom" for their kids; they literally spoil their kids with a lot of consequence-free actions with the fear of not wanting to upset or offend their kids. This set of parents act more like "best friends" than parents. In permissive parenting, while showing a lot of love and affection towards kids, they tend to be overly lenient and delicate with them.

Permissive parents:
- Show so much love and affection towards kids.
- Give the mammoth rewards for kids' minutest efforts.
- Always try to avoid kids' anger, even if it requires not correcting them.
- Unlike the authoritative, have no rule or consequences and always willing to compromise even if there is any, so as not to tamper with their temper.

This type of parenting, however, doesn't help in the building of the child's personality as it most times result in a lot of negatives like self-centeredness, very low socialization skills which make it hard for them to build and keep good relationships with people, kids brought up with this kind of method tend to become very saucy, and have no regard for authority.

The authoritarian parent. A type of parent with very high conditions and code of conduct, the authoritarian is similar to the authoritative, in the sense that they both set rules and principles, but the difference is that the rules and regulations of the authoritative are detailed, but the authoritarian's are always overly strict and without any reasons or explanations. The authoritarian parents believe that children have no rights whatsoever to question their authority, once they say "go," it is "go," there is no "go because," "go so that," whatever they say is final!

Authoritarian parents:
- Do not believe kids have a say; they believe kids aren't to be heard, only to be seen.
- Give no reason for rules; they believe they have no reason to explain to their kids why rules and regulations are being set.
- Have no problem with using punishment as a means of discipline.
- Give their children little or no chance to make their own decisions or choices.

- Makes sure rules are obeyed no matter what.
- Don't give much time to a showing of affections and emotions.

The authoritarian type of parenting has a really strong effect on the confidence and self-esteem of the kid. The fact that they are never given a chance to affect their self-assurance. Parents that find themselves in this category might want to try and be a little softer for the child's sake.

The neglectful or uninvolved parent. This is a very harmful type of parenting in where the parent has little or no involvement in the life of the kid. This actually is not very common as no responsible parent would want to neglect their children, but some parents actually think this method aids in making the children strong on their own. Causes of cases like this can include, having no clue on how to handle their children, not wanting to invade their child's privacy, having jobs that require a lot of their time, and other numerous reasons.

Uninvolved parents:
- Give little or no attention and spend less amount of time with their kids.
- Have not-very-close relationships with their kids.
- Less involvement in their kids' outside-home activities.
- This type is another type that can also affect the self-esteem of kids. Parents that find themselves in this category should do something about it, and try to adjust; if not, you might want to contact an expert for professional advice.
-

Some parents might find themselves exhibiting traits of more than one method, just be sure to choose the type that fits your kids, although the most advisable is the authoritarian parenting method.

Talking To Toddlers

The ability to communicate with our toddlers in a way that they can understand is an asset that every parent should possess, although it might not be easy, it is possible through the help of some key information that I will be sharing with you shortly. You don't want to live the nightmare of having your toddlers getting your message wrong or misinterpreted.

There are ways by which you can be sure to establish a good communication with your kids, either when you're just talking to them or when the talk is for some discipline and correction. First, we discuss the approach to employ when talking to your kids; then we move onto the part where you implement discipline.

Tips on Establishing Good Communication with Toddlers

- **Speak normally**: You might be tricked into thinking that talking to your toddlers like they do makes them understand you better, no, in fact, it might even upset them, why? Because it might seem like you're trying to mock them. The truth is, what you call "baby language" is the best result of their effort to speak as we (adults) do. They are always eager to be able to do the things they see us do, but, like every person trying to learn something new, there is a slow beginning. Now, let me ask you this, as a person trying to learn how to play tennis, will you be pleased if your trainer drops the egg(ball) to bounce before hitting it with a bat instead of serving normally? And say it's because he wants to come down your level and make it easy for you. That only reflects your incompetence, and does that not seem like mockery? You can only get better when you practice with people that are way better at it than you because that's how you discover and develop new skills and techniques, the same goes for the kids. Also, it's only hard for them to speak; it's not as hard for them to listen and hear. Although it is good to try to come to our babies' level for better understand, it can only be advised in some other aspects, not while talking.

Note: They can only learn from the original, not from the imitation of their own sub-standard version.

- **Keep it short and simple**: too many words will confuse your toddler, so, it is advised that you keep your information short and simple, for a quicker, easier understanding, but be careful not to misunderstand a toddler's "quicker" for an adult's. Excessive words can sound like gibberish to toddlers, Imagine, extracting a question from engineering, mathematics to a second grader to do.

How to Talk to Toddlers When Trying to Discipline Them

- **Talk with subtlety**: Nobody, not even toddlers, want to be ordered around, so refrain from using a commanding voice. The mind is built in a way that it tends to defend itself against an imposing or enforcing authority; this makes the kid tend to refuse instructions that sound like orders. For example, instead of shouting, "Daniel! Stop bouncing on the couch," you could use, "Danny boy, mummy wants you to sit still on the couch" a little slow, that gives a tone of subtlety. Don't ever yell!

- **Find substitutes for NO!** Why do companies change their commercials from time to time? We get tired of what we are used to. When you always say no to your kids, they get used to it, thereby reducing the effect it has on them. Instead, try and erase that sense of negativity and replace it with some sense of positivity. For example, when trying to stop finger sucking, offer suckers, and say to them, "why don't you suck this instead, we don't want our fingers to get wet and smelly."

- **Avoid making threats**: It is natural in humans wanting to dare; we like to see what comes after a threat has been made. Therefore, refrain from adding "or else" in your instructions, it calls out the inbuilt daring nature, thereby raising the tendency of refusal to comply.

- **Show seriousness**: Like adults, toddlers like to get involved when they recognize a level of seriousness. Toddlers too can be severe at times, even though they can be very playful with almost everything. For example, you want Diana to stop hitting the perfume bottle on the shelf; you don't just sit where you are and ask her to stop, rather, you get up, go closer and make your point known, the fact that you got up from where you were seated, shows a level of seriousness about that subject matter.

2

Be True To Yourself

Taking Care of Yourself

Parenting, in itself, is a tough job. Parenting toddlers is super tough. While you struggle to handle that little bundle of energy, oftentimes, you forget about yourself. We are so invested in the well-being and care of our little one that our own health and mental sanity take a back seat.

Toddlers are energy driven, curious beings. With their curious nature and ever-developing emotional repertoire, they unwittingly throw many challenges before us. Understandably, such challenging behaviors can strain our patience to breaking point and frustrate us to no end. It becomes, therefore, even more, important that you take a breather every now and then so you do not lose your own balance and control of emotions. Remember that if you lose control of your emotions and get exceptionally angry over your child, not because they have done something so unpardonable, but because you are so frustrated with the continued stress of misbehavior that a point comes where your patience breaks, you will only harm your child more. As innocent as toddlers are, they are incapable of doing something unpardonable that would deserve or justify the use of force on your part. It is important, therefore, to act before the situation reaches that boiling point, that threshold where things could tip over for worse.

Controlled Reactions

The best step that you can take as a parent is to take care of your own emotions in a timely manner. If you are working hard and struggling to teach your child emotional control and addressing challenging behaviors, it all comes to nothing if you yourself end up losing control of your emotions.

Many times, we as parents are tempted to simply shout, slap, or yell at our children. But, if you wish to be a positive parent, take care that your actions or reactions to your child are hasty and rushed. Make it a point to breathe deeply (remember the breathing exercises!) and calm yourself before addressing your child. Count at least up to ten to give yourself time to calm your mind and swallow that frustration and anger. This is an important step to practice before you talk to your child after a difficult situation or as a reaction to their misbehavior. Imagine what you could do to your child if you did not calm yourself and take the time to think clearly and with positivity before approaching them. Keeping this thought, and this realization always at the forefront of your being as a parent will help you reign in your emotions and not act rashly.

Self-Care

Beyond providing consistent and controlled reactions each time to every misbehavior, it is important to make your own self-care a priority. Allot time for taking care of yourself each day. But what exactly is self-care? It is like filling up your tank before you begin each day fresh and rejuvenated. It is giving your mind and body the rest it deserves. It is to give yourself the ability to handle your own social and emotional needs as an individual and not just as a parent. Self-care might is the last thing on your mind now when all your focus is on your toddler and giving them your best. But, you can't really give them your best when you are not your hundred percent self. Think of the safety instructions on flights. They always say that if the pressure in the cabin drops, you must put on your oxygen mask first before assisting your child. Of course, our initial instinct is first to take care of our child. But, if we do not get oxygen, we may pass out and will not be able to take care of our child or ourselves. The same goes for life. We must have our needs met so that we can care for our family properly. There are a few things that you can do to give yourself proper care. Plan to experiment with the different self-care strategies so you are able to decide what strategies work best for you.

Meditation

A short and quick meditation spell can help you feel refreshed. If you are new to the world of meditation, there are several resources available to guide you through various meditation techniques. Make a habit of meditating for at least five minutes every day, either in the morning or in the evening, so that you remain calm and rejuvenated every day. You can even include your child in your daily meditational episodes so that you both can benefit greatly from this important life skill.

Spending Time Outdoors

An excellent idea is to spend sufficient time outdoors near nature. It has been observed that simply watching the greenery for a certain period of time has a very soothing effect on the mind. Therefore, if you could squeeze time out to spend at least a little time per week at a place full of greenery, close to nature and its elements, it would be greatly calming and rejuvenating for you. Look for hillsides, riverbanks, mountain treks, waterfall resorts, or any such spots that you can easily reach for a quick refreshing trip. If once in a week is not workable for you, you could opt for other self-care techniques and keep outdoors to a minimum of once in a month or two.

Music

This is one of the easiest ways to stay calm and poised. Simply listen to any music that you like, which you are confident would calm you. You could listen to music at almost any time. Whether you are feeling stressed or not, you can simply tune into your favorite music as you go about your daily chores around the house. An advantage of using music to stay calm is there is no real need to set aside time to listen to soothing music. It can be done while you are busy with other work too.

Physical Exercise

Keeping physically active apart from all the work you do around the house will greatly help you stay fit and refreshed. A time and activity assigned explicitly for the purpose of the exercise will work positively on your mindset. If you are unable to hit the gym for some reason, simply taking a walk outdoors for at least fifteen minutes will do wonders for your positive approach to daily issues.

Maintain a Journal

If you are able to write your thoughts and feelings regularly in a diary or a journal, it would be greatly beneficial in relaxing you and emptying your mind of stressful thoughts and problematic issues. This can be a great tool to keep you positive and feeling good about your life. When things become tough, you can make it a point to just write down at least three things you are happy about and grateful for. This can become your own gratitude journaling exercise. It will help you retain a positive outlook on life and avoid feelings of excessive frustrations and annoyance.

Pamper Yourself

You could take time out to treat yourself with a few simple pleasures. These need not necessarily be luxuries. Simple things like an aromatic massage, a hot bath, some soothing music, lighting scented candles around the house, or drinking rejuvenating herbal teas can all be great ways to pamper yourself and give yourself some much-needed attention.

Spend Time with Family and Friends

If you can make time to get away from the busy schedules and the hustle and bustle of daily life to spend time with your friends, it would be a great way to unwind. Get some away time from kids by having someone watch over them while you take a much-needed breather. This will help you relax, and you will be able to get back in the groove after the retreat with more vigor and energy.

Get Away From Gadgets

Though it is usually assumed that watching something on your mobile or the television will help you relax, and it is valid to some extent, often times it is the contrary that is true. From one social app to another, you can simply feel stressed into replying to messages, emails, and whatnot. Instead, if you can spare time for a digital detox, it will be extremely beneficial for you.

3

You Matter

Children tend to suck up most of their parents' energies and time. However, You are not just a provider, a driver, a cooker, a carers. You matter. You have needs. Adult needs. And so is for your partner or any other adult helping raising your children. You need your space and time, and so does your partner. This is essential in order to be relaxed enough when reconnecting with your child.

You need to take care of your emotions with the aim of coaching your children's big emotions.

In case your parenting background has been particularly negative; for instance, you have survived narcissist parents or abuses, you need to re-parenting yourself and avoid bringing the past misdeeds into your relationship with your kids.

Attempting to raise children, especially those who tend to be disobedient or those who have been spoiled for many years, can be very difficult. It usually takes a lot of thought and self-control not to resort to the things we usually do, the parenting methods and statements that we grew up with, and the language that has been woven into us. For many parents, yelling, punishing, sarcasm, name-calling, and threats seem to be the only ways they can make themselves heard.

However, these aren't the only ways. Worse, they don't work. Child psychologists have repeatedly pointed out that punishment, yelling, and discipline tactics that aim to subjugate children are ineffective because instead of the child feeling bad for what she has done and thinking about how she can make things better, the child then becomes defensive and starts thinking about revenge. When we resort to the type of harmful ways of disciplining children that many of us grew up with, we actually deprive our children of the essential inner process of facing their own misbehavior.

How to Stop Feeling Anxious and Guilty About Your Parenting Skills

It is impossible to be the best parent, you are capable of being when you do not take time to set your mindset. Regardless of how patient you typically are or how well you can manage stress, every parent has a breaking point. This breaking point is a stressful moment, where you are overwhelmed with your little one's behavior and at a loss for what to do makes it any better. Of course, that breaking point may come easier when you have added stress from work, finances, or home life, as well as when you are hungry or tired. You see, the key to being the best parent you can be sure you are in the right mindset first. This involves taking care of yourself and being sure you have the alone time you need to recharge when it's needed.

You Cannot Pour From an Empty Cup

It is not uncommon for new parents to feel they must dedicate every waking moment to their child. They are constantly interacting with their little ones during their waking hours and desperately trying to catch up on housework when they are asleep. While there is nothing wrong with being dedicated to your baby and home life, you cannot pour from an empty cup. Even parents who are at work during the day need time to 'refill their cup,' meaning they need to take care of themselves before they have the energy stores to care for others.

Finding time for yourself is about more than hygiene or relaxation. It is about finding time to nurture your relationship with your significant other, getting away for relaxation with friends, and getting time away from their toddler. Whereas babies require constant supervision, toddlers can play in safe environments with less supervision. Allowing them to play on their own also encourages their individualism and independence. These are things that allow them to explore and develop their personality traits.

Allowing them to play on their own also allows you to observe your little one and the way they interact with their environment.

Strengthening the Bond Between Mom and Dad

Though not all toddlers grow up in a two-parent home, those that do should see mom and dad as a unified front. A major part of staying on the same page is finding time to nurture your relationship. You should feel comfortable talking to your partner about the blessings and pitfalls of parenting. They should support you in finding time for yourself to recharge. They should also be willing to spend time with your toddler, helping them learn more about the world around them, and sharing in the parenting experience.

The key to finding any type of coherence between mom and dad is having a strong relationship that you can build cooperation on. Make time for each other—not just to talk about your child, but to talk to each other and become closer. Get in the habit of relying on your partner. Be clear about your own needs and how they can help. Getting time away from your little one is also crucial for effective parenting. Parents in loving relationships need time to celebrate and grow their love to maintain a strong, supportive bond. Make the time for your partner. Of course, your toddler is more demanding and has greater needs. After all, they rely on you to cook for them, help them clean up, provide them guidance, and much more. Be sure your partner is not being pushed away in the meantime. You'd be surprised how much having a date night twice a month and spending a little bit of time without your toddler each night (even if it's cuddling and watching television) can help you bond with your partner and maintain the closeness in your relationship.

Get Enough Sleep

People often imagine new parents as those with dark circles under their eyes, unkempt hair, and stains on their t-shirt, walking like zombies in a sleep-deprived stupor. It can be difficult to be sure you are getting enough sleep, especially when your little one is not sleeping through the night yet. Fortunately, the toddler years come with an increased likelihood that your little one will not wake up for a middle-of-the-night feeding. You'll be able to get a few more hours of uninterrupted sleep than you did when they were an infant.

If you don't get enough sleep at night, find time to nap with your toddler during the day. Many new parents say this is easier said than done, as there is always something to do. Once the baby is down for a nap, it is easy to find yourself binging your favorite television show or trying to catch up on housework. Keep in mind that the television show and the messy house will still be there when you wake up. Try to at least rest your body while your little one is napping. Ideally, try to fit in some meditation or mind relations. Find some relating tracks that you love listening to and enjoy the feeling of mindfulness when your little one wakes up again. If you cannot afford a cleaner, try to do little and often. This might help you feel that you are at it, and the house is tidy (for your sanity). This also might prevent you from ending up having hours of house chores to carry out while having a toddler (or more) around. Another idea could be to stick a list of house chores to do in your kitchen and ask your partners, and/or other carers, to help tick them off the list while the day goes along. Another valuable option to consider is to see house chores as an activity to perform With your toddler(s). Toddlers love to be given jobs. We are obviously not suggesting child labor but! A simple house chores that they can be completely absorbed with while you are praising them for being helpful, can buy you that 15 mins to clean a toilet, peel those vegetables or sort the laundry. Think strategically!

Do the Things That Make Life Simpler

Some parents feel bad about taking the 'easy road' for their toddlers. However, what they don't realize is that there are things that you can do that are easier without compromising your child's care. Additionally, doing things a simpler way gives you more time. This means you have more time for doing crafts and interacting with your little one. You also have more time to yourself—which is critical to maintaining your sanity. Here are a few strategies used by those parents whom we would classify as 'experts.' They'll free up your time without sacrificing how effectively you are raising your toddler.

201

Take Advantage of Low-Maintenance Cooking

Crock Pots can be a lifesaver for parents, especially when they have errands, cleaning, or work to worry about during the day. Instead of stressing about dinner, you can throw meat, veggies, sauces, and whatever else you would like into the crock pot and let it cook on low. You don't have to worry about constantly stirring it or overcooking the meat, as this method of cooking lets many flavors meld together. There are tons of recipes available online if you don't know where to get started!

Find Things to Do That Include Your Toddler

There is nothing wrong with working out with your toddler in the room or putting them in a stroller and taking them for a jog. Another great tool plays dates. The other child will help your little one to socialize and give them something to do while you catch up with the other child's parent. This allows you to have a good time while encouraging your child's social development.

Join a Gym with a Playroom

Once your child is old enough, it can be useful to join a fitness center that has a playroom or sign up for classes designed for mums to bring their children with them, such as running buggies, mummy fit, and so on. Of course, you should always ensure the safety of the environment and the credentials of the play area supervisor before leaving your little one in their care. There are two major benefits to these types of centers. First, you get some alone time with your little one close by—but out of the way. Second, your toddler has the chance to interact and socialize with other kids in their age group.

Familiarize Your Toddler with Friends and Relatives

Children look to their parents for everything. They share a special bond from the moment they are born and all through their life. Even so, your toddler must have the chance to interact with family members and friends. These people form your support system. They are the people that you can trust your toddler with when you want to spend alone time with your significant other—or even if you just need a break. Starting these bonds early is important to preventing toddler freak-outs when mom or dad leaves the house.

Keep Your Little One Busy

A busy toddler is a well-behaved toddler (for the most part). When kids are busy, they are learning. Additionally, activities keep your toddler from falling into the trap of electronics like televisions, iPads, and other devices. You'll learn more about great activities for your toddler and family, as well as how to set limits and rules about screen time.

Set Boundaries

Your toddler is constantly picking up on new words that describe the world around him or her. While it is exciting as your little one learns new words, especially at first, it can be frustrating when they are rambling on, and you are trying to have a little quiet time. Keep in mind that your child is just now learning about all that goes on around them. They are going to have questions and want reassurance about the things they believe in the world. Their conversation is also an incredible learning experience, as they look to you for guidance on what is going on in their world.

Even though, you should help your little one as they explore, you should also get in the habit of setting boundaries for your toddler. This is especially true for stay-at-home parents and the child's primary caretaker. Let them know when you need a little time for yourself. Encourage them to play and explore on their own.

Eat a Well-Rounded Diet

On top of lacking sleep, many new parents do not eat the nutrition they need. It is so much easier to grab a handful of chips or a quick sandwich or microwavable meal, rather than preparing something healthy and nutritious. Besides, who has time to eat with all the demands that parenting has?

If you pay close attention that you binge on chips for lunch or make other unhealthy choices, you'll notice that the food you are eating is not nourishing your body. It may make you feel overfull, bloated, or sluggish. You may feel unfocused or tired. This is no way to be in the best possible state of body and mind for parenting.

Additionally, countless studies have proven that eating a healthy diet is essential for proper functioning and brain health. The foods that we eat provide the nutrition we need to thrive. Without it, parents might become agitated easier, which hinders their ability to think clearly and rationally when dealing with a cranky toddler.

4

How to Be A Positive And Mindful Parent And Reach A Guilt-Free Discipline

Are you following a gentle parenting approach? A conscious parenting approach? Or do you not have a clue about it?

There is so much out there today that is even confusing if we are talking about the same thing or there are differences between all the possible options. This book suggests applying a Positive Parenting approach for disciplining your children. Let's look a bit closer:

Positive Discipline

- **It is both firm and kind**. It promotes mutual encouragement and respect that strengthens the parent-child relationship during the teaching process. Children learn good habits by imitating their parents and other role models around them. Teaching, by example, is the best way to instill discipline.
  Be respectful and kind, even if you are upset.
  Refrain from yelling, humiliating, or calling him names to prevent him from copying you when he becomes upset over something in the future. Seeing you calm and composed while dealing with the situation teaches him that this strategy is better compared to panicking or getting mad.
  Aside from that, kindness encourages your child to become more receptive to reasoning, calm down, and cooperate. However, it is important to remember that kindness in this context is not synonymous with giving in or permissiveness. You are still

teaching him self-discipline, kindly, and firmly. You say NO but in a tone that is not mean or harsh.

Furthermore, you expect him to follow the limits you set and enforce consequences when he acts otherwise. This method helps your child practice cognitive thinking, helping him master skills that he will need to make more complex decision-making in the future.

- **It promotes a sense of belonging and significance**. Positive discipline promotes a sense of connection, eliminating deep-seated fear of being punished or grounded. It can be demonstrated by communicating your discipline plan or rules, then explaining the consequences that you will enforce if when he disobeys or misbehaves.

  If you are introducing a new rule or discipline technique, discuss it to your child, so he will know how to adjust. It should not come out of the blue. In this way, you are showing him that you are working together during the learning process. It will make him feel significant and more compliant to conform to the new rule, limit, or consequence.

  It works well with older children who already understand the science and reasoning behind the discipline. Kids below the age of three find it quite difficult to understand the consequences or make a sound judgment because the prefrontal cortex of the brain is not yet developed. For this age group, redirection strategies should be used. Parents should understand age-related behaviors and enforce appropriate discipline techniques.

- **It teaches essential life and social skills**. Positive discipline is geared toward the development of skills, problem-solving, cooperation, respect, and concern for others. All these factors are important factors for the child's development and ability to contribute to the larger community, school, and home.

- **It leads to the discovery of personal power**. This kind of discipline invites children to discover that they are capable of doing great things. They learn it when they obey and do positive deeds, or when they receive an appreciation, praise, acceptance, or a reward.

- **Its effectiveness is long-term**. Positive discipline prepares your child to adulthood. What he is learning now will effectively help him thrive and survive in the future.

The Core of Positive Discipline

To fully comprehend the rationale of Positive Discipline, it is important to understand its context as an approach to instill child discipline. It originates from "discipline," the Latin word which means teaching and comes from another term "Discipulus" or pupil. It is about teaching and providing vital learning that the pupil can use in his lifetime. But over the years, discipline becomes synonymous with punishing and not teaching.

There is no such thing as bad kids, only bad behavior

At the core of Positive Discipline is the general statement that "there is no such thing as bad children, only bad behavior." It is important for parents to bear in mind that kids are naturally good, and they have episodes of acting up due to certain reasons that they cannot voice out, especially when they are young and do not know how to process their emotions.

There are two factors behind the challenging behavior of your child-the sense of not belonging (connection) and the sense of significance (contribution). When one or both of these basic needs are not satisfied, the children find a way to fulfill it, even if it requires negative action. Dr. Dreikurs aptly put it by stating that "A misbehaving child is a discouraged child."

Calling the child as "bad" for doing something negative is not healthy for his self-esteem. It usually starts when your kid continually misbehaves or throw tantrums, and you are exasperated. While trying to calm him, you slip and label him as a "bad boy" unintentionally. You can forgive yourself after that slip and quote the famous cliché that you are just human and commit mistakes, but if you keep repeating it every time he does something wrong, it will be engraved in his mind and damage his self-worth.

Positive Discipline aims to help parents learn to objectify the behavior and cut the "bad cycle." For example, instead of telling your child when he hits his younger sibling that "that's bad" or "you're such a bad boy," you may say "it is not okay to hit your brother when you are angry because he does not share his toy" and then let him understand the harm that might happen to his brother. When you objectify his behavior, you are teaching him the cause and effect. By directly addressing the "bad behavior" without using the term "bad," you are encouraging your child to make better choices and avoid hurting other people.

Show the child how to resolve the problem, instead of pointing out that what he did is wrong

Redirecting the behavior of your child requires more than saying, "Don't do that" or "No." It needs skills to teach him right from wrong using calm actions and words. For instance, you catch your child before he can hit his little brother, instead of saying "No hitting" or "Don't hit," tell him to "Ask his brother nicely if he wants to borrow a toy." By giving him an alternative way to get the toy, you are showing him that asking is more effective than hitting.

If he already hit his brother, it is a must to be creative with your response. One good way is enforcing a non-punitive time-out, which technically is about removing the child from the stimulus that triggers his behavior and allows him to calm down. You can cuddle him when he is very upset, let him play in his room, or ask him to sit with you. After his emotion subsides, start explaining (not lecturing) why his behavior is inappropriate. Encourage your child to give other positive options that he believes will give him the result he wants, without hurting anyone.

To change his behavior, use discipline as a teaching tool. Rather than telling him not to hit his little brother, show him the correct and acceptable behavior that will resolve the conflict and prevent him from repeating the mistake.

Be kind, yet firm when enforcing discipline. Show respect and empathy

A child may insist that what he did was right, hence the importance of enforcing safety rules and consequences to prevent similar incidents in the future. Listen to his story as to why he did it and win half the battle by displaying empathy, but still impose the consequence of his action to make him learn from his mistakes. Empathy makes your child feel understood, lessening his resistance, and heightened emotions.

However, even when you are disciplining your child, be respectful, and when you overreact, apologize. It will teach him to respect you more and the people around him. You should behave the way you want your child to behave while showing your parental authority.

Look for the "why" behind this behavior, especially when you observe that there is a pattern. Sometimes, hitting a sibling is a silent message that he is jealous of the attention you are giving to the younger child. Whatever the cause, resolve the issue early to make your child feels secure and loved. Treat the root cause and not the symptoms.

Offer choices, whenever possible

Giving your child positive choices works like magic when disciplining him. An example is when you are trying to make him sleep, and he still wants to watch TV, instead of getting angry, provide choices. "Do you like to go to bed now or in ten minutes? Ten minutes? Okay, ten minutes and then off to bed."

This approach is a win-win solution because he gets to pick the option that is okay with him, and you are offering choices that are advantageous to you. For example, you are about to go to bed, but your child doesn't want to sleep yet, you can give him/her choices like: "You want to sleep now, or I will read you a bedtime story?" By not forcing him to do something and letting him choose, you prevent power struggle. You allow him to take charge and show autonomy within your parameters. To successfully use this technique, provide palatably, but limited choices. Eliminate options that are not acceptable to you and honor what he selects.

Use mistakes as learning opportunities for your child

Use every misbehaving episode as a chance to learn invaluable life lessons. Often, the child misbehaves to achieve what he wants or when he is bored. For instance, he throws and breaks toys when he does not like them anymore. Instead of scolding him, use the opportunity to teach him the idea of giving them to his friends or donating them. If he is bored, provide other interesting activities. This will teach him the concept of displacement or finding ways to be productive and prevent destroying his properties. By empowering him with alternatives, he will be adept at making wise choices, even if you are not with him.

Use mistakes to teach your child about right and wrong. He needs to know why he is wrong, or he will continue using the act to get what he wants from you or the people around him. Just be careful not to give long lectures that will make him feel bored. Use past examples of misbehavior to strengthen your points.

5

The Science behind the 'Happy Mind'

What is Mind?

The research findings of how our brain rewards efforts which enhance the ability of our species to survive, surely, we're living in the happiest era in the history of mankind. After all, wild capitalism is parallel to wild nature in terms of brutality. In the modern world, we are constantly faced with the quest for survival. We set off to work early in the morning and return late in the day. In between times, we are constantly engaged in struggling to make ends meet.

The human brain emerged approximately 2.5 million years ago. Then, when few people were around to witness it, it tripled in mass, reaching the 1,500 grams of the modern human brain from that of Homo Habilis' 560 grams. All this progress took place during the so-called 'hunter-gatherer' phase except for the last 10 thousand years after mankind settled.

Therefore, within this period, survival challenges and their respective resolutions have shaped the human brain. As a result, we are trying to find our way through the modern world's super complexity using a control system designed for the primitive era.

Our out of date factory settings are the root cause of many of the problems we currently face—including unhappiness. However, unaware of this situation, we have become smug enough to believe that we have a perfect brain compared to other living creatures—a conviction that collapses like a failed soufflé under the lightest of scrutiny. Our fondness for sticking with our inbuilt conditioning makes us fall, time and again, in the same pit.

During my research, I came across a rich seam of data about lottery billionaires—clearly the popularity of the subject. I discovered a regular pattern in the lives of these billionaires. The moment they are in the money, they chase after the life they've always dreamt of naturally. In many cases, the unbecoming demands of relatives and friends forced them to leave their familiar surroundings, break with their past, and start a new life elsewhere. Surprise, surprise, they end up struggling to become a part of this new environment. Many are either defrauded or betrayed by their new friends and spouses.

Consequently, they exhaust their riches, ruin their social relations, and end up worse off than when they started. It's a bleak thought, I know, but regardless of their country or culture, young or old, educated or not, they followed a similar downward spiral to unhappiness, with some making the same mistakes over and over again. As in the case of the guy who hit the jackpot 3 times and still ended up polishing shoes.

The brain is fairly magnanimous in this regard and rewards our best efforts with a blast of another substance in its chemical arsenal: dopamine. We are relieved, grateful even. We feel good and happy. Therefore, while cortisol helps us withdraw from life's less enjoyable moment's dopamine gets right in there and points out what needs to be done for a better life, then sets us in motion.

If what we do is recognized and appreciated by others, our brain triggers a third hormone called serotonin, boosting our happiness once more. When we choose to work for the common good and contribute to the well-being of others rather than pander to our own self-interest, a fourth hormone named oxytocin kicks in. And takes us to an entirely different dimension. Confidence generated by oxytocin strengthens our resistance to challenge. In short, even though we are always rewarded for overcoming challenges on our own, the grand award comes if we function with the people around us and when our resolutions are accepted by them as well.

And of course, there is the dimension of physical endurance. In response to hard physical effort, the brain deploys another hormone: endorphin. This attenuates muscle pain, and endorphin allows us to continue our activities without performance loss. Although the primary function of endorphin is to mask physical pain, it also counters the effects of cortisol. That's why at times of stress, leaping about a gymnasium in our Lycra leggings helps us feel good.

What Caused a Happy Mind?

We descend to earth in the second square, babies totally dependent on others. To survive, we need someone to feed us, put us to sleep, take us to the doctor when we're sick. In short, we need to be completely taken care of. Taking care of these demands isn't easy for our parents, but thanks to oxytocin, they take great pleasure in taking care of us. Besides, oxytocin enhances a solidification of mutual trust and affection; it makes us a family. Many people marry and have children so as to amass enough joy that oxytocin can provide them with.

Our struggle for independence starts the moment we are born. Our desire is to escape the Second Square and move into the Third. At first, achievements such as learning to speak, crawl, and walk fill us with hope. Everything we do is applauded by our family, and this triggers the release of serotonin, which evokes feelings of superiority.

We begin to think that we have the power to dominate and get everything we want. The bubble bursts when other kids get involved. The happy chemicals supplied unconditionally by our parents in our inner world cannot be found in the outer world. Even though we can't name them, we discover that dopamine comes from success; serotonin from appreciation and oxytocin from establishing strong friendships. That's how our battle to move to the fourth square kicks off. Showing others how important we are and proving ourselves becomes our priority. We strive to trigger these three chemicals. Some add endorphins to their happiness cocktail, with sport become an integral part of their life. These types can often be found running up mountains, white water kayaking. If over time, we establish relationships based on the trust we may manage to transfer ourselves to the fourth square. We can easily activate the happy chemicals because the contributions and support of others help us achieve success earlier. Besides, we will have people around us to appreciate our accomplishments, and their presence gives us a feeling of security in hard times.

Those who fail to gain such support over time may give up their efforts to establish meaningful relationships and end up back in the third square. Achieving success and feeling superior to others becomes their top priority and purpose in life. They are often surrounded by false friends (the worst kind). In successful times, they cannot find anyone to congratulate them with sincerity.

They accuse those around them of jealousy. Their bitter feelings prevent them from enjoying the pride and joy for their achievements. They hide their fragility and craving for love behind a mask. Some hide their true feelings with fake smiles to present a rosy picture to others. Yet, nothing they do can substitute for the serotonin and oxytocin gap; they can't find true happiness. In short, the people in this Square might be gloriously successful, but not as happy in the true sense.

What about those who fail to make any personal achievements—the people in the Third Square? They have two choices. Those who choose to obey go back to the Second Square. They win the love of people whom they see as their protector and leader by pampering them. Gaining the support of powerful people gives them a sense of security. However, failing to accomplish something on their own eats them up and leaves them with a feeling of lowliness. They may lead to a peaceful but unhappy life.

6

How to Have Thriving Thoughts?

Gratitude

Practicing gratitude places the focus clearly on what you have as opposed to what you don't have. There are many reasons we are encouraged to do this. For starters, whatever you concentrate on increases in your life, just as whatever you focus on when you take a picture clearly defines the subject and quality of the photo. What you bring into focus in your life, you talk about, you think about, and you end up drawing to you. If you focus on poverty and bills and lack, you attract more of that. Most people don't realize that they continually communicate with God. You put out your energies, and he answers. The subconscious does not know imagination from reality; it only knows what you think about all the time and how you feel about it. So it figures, if you obsess about your crummy relationship with your spouse, you're terribly disobedient children or your ramshackle house, that must be what you want, and it takes you at your word and sends you more of it.

There's a little saying, "Count your troubles; you'll be sad; count your blessings; you'll be glad." It's relatively simple. Instead of always complaining about your disobedient kids, start being thankful for them, for the way they think, for the opportunity to raise them, and for their strong and varied personalities. Rather than worrying about how everything has gone wrong with your house, try to thank God for a roof over your head and concentrate on the charm, the affordable house payment, and the fun you have decorating. And even though your spouse may not be perfect, he or she does have great qualities, and there are surely things that you appreciate about being married. Start being thankful for those things and see how quickly your life seems to change.

The amount of happiness and joy you have in your life is directly related to your ability to acknowledge what you are grateful for. Studies have shown that among the leading characteristics of strong families is the ability to express appreciation: not only for what each does but for who they are.

I recently met with a husband who told me that his new wife changed his life because she expressed her thanks to him for everything, even the small things that we tend to overlook. It has made a huge difference in their marriage—as well as their outlook on life. Even when you are not in the presence of your spouse or kids, talk about them in a positive way. Convey to your friends and coworkers how grateful you feel for them. Your outlook and attitude determine the direction of your life—not the external things that seem annoying or wrong at the moment. You captain your own ship. You select the course of your life. You are not a victim in any way—unless you choose to put yourself in that role. A victor sees where he or she is going and enjoys the journey. Gratitude helps you get there. As a matter of fact, you can't get there without it. You will keep circling and circling, getting tossed around on the waves you focus on.

This is what happened to Peter in Matthew 14. The wind and waves were crashing all around, but Jesus walked on the water. When Peter wanted to walk on the water, Jesus told him to get out of the boat. For a moment, it seemed like he would be able to do it, but his focus changed from Jesus to the chaos and danger swirling around him, and he began to sink. That's when we begin to go under too. When we take our eyes off of the good and focus on what bothers us, we spin down a spiral of despair that sucks us under.

What you focus on increases. Don't wait, always looking toward the future for what you will be thankful for one day. Be thankful for what you have today. Make a practice of being grateful. Make a mental list before you get out of bed in the morning or before you drift off to sleep at night. Write a gratitude list when you feel overwhelmed and tempted to get anxious or depressed. What is working; what do you have? Focus on that. It's important to be thankful in all circumstances. Without our trials, we would not grow. Without those challenges with our children, we wouldn't recognize our own weakness. Our spouses and children serve as our best teachers. They show us where we are now and where we still need to go.

You may think that you are fine the way you are: that you don't need to grow. Yet consider the laws of nature. Anything that stops growing is dying. The same goes for you and your relationships. I know it's much more comfortable to just be the way you have always been and do things the way you've always done them, but are you really happy that way? From what I have seen as a therapist, I tend to agree with Henry David Thoreau when he said, "The mass of men leads lives of quiet desperation." Chances are: you are one of them. This need not be true! Start to see things in the encouraging and bright light of gratitude. It takes no time and no special skills, and you can start immediately.

Now you might say, "Yes, but you don't know my situation. My life is filled with troubles. I can't just turn into a 'Pollyanna' and expect them to disappear." All I can say in response to that is that it's up to you. You can stay where you are, but you don't have to. You can always find plenty to be thankful for. And not only will it benefit you to begin this practice, but it will benefit your kids even more because you will teach them to start this practice early in their lives, and their lives will be that much better because of it. So if you don't do it for you, do it for your kids.

Kids who are taught gratitude are less likely to have the "entitlement" mentality that we see so often today. When a child feels content, he or she experiences less stress and resentment, resulting in better overall health. As we all know too well, stress hormones released into the body that has no outlet for release impact your immune system, your heart, and other organs, and they decrease your resistance to disease.

Over the years, there are many suggested ways for clients to make gratitude, fun and memorable and to strengthen it into a habit. For example, give each of your kids a roll of toilet paper (or paper towels, shelf paper, or whatever you might have handy) and have them fill out each square with things they are thankful for. You can give a little prize to whoever thinks of the most.

A Note About Competition

Competition is not the enemy. It can be used to spur each other on to greatness. The important thing about competition is to promote good, healthy principles of sportsmanship. Competition can be harmful when used to pit one sibling against the other. "Why can't you be more like your sister?" "David gets good grades; what's wrong with you?" "Annie is definitely the prettier of the two girls." "Dustin is clearly the athlete; Josh seems to only like art. I don't know what to do with him." These statements clearly foster harmful competition, creating a space for kids to feel resentful toward a sibling because Mom obviously prefers one over the other.

Creating a fun atmosphere that nurtures good-natured competition can encourage a child to be the best he or she can be. Games to promote certain characteristics (such as gratitude) can help. Encourage kids to find nice things to say to each other—to express thanks even for the little things. Writing thank-you notes is another way to do this. Such a habit teaches kids not only to be focused on what they get but to express gratitude to the giver.

Thanking God for all your blessings is so much more pleasant than praying for him to make you well when you get sick; yet, unfortunately, that is what most of us do. We forget to acknowledge the good things in our lives, but when we get in trouble, we run to God and ask him to fix it. Perhaps if we practiced active gratitude for our health, our good appetites, our strong bones and muscles, our prosperity, our skills and talents, and our relationships, we might be less likely to get sick in the first place.

Studies have shown that people who practice gratitude regularly are less likely to show symptoms of depression and experience higher levels of life satisfaction than those who do not. Having higher levels of life satisfaction leads to a better quality of sleep, which is important in maintaining a healthy lifestyle. It is obvious that it feels more fulfilling and less stressful to be in a relationship with someone who appreciates you than one in which you feel taken for granted.

Since gratitude leads to greater contentment, you will be less likely to judge others. This leads us to our principle: limit judgments.

7

Happy Parent Happy Children from the Start

Integration is the key: Between the parents and their child. It is about a balance between "no too much", "no too little" differentiation. Lack of differentiation: parents that don't go to the gym, don't work, don't have me-time, etc. Their life is only about the kids and this may because children might not develop fully and the effect is in all aspects of life from the 'bedroom' to classrooms etc. The opposite is too much differentiation.

How does the relationship with your kid/s shape the way your kid develop their mind and build relationships around them?

Consciousness and integration need to be joined.

Empathy overreaction. Go and meet them right there. Be present even if just for 10 mins a day. Always talk about your kids about how amazing they are, talk to your friends about your struggles only when the child is not present.

Boundaries and routines with a 12- to 18-month-old are very important. Routines are imperative to all child learning and a critical part of healthy development. This is because routines contribute to the child's sense of safety. They also invite repetition, which is critical to brain-building. Plus, behavioral routines like teeth-brushing and physical activity can even influence long-term health. Let's start with play and sleep—two of your 12-month-old's most valuable routines.

Maybe you are not paying attention to your young toddler's routines because you are very busy or "going with the flow." You might also have your child in daycare and simply not know much about their schedule during the day. That's okay. Skip to Noticing Your Toddler's Schedule in this section and begin there. Determining your child's schedule is as easy as making a record of their play, eat, and sleep times each day and then stepping back and noticing any patterns. Once you notice your child's typical metabolic patterns (when they are hungry) and sleep patterns, then you can begin to become more predictable and intentional about the routines discussed in the following sections. Predictability and intentionality are very important in creating the kinds of routines that facilitate your child's health and well-being.

Playtime

Playtime is one of your child's most treasured routines. At this age, your child needs a minimum of four 20-minute periods of dedicated play with a responsive, valued caregiver. It is very important that you set aside several moments to stop what you are doing and engage your child in attuned, responsive play. You should also be playfully engaged when you are simply in the room with them but busy doing other things. This exercise is an opportunity to expand on the skills that are most important during the dedicated playtime moments. We call this "floor time" because parents should be on the child's level.

Parental Authority

Authority is the foundation on which your discipline depends. Without respect for your authority, your child is not likely to give consent to what you want. His respect for your power can base on love, so your child goes along with what you want because he values you and your relationship. Or that respect can be found on fear, so that your child dreads knowing what will happen if he or she doesn't go along with what you want, because of the hurt you might inflict.

Parental Modeling and Example

You are the most important teacher your children will ever have. You set the Mold in terms of what it is to be an adult in this world, and they will copy you in many ways. You will see that, even as they are well into their adult years. Of course, you don't have to be perfect, but do the best you can in being an honorable human being, and discipline issues will somewhat fall into place.

Fear-based authority can be costly to your relationship. Children learn to use distance, distrust, and deception as strategies to keep the scary power at bay. If you want a close and trusting relationship with your children as they grow, do not resort to threat, force, or intimidation to get your disciplinary way. Instead, create a safe connection of sentimental value that your child can truly respect.

Why It's Important

Your child must give you consent—that is, agree to do what you say—for your authority to take hold. However, parents should not ask their child for permission to be granted this authority in the family. Parents must assume power if they expect it to give. They must act like they are entitled to it. They must work in charge. They must expect to be respected, asserting authority in a manner that encourages the child's respect—not by abusing the power of their position.

The influence of your authority is less dependent on your power to dole out positive or negative consequences than you might think. It's more a matter of conveying a firm and confident attitude: "I mean what I say, and I will do what I can to help you behave responsibly." This attitude communicates the firm belief that, among other responsibilities, your job is to establish and enforce rules for the safety and well-being of the child, and that those rules shall obey.

Fact

A family is not a democracy with elected leaders, where each family member has an equal vote. A family is a benevolent autocracy, where those with caretaking responsibility—the parents—are in charge of governing those who are dependent on their direction and support—the children.

A parent who wants to be his children's friend, or who feels insecure or uncomfortable assuming authority, is soon going to be exploited by children who come to understand how much power they have in the family. Unable to set practical limits and to make practical demands, this parent increasingly lives by the children's terms. Children now set the behavioral plan in the family by dictating wants or threatening upset if their desires deny. The parent tries to please, tiptoeing around unpopular issues, not wanting to upset the children, indulging them to avoid conflict, placating them to keep the peace. This is the worst-case scenario— when a parent is unable or unwilling to assume authority.

The Dangers of Not Having Authority

Why would parents not assume authority? Some people grew up with such stern or harsh parental authority that they go to the other extreme to avoid inflicting similar suffering on their child. "I don't want to do to you what my parents did for me." Some people fear to assert adult authority because it creates inequality with their child. "I don't want to be your boss if it gets in the way of being your friend."

Some parents crave their child's approval. "I can't stand your being displeased with me." Others lack the confidence to assume adult authority. "I don't know how to take tough stands and make them stick." Some parents never had a model of sufficient parental jurisdiction to follow. "My parents were Hands-off—they never made me do what I didn't want and never stopped me from doing what I did."

By not assuming meaningful authority, parents risk encouraging their child to gather more power to control himself and the family than is healthy. Parents risk eroding their effectiveness and self-respect as parents. They also risk shaping a self-centered child who may have problems accepting healthy limits in relationships and abiding by standard social rules.

Imagine that your child begged for a real live rabbit for Easter. Now a few weeks down the road, when you remind your child about caring for the rabbit, she attempts to place the responsibility back on you, as she's "too busy." Do not let this happen. Stand firm, even if it makes you momentarily unpopular. An agreement is an agreement, and this is part of your authority, to enforce the agreement.

Authority is part of the leadership that comes with the job of parenting—directing aspects of the child's life, enforcing adherence to those directions, and gradually turning over more power of authority as he grows older and learns to lead himself responsibly. This, of course, is the parents' ultimate objective: to put themselves out of the parenting business when the adult child is ready to assume responsibility for becoming the governing authority in his own life.

Establishing Parental Authority

If you feel uncomfortable asserting authority, can you learn to exercise this responsibility? Yes. You can practice several simple authority behaviors that all communications that you are in a position of authority. Simple acts of power include:

- Requesting information or asking questions about the child's life: "I want to know."
- Confronting issues in the child's life that you want to discuss: "We need to talk about this."
- Making demands for actions to be taken: "You need to do the following before you go."
- Setting limits on freedom: "You're not allowed."
- Expecting that agreements and promises are kept: "I will hold you to your word."
- Repeatedly insisting that an activity accomplished: "I will keep after you until you get it done."
- Applying consequences (both positive and negative): "You have to work off the damage that you did."
- Advising the child on the best course of action: "In my opinion, this is what you need to do."
- Controlling what kinds of support you will give and what kinds you won't: "We won't buy you those kinds of clothes."
- Making judgments about what is going right and wrong in the child's life: "In our judgment, you handled that situation very well."

By practicing behaviors such as these, with sincerity and without backing off, parents will establish their authority. Do not use threats to assert your power. A genuine threat inspires fear, while an empty threat is like a broken promise. It causes the child to lose trust in your word. Commitments work well than threats: "If you choose not to do what I asked, then I will do what I said." Fear and threats are to minimize, as this is not the true meaning of discipline and authority. You usually will not have to resort to punitive measures.

The Authority That is Positive

Authority is not just about correction. Another side of authority is contributive. As a parent, you exercise contributive authority by providing positives in your child's life that you control—resources, permissions, encouragement, help, support, advocacy, protection, knowledge, instruction, coaching, and praise, for example. Generally speaking, the more you have to correct, the more you should also demonstrate the positive, contributive side of your authority. Otherwise, your child will begin to feel that your influence is all negative when it is not.

Contributive authority is particularly important in second marriages where one partner is now stepparent to the other's child. Before the stepparent even thinks of exercising corrective authority, he or she should establish a base of contributive power with the stepchild. In the beginning, the biological parent should be the one providing any correction. The stepfather or stepmother needs time to build up a solid base of real authority before beginning to enforce corrective discipline. If the stepchild has been given no favorable jurisdiction on the part of the stepparent to accept, then he or she is unlikely to take the negative.

8

Establish Respect

Respect, although is commonly used, can be a controversial and unclear idea when you think about it or when trying to put it into practice.

First of all, Respect for what?

It can involve multiple values and principles. What are those? Are they Universal? Or are they particular to you or your family, community and/or nationality?

What are you going to teach your children that you have been taught (by your family or life experiences) and what you want your children to learn that you wished was introduced to you?

What are your values? And which one is important for raising respectful and responsible children? Some core values that many parents think are actually very important are: respect for others, kindness, diversity, gender, anti-racism, social justice and fairness, empathy, respect for the environment, clean eating, active lifestyle, mindfulness, and so on. Have you thought about your most important values and how to pass them on to your kids in an appropriate manner so that it feels natural to them to act in certain ways? For instance, let say you care about the environment, and you want to instill good manners and respectful behaviors in your toddler. It should follow that when unwrapping a snack, should be natural for your kids to handle you back the wrapping paper or to look for the bin. In order to teach that behavior, start at home by encouraging your kid to mimic you and invite them to use the bin every time they have a wrap to throw away. Let them familiarize themselves with the idea of recycling by drawing their attention to the rubbish tracks (that most of them love anyway). Ask them to help you with the recycling and bins in your house. When you are at the park or outside in general, comment on the beauty of trees, plants, and flowers and introduce them to the wonderful job they do for us. Trees provide us with the air that we breathe, shade for our picnics during the hot days, a shelter for little animals like birds' nest or squirrels. Flowers provide the pollen for our honey and so on. If and when your toddler pulls leaves from the bushes or plants or kicks a tree, intervene on their behaviors and explain that it is unfair and disrespectful. This is just an example of how you should proceed in order to establish respect in your little ones. Proceed in the same way for any other topic you feel is important to you, your family, and that is important to learn about in those early stages.

Patience and consistency are the keys.

Can little people get values? The answer is: the earlier, the better. However, you should aim to have a clear overarching frame agreed between you and your partner and relevant carers (or just with your-self if lone parent) about what are the core values and principles that your children must learn from early stages.

Remember, though, respecting children means respecting their stage of development, not reacting as if they were our peers.

Lead by example: if you snatch toys from your child to let him/her sit down for dinner, you should not be surprised if it does the same with other children.

Many parents stay at work all day and resent leaving their children at home with no activities to do. If television is not an option, this should be agreed with carers, and the greatest tip of the pedagogue is to create a daily agenda with the tasks that children must do after school.

Write down on a paper, the activity and time that the task should be completed. Vary activities each day. You have to be a bit methodical with the child. Leave a clear and objective list with bath time, television (if any), structured activities, and unstructured play time. Create a consistent routine, teach him how to organize room space. Organization is very important.

Another good tip is to set aside time for free activities. The little ones are going to adore this!

Are days when your little angel looks more like a little devil?
Here are some good practices for educating and disciplining your child, which have been gathered from across viewpoints, training, and curriculums:

Educating and disciplining children implies, among other things, establishing clear rules and limits. This is not always easy, even more so these days, but if parents adopt positive educational practices early on, it is possible to prevent future difficulties and problems. Cláudia Madeira Pereira, a clinical and health psychologist with a doctorate in clinical psychology, points out some good practices that will make this task easier:

1. Talk to Your Child

Even if you are exhausted after a day at work, take some time out of your day to talk to your child. At dinner or before going to bed, ask him how his day was, using phrases such as "Tell me what you did today," "Tell me about the good things that happened today," or "Did something bad happen?"

If your child is having a bad day, he can resort to several solutions. First, allow him to speak and listen to him without judgment or criticism. If you prefer, look for positive aspects that you can highlight and praise. Also, tell him about "what" and "how" to better deal with similar situations in the future.

2. Pay Attention to Good Behavior

Sometimes children learn that bad behavior is the best way to get parental attention... This is especially true for children whose parents pay attention to them only when they misbehave, even if that attention is negative, scolding them and rebuking them.

In order for your child to see that the best way to get their attention is through good behavior, praise him, her, and/or offer affectionate gestures (giving him kisses and hugs) whenever he does or even tries to do something good, such as helping set the table or doing a message, for example.

3. Promote Your Child's Autonomy and Responsibility

Some tasks, such as dressing in the morning, can be difficult for children. Even though it would be quicker for you to dress your child, you would prefer to encourage their autonomy and responsibility. Help your child by giving short and simple instructions on how to do the tasks.

To do this, use expressions such as "Take off your pajamas," "Now put on your shirt," or "Finally, put on your pants." Finish with a compliment, using phrases like "All right, you did a good job!" Sometimes it will not be enough to tell your child what to do; you may need to show him "what" and "how" to do it.

4. Establish Clear Rules

Be clear with your child about a set of rules. First, explain the rule succinctly and concretely. Second, make sure your child understands the rule and knows what is expected of him. In order for your child to be able to respect the rules more easily, try to give clear and simple directions, empathically and positively.

Phrases like "It's time to go to bed. Let's go to the room now, and then I'll read you a story," usually work. It is common for children to challenge the rules in the early days, but stay firm and consistent. Repeat as many times as necessary so that your child realizes that the new rule is to be followed.

5. Set Limits

When you need to correct your child's behavior, try to be patient, and stand firm. Tell your child that a certain behavior must stop, explain the reasons, and inform him of the consequences of not obeying. In that case, preferably use phrases like "If you keep doing, then..." Immediately and consistently implement the consequences whenever bad behavior occurs.

But do not resort to punishment or physical punishment (such as beating), as they only aggravate children's behavioral problems. Prefer to take a hobby or an object appreciated by your child for some time.

6. Stop the Tantrums

Although it is not easy, try to ignore the tantrums, not paying attention to the child at such times, as long as there is no danger to the child, of course! If possible, step back and pay attention to it only when the tantrums stop so that your child realizes that they can only get their attention when they stop throwing tantrums. At that point, prepare yourself, because your child will put him to the test.

At first, it is normal for tantrums to get worse. However, by systematically applying this method, the tantrums will eventually disappear. Remember that what you want with this is that your child learns that tantrums are no longer a good way to get what you want and that the best way to get the attention of parents is to behave well.

To achieve this, you must be aware of your child's good behavior and value these behaviors whenever they occur, for example, by giving a compliment, a kiss, or a hug. If you do, the child will feel more accompanied.

Open Communication is the Key

Communication is important in any relationship. It is also a good way to express love. Although it is good to exercise your authority as a parent when you communicate with your child, sometimes, you should lighten up a bit and just have fun and relax. Instead of talking about changing some undesirable behaviors, talk about pleasant stuff, and have a good laugh with your child. There are moments when the best way to solve a problem is simply by not giving it any attention by talking about other things that are positive in nature. By communicating with your child, he will not just feel loved, and you will also get to understand him better, and perhaps, you will also know the reasons behind his tantrums and other frustrations.

Listen

If there is one skill that all good communicators value the most, it is able to listen. Remember that communication is a two-way conversation. Therefore, do not just focus on doing all the talking. Instead, let your child talk and express himself. When he or she feels that you are listening, he or she will be more open, and it will also lessen his or her frustrations. Listening also means being open. Do not get mad at your toddler if the reason behind his or her misbehavior is not clear to you. Perhaps, he or she might start biting simply because he or she is teething. In such case, you cannot blame your child for biting.

Children act out mostly when we are frustrated, angry, stressed, and so on. Talk to your child about your feelings. E.g. 'mommy did not sleep a lot because of the baby, so mommy feels grumpy today' and so on...

Do not shame your child because of their tantrum, but comment on the situation 'you are very tired and this is why you are hitting and not sharing. Let's go home now.' And then go home NOW.
Always give hugs, kisses, and say, 'I love you.'

Raising psychologically, socially, physically, emotionally, and mentally healthy children are not about setting high expectations and strict rules. Instead, it is about showing children unconditional love, healthy communication, and reasonable expectations. It is about balance and providing the right environment that will nurture his total development.

Administration

The relationship between the parent and the child is central to the development of physical and mental health, cognitive and social-emotional functioning, as well as academic success. Aside from giving the basic needs, parents are also expected to chart a trajectory which promotes the toddlers' overall health and well-being. The child's experiences during toddlerhood impact the course of his life. His brain is developing rapidly during this period and assimilating what he sees, learns, hears, and experiences. He relies on his father and mother to survive and thrive. For a young child, his parents are the most important people in the world.

Parenting is regarded as the primary mechanism of socialization, which makes parents as focal persons to train kids, help them meet the demands of the environment, and teach them to take advantage of various opportunities. These vital tasks are continuing processes to help them survive and thrive.

The parents' main responsibility is to introduce children to the social world, helping them find their place and value in society and develop healthy self-worth by making the right choices. The way parents cope with the challenges of parenting enriches the lives of children, shaping the circumstances that help them build and refine their raw skills and knowledge.

One of the central aspects of development is attachment security, which influences the child's self-esteem and confidence that no matter what happens, his parents or caregivers will nurture his needs. The quality of attachment is dependent on how parents interact, communicate, and respond to these needs, especially during low moments. Consistency, appropriateness, and immediate response are also defining factors of good parenting. Children who are securely attached to parents have a more solid foundation that helps them establish strong relationships and empathize with others. Those with unsecured attachment have insecurity, disruptive social and emotional issues, and mental health disorders.

The Power of Empathy

Being an empathetic parent is the best gift a parent can give to their child. Your empathy for your child will let them understand that you actually 'get them.' Just like adults need someone to show confidence in them and acknowledge their feelings, so do young kids, especially toddlers. We need an understanding shoulder to lean on and cope with our time of distress. That shoulder will only be supported when the person understands where we are coming from and what the reason for our present situation is.

Toddlers are no different. They need us, parents, to be those understanding shoulders for them. We can become such strong support for them only by showing empathy. It is essential for kids that we understand them and their needs. For toddlers, their emotional needs and their feelings are of paramount importance. For us, a crying, whining, screaming, thrashing child might be just that, a child behaving undesirably. More so when according to us, they are doing so for no real reason and 'nothing.' But for them, it is hugely important. How many times have we encountered parents who defend their ignorance of their child's needs by saying it was 'nothing'? For us, it indeed might be nothing, but to them, it is as essential as the world.

Being empathetic toward your child gives you the space to see the world through their eyes. It makes space for your feelings without any judgment. Empathy is the great affirmation that toddlers need that tells them, "I understand how you are feeling. It's alright. Your feelings matter to me."

Empathy lets your child feel connected to you. It gives them a sense of belonging and security. They will be more at ease, knowing you are someone who understands them. It will bring more confidence in your relationship with your child. Children who have empathetic parents are more comfortable to "manage" and workaround. They live with the knowledge that they have support to fall back on bad days. If the parent is always critical and lacks empathy, the child will retreat within themselves. Such parents may be unable to foster a relationship based on trust and confidence with their kids. Such children will build resentment toward parents as time goes by. Empathy gives them the validation their feelings need.

The very first step to validate is welcoming of their mistakes. You are not accepting their behavior, instead of appreciating the fact that they are humans and will make mistakes just like you do. We taught from our early childhood that mistakes are bad, and the ones committing errors are wrong. We explained that making an error is akin to failure. What we need to realize is that children are innocent. They aren't bad; they are pure. But when we are not welcoming of their mistakes, we are saying the exact opposite to them. When you are accusatory in your approach, kids resort to hiding and covering up their mistakes because they fear you. Hiding mistakes can never be a good idea, as one lie would need a hundred more to hide it. This is not a good trait to encourage in your child. When you hide wrongdoing, you can neither rectify it, nor can you learn from it to avoid it in the future. Instead, be welcoming of their mistakes, guiding them gently as to how they can correct them with empathy. This is what validation gives them; a chance to get back up from their failures, learn from them, and try not to repeat them.

Validation versus Acceptance

Many parents confuse validating their child's behavior with accepting their behavior as correct. These aren't the same. Validation is simply to affirm the feelings of your child as something worth taking note of. You give their emotions the respect they deserve without brushing them off as inconsequential and meaningless. One of the biggest criticisms of the theory of empathy is that it encourages the child to feel confident about their mistakes and urges them to continue their bad behavior. This also isn't true.

Validation is not equal to condoning bad behavior. You are validating the way your child feels, but not the way your child behaves. While you are empathetic toward your child by telling them how you understand their feelings and as to why they are angry or upset, you also firmly establish how you do not support or condone their bad behavior. See the following as an example.

A three-year-old is upset that her older brother has finished her orange juice. They both get into an argument, and she throws the empty juice carton at her brother who ducks, and the empty box lands on the side table, holding crockery, breaking a glass quarter plate, and smashing it to pieces on the floor. Here their quarrel and argument have resulted in a broken plate and the danger of strewn glass pieces all over the kitchen floor. Any caregiver would be angry. She was in the right by being upset, but was the ensuing argument and throwing things appropriately? How must the parent react? How would you react?

What the child needs here is for us to understand that firstly she is simply three years old. Just two years older from being a no-idea-what's-happening infant. Only one year earlier from being able to talk. That is still a very young age for us to be taking them to the task. So, what do we do? What that child needs are a hug and a rub on the back that tells them you understand. If it is a sensitive child, they would be crying even before you look at them. A more hardened child is bound to melt into your arms and cry when you give that hug. Why is this so? Because at this tender age, kids are too innocent of fostering any real hatred or negativity. Their guilt will bring those tears on. At this point, they are overwhelmed by the loss of their juice and the loss of their own emotions. You would only be hurting them more by scolding or yelling at them.

Once they have calmed down, the crying has subsided, and they can look at you without being uncomfortable, now is the time to tell them it was wrong gently. By this time, they know that already. But you have to lay down the rules when your child is calm and in a receptive enough state to listen and acknowledge what you are saying.

"I know you were upset. You were angry; your brother drank your juice. But, dearest, what just happened wasn't fine. You mustn't throw things at each other. We talk about and solve our problems. We do not throw things at each other. That could have seriously hurt someone."

This much is enough to let the message sink in. But this message will only get in mind when you have held them and rubbed their backs, giving them that much-needed hug. That simple, empathetic gesture broke the barrier between the parent and the child. It is what made the child more accepting of their follies and the given advice. Of course, you mustn't forget the older brother or his part in this whole scenario, but for now, our concentration was the vulnerable little girl of three.

Validation is like saying I get how you are feeling. I don't agree with what you have done, but I understand why you have done it. You can and must set behavioral limits while being empathetic at the same time.

Strategies on How to Empathize with Your Toddler

If you are looking to be empathetic to your child's feelings, there are a few things to keep in mind to convey the right message of understanding effectively.

- Bring yourself to their level. Either bend down or kneel so that you both are at the same level.

- Look your child in the eye and truly listen to them. Put away any phones or electronics, or any other chore that you might be doing, to give them your undivided attention.
- Reflect and repeat what they say. It is always a good thing to happen what they tell you back to them. Doing this accomplishes two things. It tells them you have understood what they are saying and also opens for them a chance to correct you if you have in any way misunderstood them.
- Describe how they look and give those words to help them tell you how they feel. For example, you may say, "You are pounding the table with your fists; you look angry!"
- Ask them appropriate questions, so you know you are understanding them correctly and validating their feelings and not the souls you have chosen for them. For example, you might say something like, "You look sad, are you sad?" And then you let them agree or disagree.

9

Let's Talk About Discipline

D iscipline means to teach no punishment, but it also means solid clear limits and consequences for behaviors that are or can be dangerous (play with knives or sharp objects/ crossing the road, pushing others, etc.). For long-lasting behavior change.

The beginning of all effective discipline is parental self-control, thoughtfulness, and intention. At 12 to 18 months, when a child's ability to inhibit their behavior has not yet developed, there is no real necessity to discipline them for any reason. You can express boundaries and celebrate target behaviors—but scolding them for developmentally appropriate behaviors like wandering and mess-making should not be something a parent does at this stage. It is appropriate to prohibit certain behaviors by offering simple course correction or redirection, but anger about your child's poor self-control should be off the table.

Remember, discipline is much closer to the word "discipleship" than it is punishment. And yet, punishment is the word most parents closely associate with discipline. From zero to three years of age, it is especially important that we make sure all our discipline is rooted in teaching, connection, and care. During this time, while your child might be coloring on the walls and throwing food on the floor, make connection priority. Always share your expectations for their behavior in a way that expresses a benevolent understanding of both their limitations and their desires.

Effective Discipline vs. Punishment

Punishment has a punitive nature and does not change the behavior of a child. In many cases, punishment can even make the situation worse.

The child only suffers and learns nothing. Unfortunately, punishment also tends to subject the child to humiliation, serious discomfort, anger, more frustrations, and anxiety, among others. On the other hand, effective discipline is both safe and healthy for the child. Although punishments are also used in an effective discipline strategy, such punishments are mild and only play a part of the whole strategy. Last but not the least, punishment controls a child while discipline guides a child, allowing him to learn from his mistakes and grow beautifully.

Say No to Spanking

Although spanking can be traced back to ancient times as a way to discipline a child, various studies today show that it is not effective. In fact, spanking can even make the situation worse. Spanking a toddler tends to make the child more aggressive, and it does not teach him the right conduct.

Spanking is based on pain. The theory behind it is that a person would not continue doing something that harms him. For example, if you touch a hot stove with your bare hands, you will get hurt, remove your hands immediately, and would no longer dare to do the same action again. Although this sounds logical enough, disciplining a child is not as simple as avoiding getting burned by a hot stove. When you discipline a child, you have not just tell the child what not to do but also what to do. Discipline teaches a toddler positive behaviors, which leads him to take positive actions.

Another thing that makes spanking harmful is that the child tends to lose trust in his parents. Your toddler looks up to you for support, comfort, and care. If you become a source of pain to them, especially if it happens a lot of times, then your child would tend to step back and put a shield around himself. This naturally damages the parent-child relationship.

If you are a parent who is used to spanking your child probably because that was how you were "disciplined" when you were young, or maybe because you simply thought it was the best way to save from child from being a bad person, here are five ways that you can do to stop yourself from spanking your child and be a better parent.

Learn to Use Words

Use words instead of physical aggression. Control yourself and talk calmly without scolding, and be sure to use words that your child can understand. Toddlers have a short attention span and cannot analyze things as good as adults, so keep your words short and simple. Since you communicate with words, you must also listen to your child. It should be a two-way conversation so that there will be understanding. It is also likely that there will be fewer problems if your child feels that you are listening to him. Just as you get exasperated when you feel that your child cannot understand what you are saying, your child also feels terrible when you do not listen to him.

Shift of Focus

Many times, all it takes is a shift of focus. Instead of focusing too much on the negative, focus on the positive behaviors. By giving all the time to positive things, there is no opportunity for the negative behaviors to even manifest themselves.

Let Him Learn On His Own

As people always say, "Experience is the best teacher." This is also true for toddlers. There are times that you do not have to spank your child just for him to learn. By simply letting the normal flow of things to unfold by itself, your toddler can learn from his own actions. For example, if he continues to play with his toy despite your warning roughly, the toy can soon break. This will teach your toddler a good lesson, which is more effective than simply spanking and hurting your child. But, of course, if there is a risk that is threatening to the life and well-being of your child, then you should intervene immediately and explain to your child the possible serious consequences.

Take a Timeout

Take a timeout. Except that this time, you should be the one who should take the timeout. Just before you lose your cool, give yourself a break. Step back for a minute and cool your temper. It is important to note that you should not face your toddler when you are not calm and centered.

Unfortunately, if you are in a public place and you cannot step back and leave your kid alone, the best thing you can do is to pray and think of happy thoughts.

Have the Realization That Spanking Does Not Help

Time and again, various studies show that spanking is not a good way to discipline a child. In fact, spanking can only make things worse, and it does not make you a good parent. Therefore, instead of spanking your child, think of more ways that are positive and constructive on how you can correct the wrong behavior.

Four Pillars of Effective Discipline

The most effective techniques to discipline a child are characterized by four factors, which make them not only effective but also safe and healthy for the child. Unlike punishment, the four pillars of effective discipline promote childhood learning and welfare.

1. It builds a positive parent-child relationship

An effective discipline should be supportive of the relationship between the parent and the child. Unlike punishments that are based on fear, effective discipline is based on understanding, love, and support. You should keep in mind that toddlers are very sensitive, and their early childhood relationships have a great influence on their brain development, as well as on their behavior. By building up a positive relationship with your toddler, he will not only learn the right conduct but also enjoy a strong bond of love and trust with you.

2. It is safe

The safety of the child is of utmost importance. This is another reason why smart parents frown upon the use of punishments that involve bodily harm. Sometimes, the punishments can turn into cruelty and no longer serve the best interest of the child. Not to mention, many of such serious punishments are inflicted when the parent has already lost his patience and control of the situation.

3. It has reasonable expectations

Discipline teaches the child the right and proper conduct. Therefore, you should also consider the age and brain development of your child in making your expectations. Positive behaviors should be continuously enforced, while negative behaviors should be suppressed as early as possible. Be sure to take notice every time your child demonstrates good behavior, or at least try to do so.

4. It is composed of multiple techniques that are safe for the child

Effective discipline is a system of techniques or strategies. A certain technique is used depending on the situation. And, again, this pillar highlights the importance of the child's safety. Every challenging behavior should be taken as a learning opportunity, which can allow the child to learn and grow. As a parent, you must be able to approach the problem directly in a calm manner.

Is it Too late?

Some people think that it is too late to exercise discipline and that their toddlers can no longer change. It is worth noting that toddlers experience rapid changes. In fact, change is part of being a toddler. Either you turn a bad behavior into a good behavior, or let the bad behavior get worse. Of course, as a loving parent, you only want what is best for your child. So, if you are one of the many who think that it might be too late to begin using some discipline, then it should be clear to you by now that it is never too late to do so. Scientifically speaking, it is best to help your child grow in a positive light while he is still a toddler. If he gets to bring certain bad behavior up to his adulthood, they will be more difficult to correct.

What if It Does Not Work?

Another common dilemma shared by most parents is what if nothing changes even if they try to discipline their child? There are certain points to consider. First, there are many techniques that you can use to discipline your child. Second, you would not know if it will work unless you take the action to do so. Third, changing a bad or inappropriate behavior takes time and effort. Fourth, toddlers usually have more than a single behavior that you should try to improve. By applying a form of effective discipline, you can at least help him change some of his bad behaviors. If you are lucky enough, you might put right all his inappropriate manners. Fifth, exercising discipline increases the chances that your child will grow as a good person. Sixth, change happens not only in toddlers but also in adults. Therefore, there is no good reason to think that you cannot change your child's behavior. At the least, you can be able to teach him some good manners. Last but not the least, it is your responsibility as a parent to do everything for your child, to make him grow the best way you can.

All kids need boundaries. Boundaries are not only a great way to teach your toddler good behavior, but they also help him feel safe and secure. The tricky part about boundaries is setting and enforcing them. This becomes a little difficult, especially if you want to avoid bribing, threatening, or coercing your child to listen to you. You must be calm and set firm limits for your child. This is a simple exercise you must repeat time and again, without any inconsistencies. There are no timeouts when it comes to parenting - you are in it for the long haul.

10

Taming Tantrum and Growth Spurts—A Toddler Style to Ask For Attention

Brain Development and Why it Matters

Cognitive, social, and emotional development between 12- and 36-months old children. What to expect?

	Brain Development	Social/Emotional Development
by 12 – 18 months	- Expresses 'no' - Expresses desire (i.e. through pointing) - Recognizes everyday concrete objects such as bottles, blankets, and books - Can follow single-step verbal commands such as 'sit down' or 'come here.'	- May begin to have temper tantrums - May begin to show a fear of strangers - Shows affection for others - May cling to mom, especially around strangers or in unfamiliar situations - Uses

		pointing to share interesting finds with others - Begins to explore by venturing out alone, usually as long as a caregiver/ parent is present

18 Months – 2 Years: Your little one is well into toddlerhood. By now, he is starting to speak in short sentences, show an increased interest in other children, engage in simple imaginative play, and follow more complex instructions. He can also recognize the names of objects or pictures of objects and point to them when prompted. By this age, he is able to experience the full range of emotions. Thanks to his burgeoning independence, more fully developed emotions, and lack of impulse control or emotional regulation, tantrums and refusals will begin to occur. Discipline strategies will continue to be focused on keeping your toddler safe and healthy while helping them to develop self-control. Check out the table below for a more in-depth look.

		Brain Development	Social/Emotional Development
s	by 2 year	- Points to things or pictures when they are named - Able to form short sentences (2-4 words) - Begins to be able to sort basic shapes and colors - Begins to play	- Mimics the words and behavior of others - Gets excited when around other children - Increases in independence - Shows defiant behavior - For the most part,

	rudimentary make-believe games - Can follow instructions with two steps	plays next to other children rather than with them, but is beginning to include other children in simple games such as chase	

2-3 Years: By now, your toddler is exhibiting increasingly complex cognitive abilities, including following more complicated instructions and completing simple puzzles. He is also able to hold short conversations with full sentences and demonstrates the enjoyment of and empathy for others. He's grown more socially independent, separating from parents with greater ease. The terrible twos have arrived full force, and you can expect more resistance when your toddler is tired or doesn't get his or her way. As with all stages of toddlerhood, discipline will continue to focus on health and safety, but now you can begin to introduce more concrete life skills such as sharing, turn-taking, and better emotional regulation.

		Brain Development	Social/Emotional Development
ars	by 3 ye	- Can follow instructions with 3 steps - Can hold a short conversation using 2 to 3 sentences - Can play with more complicated toys that include moving parts - Engages in imaginative play with people and toys - Can complete very simple puzzles	- Copies the behavior of others - Shows affection for others - Engages in turn-taking during games and other activities - Shows concern for friends or family in distress - Understands possession ('mine' vs. 'his' or 'hers') - Shows a wide range of emotions - Able to explore comfortably without a caregiver's presence, at

| | | least some of the time |
| | | - May be upset or uncomfortable with changes in routine |

3-4 Years: The skills that began to appear between 12 and 36 months will continue to develop, leading your toddler to be able to engage in more complex cognitive activities, such as memorizing nursery rhymes and beginning to conceptualize things like time and contrast. She may also show an awe-inspiring degree of creativity as she engages in imaginative play with herself, her toys, and others. By now, she's probably learned a degree of self-control when it comes to emotional regulation and is having fewer/shorter tantrums. She's made strides in impulse control, although it's still very much a work in progress. She has also learned to meet basic behavioral expectations, such as not throwing food, not hitting, and cleaning up toys. During this stage of development, discipline will become more focused on helping your toddler to learn the foundations of critical life skills such as cooperation and conflict resolution.

	Age	Brain Development	Social/Emotional Development
rs	by 4 yea	- Abel to recite simple songs and poems from memory - Abel to tell stories and make predictions in a story - Understands the concept of counting and may be able to count - Begins to understand the concept of time - Understands the concept of 'same' and 'different.'	- Becomes increasingly creative with imaginative play - Enjoys playing with other children more than playing alone - Is able to cooperate with other children - Not always able to tell what's real and what's make-believe - Talks about likes and interests

As you can see, the toddler years are a crucial time for the brain and social development. As your child moves through each stage of toddlerhood, there some important supportive and risk factors to keep in mind to ensure your little one's optimal brain and social development.

Supportive factors are environmental, situational, and interpersonal influences that contribute to and/or support healthy development. Risk factors, on the other hand, may have an unhealthy, detrimental, or damaging effect on your child's brain and social/emotional development.

The table below lists some of the supportive and risk factors to look out for. Supportive factors should be encouraged within the home, and risk factors minimized or eliminated.

Supportive Factors	Risk Factors
- Responsive caregiver interactions (caregiver interprets and responds to toddler's emotions/needs in an accurate and timely manner) - Loving interactions - Hugs - Adequate nutrition - Healthy sleep - Time for safe exploration in a caregiver's presence - Structure and routine	- Lack of loving interaction from mother or primary caregiver - Invasive or unresponsive parenting - Too much 'screen time' - Poor nutrition - Poor sleep - Stress in the home - Abuse of the toddler - Abuse in the toddler's presence

Now that we've gone over some of the exciting developmental steps you can expect to see throughout toddlerhood, it's time to move on to the next aspect of our discussion on toddler discipline: Limits!

What is a Tantrum?

Temper tantrums are frustrating. There is no way around it. However, they are not some majorly negative factors to consider—rather, they are learning experiences for everyone involved. Your child does not know better than to throw those tantrums. They happen when your child is feeling incredibly emotional, but is unsure about how to handle those big emotions that are roiling around inside him or her. For that reason, you should approach tantrums with grace and understanding—you should be willing and able to recognize that your child is not throwing this massive fit to hurt you, but rather because he or she feels entirely out of control.

Tantrums can range greatly from kicking and screaming to hitting or holding one's breath. Some children, particularly the stubborn ones, will hold their breaths until they finally end up passing out due to oxygen deprivation. While alarming to watch what happens at the moment, it is not putting your child at any real risk, and your child's body will take control before he or she can do any real, lasting harm.

Most often, these tantrums happen between the ages of 1 and 3. During this time, your child is going through a major period of development. Everything is new to your child—he or she may be learning how to interact with the world. There is the development of the concept of autonomy during this age as well—your child is finally beginning to recognize that he or she is their own independent person. Your child wants to interact and do so much, but they cannot communicate. They may want to impulsively do things that you know are harmful, such as jumping off of a counter, and when you stop them, they throw a fit. They cannot comprehend the reasoning behind why you say no at this point in time, and they find that they get overwhelmed by that frustration, disappointment, anger, or sadness that follows.

Reasons for Tantrums

Your Child Wants Something

Perhaps the most common reason for a tantrum is that your child wants something. They may want something that they cannot have at that moment, so they throw a big tantrum over it. Perhaps they want an ice cream cone for breakfast, but you know better, so you tell them no. They then throw a big fit because they are disappointed and angry.

Your Child Needs Something

Sometimes, the tantrum actually comes from an unmet need. They may be overly tired, overly hungry, thirsty, or need a diaper change. They need something and are struggling to communicate that need. If that need goes unmet due to not understanding it, the child may meltdown into frustration and tears.

Your Child Wants to Avoid Something

Sometimes, the tantrum is due to avoidance. You are trying to get your child to do something that he or she does not want to do, and instead of accepting that at face value, your child instead decides to cry and scream about it. For example, it may be bedtime, but your child is throwing a big tantrum about being put in the crib. Your child is looking for autonomy here and is attempting to assert his or her own will.

Your Child Wants Attention

Occasionally, if you have not been paying attention to your toddler and he or she wants your attention, a tantrum will arise. This is primarily due to the fact that toddlers operate under the assumption that even negative attention is better than no attention. If you have not been giving your child the attention that he or she needs and craves, you run the risk of having your child throw a tantrum just to get your eyes on him or her in the first place.

Your Child Can't Communicate

Sometimes, the tantrum comes down to just not being able to communicate wants and needs well. Your child has all of these big feelings that he or she has not yet learned to cope with, and because of that, they can become explosive.

Parent's Guide to Dealing with Tantrums

With those points in mind, you may be wondering how you can deal with tantrums as they arise. After all, ultimately, it will be your reaction to the tantrum that determines how the child learns to cope with them. You must be willing and able to regulate your own behaviors in order to ensure that, at the end of the day, your child learns how to self-regulate. You are setting the stage for whether your child learns that tantrums are acceptable, how to handle tantrums, or how to self-regulate. When you are dealing with a child that throws tantrums, try to remember the following:

1. It is okay to be upset: Remember, tantrums are not fun for anyone. It is normal that, at the sound of your child screaming, you feel stressed out. That is a normal biological reaction, and you are biologically predisposed to trying to make your child stop crying and screaming. Remember that it is a very normal reaction to be upset, but that being upset is not an excuse for you to lose your temper as well.

2. Remember to take a deep breath: Before you begin dealing with your child, try to practice the rule of stopping to take a big, deep breath. This will help you clear your own head and keep yourself from doing something that you will later feel guilty about or regret. You will also be teaching your child good self-regulation skills that will be developed further later down the line by showing him or her how you treat the situation.

3. Remember that your child is having a hard time: Many parents may find themselves asking why their children would do this to them. However, this is the wrong way to look at this situation. Your child is not trying to give you a hard time—he or she is having a hard time, and right at that moment, the only way that he or she knows how to deal with those big, strong emotions that are burning inside is through that tantrum.

4. Stop to figure out why the child is throwing a tantrum: If you know that your child regularly will have a tantrum when he or she is overtired, you can begin to avoid running into that problem. If you can identify common triggers for a tantrum, such as being hungry or tired, and it is a practical thing that you can avoid, you can make it a point to avoid those pitfalls. If you know that your child gets overtired and throws fits when he or she skips naptime, you may make it a point to make naptime entirely sacred, and nothing short of an emergency will make you leave the house during that time.

5. Don't be embarrassed: If you have children, chances are, you have had a public tantrum at least once with your children present. If you have not, then your children are probably either too young to cause those sorts of tantrums, or your time is coming sooner rather than later. The vast majority of children will have some sort of public meltdown at some point over something—it is just a matter of time. This means that those parents around you know what you are going through. They know the frustration and anger that you are feeling. Don't be embarrassed if you get a rude stare or comment if your child throws a fit in public—it happens. It comes with the territory. Don't let other people distract you or make you feel bad, or you run the risk of otherwise struggling.

Redirection to tame tantrums

Perhaps one of the best skills that you have on you as a parent is the ability to redirect during a tantrum. This is particularly true when you are dealing with a child that is quite young—they are throwing a fit usually due to their emotional side of their brains being on auto-pilot at that point in time. Your child has the ability to think in a rational, calm manner, and an ability to think emotionally—we all have this. When the emotional side is running rampant and taking control of the situation, we are not making good decisions. We are acting in ways that are impulsive, and with that, impulsiveness often comes to all sorts of other problems as well. Our choices can wind up having all sorts of unintended repercussions that we were not ready to deal with.

If adults can fall for these same habits, then it should come as no surprise that your child can, as well. During these periods of time, when the child's emotions overwhelm him or her, they are unable to think with the rational parts of their minds. The emotional side has taken control during this time and is going to overwhelm their thought process and actions. This is exactly what happens in a tantrum. Your child is probably feeling some very big, very strong feelings that he or she does not know how to cope with, and because of that, he or she really struggles to make the proper progress needed to calm down.

When your child is mid-tantrum, however, you can usually re-engage with their logical side of their mind, pulling that back to the surface rather than allowing it to be stifled by emotional impulses. This is precisely what you will be doing when you are making use of redirection. You will be attempting to do or say something that will sort of cause the logical half of the child's mind to stop and pay attention—you want that logical half of the brain to reengage and control the individual.

The Most Important Things Are Them Be Safe and Feel Loved, Not Well Behaved at All the Time

We are uncomfortable with our children's big emotions, particularly in public. We shame them; we belittle them, etc. It makes feel we are not doing a good job, but their brain still developing, it is normal that they will misbehave. We cannot control them, the environment, etc. If you want to control them all the time, you are breaking their will power. You break their joy.

Handling Behavior Problems

Children express their frustrations with various challenges through tantrums. Maybe your toddler is having difficulties in completing a specific task? Perhaps they don't have the right words to express what they feel? Frustrations play a major role in triggering anger that leads to tantrums. Let's look at various ways to handle tantrums in children.

Take the right steps to prevent the tantrums.

Schedule some frequent playtime with your little one. Allow them to choose the activity and make sure the child gets complete attention from you. Sharing a positive experience will offer your child an excellent foundation to calm herself down whenever they get upset. Check out the opportunities that will acknowledge her excellent performance. When a child receives favorable attention for the desired performance, they'll then form a habit of doing the same.

You can also create good tactics to deal with the frustrations immediately, like taking a deep breath. It's also essential to fess up after being angry over something. That's because your child needs to know it's OK to make mistakes once in a while. Make sure you know the things that lead to the tantrum and plan well. If the child gets frustrated when they're hungry, try to carry some healthy snacks. If the child starts grumbling when tired, try to make sleep time a priority.

Speak Whenever the Child Yells

Your toddler will match the tone of your voice since they want to get your attention. Bear in mind, and they're feeling angry and sad might assist you to remain calm. Whenever they lose control at a public spot such as the movies, take the child outside. Allow them to sit on the bench or in the car as they settle down. For most children, having such choices will help, mainly if the lack of control causes the outburst.

During a post-tantrum, try to follow through with the first demand that caused the outburst. If the child became frustrated because you asked them to collect the toy, they could still get it when they're calm. If the child started screaming because you didn't allow them to have a cookie, then give the cookie once they stop crying. When the child follows through and collects the toy, applaud the child. That's because it's a positive habit you'll want to instill in them.

Know Why Your Toddler Reacts Strongly

While your child can use words to express what they want, that doesn't imply that the tantrums have ended. They're still learning ways to handle emotions, and a slight disagreement will make them frustrated and sad. Since your toddler values their growing independence, requiring your help might be frustrating. They might break down when trying to complete a challenging task such as tying shoelaces and finds out they cannot do the job alone. Even though tantrums tend to start with anger, they're always deep-rooted in sadness. Children might get lost in how unjust and huge a situation becomes, so they struggle with how to do the task successfully.

Attempt this one tactic for tantrums for children under two and a half years. In most cases, children within this age bracket have 50 words in their vocabulary and can't link over two words together at a time. The child's communication is limited, but they have countless thoughts, needs, and wishes that must be met. When you fail to understand what they want, they tend to freak out to express their sadness and frustration. The remedy for this is to teach the children how to sign some words like milk, food, and tired. Empathizing with your child is another method to deal with outbursts. It assists in curbing the tantrums.

Give Your Child Some Space and Create a Diversion

In most cases, a child is supposed to get rid of the anger. So, just let them do it. This method will help your child know how to vent in a non-destructive manner. They'll have a chance to release their feelings, get themselves together, and recover self-control. Your child will engage in a yelling contest or fight with you. This approach can work in tandem with ignoring it a bit.

This entails a definite mental switcheroo. Try to get your child engaged and interested in other things to make her forget about the bad experience. Make sure your backpack or purse has all kinds of distractions such as toys, comics, and yummy snacks. Once your child starts throwing tantrums, get the distraction out to catch your child's attention.

Note that a distraction can assist you in warding off a huge outburst before it occurs, provided you catch it in time. If you realize that your child is about to yell at the store since you don't want to buy them what they want, try to switch gears and enthusiastically say something such as, "Hey, do we need some bread. Do you want to assist me in getting a kind?" children tend to have a short attention duration, and this makes it easy to divert their attention. When doing this, make sure you sound psyched as it will make your child know it's real. They'll tend to forget about what made them feel sad and focus on the better things.

Offer a Big and Tight Hug

This might feel the hardest thing to do when your toddler is acting up,

254

but it'll assist them to calm down. This should be a big tight hug and never say anything when doing it. Hugs will make your child feel secure and allow them to understand you care about them, even though you don't support the tantrum habits. In most cases, a child needs a safe place to release one's emotions.

Give Them Food or Suggest Some R&R

Getting tired and being hungry is the leading cause of tantrums in children. Since the child is on the brink emotionally, an outburst will quickly occur. Most parents keep wondering why their child has meltdowns that occur during the same time every day—for instance, many toddler's tantrums before lunch and in the evening, which is never a coincidence. If you're experiencing this, make sure you feed your child well and give them enough water. After that, let her veg, whether it involves taking her to bed or letting her watch TV.

Give the Child Incentive to Behave

Some situations tend to be trying for children. They can encompass sitting for long hours in a restaurant when eating or staying calm in church. Irrespective of the scenario, the tactic is about noticing when you're asking for too much from your child. Also, remember to give them the incentive for the excellent work done. While heading to the restaurant, for instance, tell her," Maya, mom wants you to sit and take your dinner nicely. I know you'll do that! And if you behave well, you'll play your video games when we get home. This type of bribery is perfectly provided. It's done as per your terms and before time and not under pressure in the middle of a tantrum. In case she begins to lose her temper, remind her about your promise. It's great how it'll suddenly guide her back into shape.

Laugh it Off

As a parent, you fear public tantrums for various reasons. You're probably afraid other people will brand you a bad parent, or that you're raising an out of control child. However, that might lure you into making some choice that will result in deep fits. Children are always smart, even the little ones. If you get stressed and angry, allow them to find the best way to end the outburst before many people begin staring, they'll learn on her own. The best thing is to suck it up, put on a smile, and pretend that everything is OK.

Get Out of That Place

Getting your little one away from the place of a tantrum will subdue the outburst. Additionally, it's an ideal strategy when you're in public places. When your child starts yelling over candy bars or a toy they want, take the child to a different place within the supermarket or even outside until they stop crying. Shifting the place will likely change the behavior.

12

Tools for More Cooperative Children

Peaceful, Patient, and Positive Parenting

In certain situations, maintaining calmness, patience, and perseverance can be very difficult. However, it is possible. The only thing that gets in the way is how you, as a parent, look at your child's unpleasant behavior.

Children are small figures in an adult's world. Each of them is born with their own temperament and their right to choose what to do, whether it is useful or harmful to them. Since children speak in "other" languages, it is sometimes difficult for parents to understand them. From the parents' point of view, their little ones are too immature to make any decisions at all. However, it is true that, regardless of the consequences, children have the right to choose what they will do at certain times. You must be patient through this process. And that is not easy.

It's hard, but necessary to maintain calmness. If a parent thinks the child is "unresponsive" and that they "can't take the child's behavior anymore," then it is entirely normal for them to lose their patience, and in a large number of cases, lose control as well. Many parents then shout at the child in order to change the child's behavior.

A common feature that occurs in these cases is: Parents have lost their patience and lost their persistence.

However, if you step away from this unpleasant situation which makes you feel angry at your child, and you look at it objectively, you won't see the child's perspective as "insignificant" or see him as "misunderstood" but will see that he needs something. From this perspective, you can use logic and try to find out exactly what your child needs and what you need to do to help him. So, as you do this, you are constantly and patiently "reading" your child.

So, What is Patience?

Being a persistent and patient parent means putting in consistent and constant work to develop quality and constructive communication with your child because you must reach your child's inner self and feelings. One of the positive side effects that you will achieve as an efficient parent is that with all of your patience and understanding as you manage the child's behavior and help them, one day, your toddler becomes an emotionally intelligent and responsible person.

The essence of positive discipline is to learn to change yourself instead of trying to change others and to make others want to change. If you're busy trying to control your child, you are not thinking about the ability to solve problems by controlling your behavior and making decisions about your actions, rather than trying to correct your child's behavior.

It is easy to fall into the temptation to repeat what you have said, to remind the child of something, and to explain it instead of just doing what you have already told. Careful and resolute parenting gives parents the opportunity to spend time developing the great features that their child possesses, talks with them on many interesting topics, and giving them an explanation of how things work in life.

Punishment: Toughness through Love. Should I Punish a Child?

Apparently, most parents think you should punish a child. But it is important to define the concept of "punishment." Punishment can be a strict tone in your voice, temporarily depriving the child of positive interaction, sweets, or any privileges that are reserved for obedient children.

We don't even contemplate using physical punishment, and when parents have outdated ideas about the admissibility of corporal punishment, we hope that they can be immediately corrected!

Of course, it's hard to imagine a mother who has never raised her voice in her life. But we can imagine the surprise of an angry mother when in response to a slap her own child turns around and does the same thing!

If you punish children physically, you risk making them angry, and depending on the individual characteristics of their personality; they will not only remember everything in detail but may also want to get revenge!

Imagine a situation where the child doesn't think about the consequences of his actions or forgets what you have told him earlier. Even if the child did something deliberately disobedient, do not lower yourself to his level, and respond in kind. Be patient, and be wiser.

Punishments Don't Help Much

If we take into account that the punishment causes a negative emotional state and causes the child to feel embarrassed, frightened, and insecure, we can understand that punishment does not motivate the child to learn from the situation. That is why it is useful for parents to make a decision about what their parenting goal is: absolute obedience or a relationship of trust.

What Punishment Can Do?

Punishment implies a loss of opportunity for experiential learning, but also causes a loss of opportunity to create a relationship of trust between you and your child. If the child fears punishment, he will not feel encouraged to learn, to draw conclusions, and later to develop responsibility.

How to Replace Punishment with Positive Parenting

A positive approach to parenthood implies an understanding of the child and of his or her behavior, paying attention to how the child feels.

What does that mean practically? Seeing what is behind a child's behavior means seeing the real cause, understanding it, and offering the child an alternate solution to negative behavior.

Adults mostly only see the "final product"--the unwanted behavior that they want to correct, or a symptom of the real cause. If they want the child to learn something and that isn't working, it is up to adults to explain to the child the consequences of his negative behavior: Natural consequences ("You are cold because you do not want to wear a sweater.") and logical consequences ("We are late for the birthday party because you wanted to play even though the clock was ringing and telling us it was time to go.").

Positive parenting creates a space for learning without guilt, shame, and the fear of punishment.

Children learn by making a series of efforts and mistakes. The whole process of a child's upbringing and learning is a series of attempts and mistakes until they master some skills. The role of the parents in this process is to provide direction and leadership. You must be a teacher to your children first of all, but a patient one.

The part of the brain that is responsible for reason, logic, and the control of impulses is not fully developed until adolescence. "Immature" behavior is normal in "immature" human beings that have "immature" brains. This is a scientific fact, and whatever you feel as a parent, and however you behave in these situations, you will not change that.

Parenting is difficult and requires the patience to repeat the same thing hundreds of times. Being a child is also difficult because it requires strength and persistence to repeat the same thing hundreds of times until it is learned. This process cannot be accelerated, skipped, or eliminated. The only thing a parent can do is change their perspective and accept that some things are slow and annoying, and have to be repeated many times. Some parents have days when they feel discouraged because they have to repeat the same thing day after day. But that is also a great part of parenthood.

Children learn about the world from their parents, and learning isn't just about gathering information. One of the most important things in your child's process of learning is learning how to live in the society in which he or she is growing up and learning the rules to function in that society. Kids have to know when it is proper and better for them to limit their autonomy and self-expression, and they have to know that they are able to do it. Then, they have to learn how to tolerate frustration and handle frustration and to be consistent in spite of it.

If we allow them to, children will try to solve the problems they face in their development and upbringing. Parents often begin to scold or criticize the child, not expecting the child to attempt to solve the problem. If the parents were more patient, they would be surprised how much their children are actually capable of making conclusions and solving the problems they face.

Being heard is therapeutically powerful and allows us to think about things clearly and find a solution. The same goes for children. Sometimes it's enough just to listen to a child when they talk about the problems they are having because they often come up with solutions that resolve the problems.

Fear and control are effective in the short term, but a child can become either completely blocked in his development or can begin to provide resistance to parental pressure through defiance and rebellion. Depending on the type of interaction a child has with his or her parents, the child forms a picture of himself and a sense of self-reliance in his roles in life. A blocked, non-progressing child has a lesser perception of his value, which can lead to isolation or to its opposite: aggressive and rebellious behavior.

Children should understand the importance of thoughts and emotions, not just behavior, because it will enable them to function better in relationships with other people and to deal better with problems. That is why adequate control of their emotions is an important skill and one of the most important goals of parenting.

The words of parents and their assessments of a child are a mirror for that child. Children will see what their parent's exhibit. That then becomes their picture of themselves, and they live with that. That is why it is very important to be specific and accurate with criticism. Criticism should be

261

expressed with body language, which expresses regret rather than disapproval toward the child. A parental look full of condemnation and criticism will be internalized by the child, and we want to love and accept our children. This strong support for them will be the seed and the core of their happy life and success.

However, you shouldn't give your child unlimited freedom; you do need to discipline them, of course. But, how? Disciplinary measures respond to the child and his abilities and support the child in developing self-discipline. Discipline aims to positively target children, recognizing individual values, and building positive relationships. Positive discipline empowers children's faith in themselves and their ability to behave appropriately.

Discipline is training and orientation that helps children to develop limits, self-control, efficiency, self-sufficiency, and positive social behavior. Discipline is often misunderstood as punishment, especially by those who apply strict punishment in their endeavors to make changes to children's behavior. But discipline is not the same as punishment.

13

Take a Deep Breath and Self-Regulate (As for Everything in Life)

Slow down against your impulse to get irritated. Become present, look at your child, and connect.

Many parents attest to the reality that disciplining a toddler is like facing constant uphill battles. These little bundles of delight can turn to extremely stubborn kids who test the patience limits of caregivers and adults around them.

It is also the phase of childhood where they begin to assert their independence. One of their first words is "No," affirming the toddlers' love to do things in their way. They enjoy running away to escape. Normal toddlers are full of energy. They run, jump, play, explore, and discover everything that interests them. They love to use the sense of touch, exploring things with their senses. Because toddlers are easily stimulated by what they see or hear, their impulsive nature can make them clumsy and touch things. Parents need to teach their children safe ways to touch or handle things and not to touch hot objects.

Although raising a toddler entails a lot of hard work, seeing your child grows and develops his skills is fascinating. However, because of the developmental changes that rapidly happen during the toddler stage; it is necessary to use a disciplinary approach that will foster the child's independence while teaching him socially appropriate behavior and other positive traits.

All too often, there is an assumption that parenting techniques apply to all, and kids will react or respond in a similar pattern. But every child has his own set of traits. They are in his DNA, which he inherited from his parents. Some toddlers are shy or even-tempered, while others are outgoing and have aggressive natures.

By understanding the child's special personality and natural behavior, you can help him adjust to the real world. It is necessary to work with his personality and not against it, taking into account the following factors that you need to consider when disciplining your toddler. Giving proper care and nourishment, providing positive and healthy activities, and instilling positive discipline is vital to his physical, mental, emotional, social, and behavioral growth...

Temperament and Behavior

Temperament is defined as the heritable and biologically based core that influences the style of approach and response of a person. The child's early temperament traits usually predict his adult temperament.

The child's behavior is the outcome of his temperament and the progress of his emotional, cognitive, and physical development. It is influenced by his beliefs about himself, about you, and the world in general. While it is inborn and inherent, there are certain ways to help your toddler manage it to his advantage.

Nine Dimensions or Traits Related to Temperament

1. The activity level pertains to the amount of physical motion that your toddler demonstrates, while engaged in some activities. It also includes his inactive periods.

   - Is your child a restless spirit who cannot sit still for so long or want to move around?
   - Is your toddler the quiet, little one who enjoys playing alone or watching TV?

2. Rhythmicity refers to the predictability or unpredictability of physical and biological functions which include hunger, bowel movement, and sleeping.

- Does your child thrive on routine and follow regular eating or sleeping patterns?

- Does he display unpredictable behavior and dislike routine?

3. Attention span and persistence are the skills to remain focused on the activity for a certain period.

    - Does your toddler stick to complete a task?
    - Is he easily frustrated and look for another activity?

4. Initial Response (Approach or Withdrawal) refers to the reaction to something new and unfamiliar. It describes his initial feelings to a stimulus like a new person, place, toy, and food. His reaction is shown by his mood or facial expressions like smiling or motor activity, such as reaching for a toy or swallowing food. Negative responses include withdrawal, crying, fussing, pushing away, or spitting the food.

    - Is he wary or reluctant around unfamiliar situations or strangers?

    - Does he welcome new faces and adjust comfortably with new settings?

5. The intensity of the reaction is associated with the level of response to any event or situation. Toddlers respond differently to events around them. Some shrieks with happiness or giggle joyfully, others throw fits, and many barely react to what is happening.

    - Do you always experience trying to guess the reaction of your child over something?

    - Does your child explicitly show his emotions?

6. Adaptability is the child's ability to adjust himself to change over time.

- Is your child capable of adjusting himself to sudden changes in plans or disruptions of his routine?

- Does he find it difficult to cope up with changes and resist it as much as he can?

7. Distractibility is the level of the child's willingness to be distracted. It relates to the effects of an outside stimulus on your child's behavior.

- Can your child focus on his activity despite the distraction that surrounds him?

- Is he unable to concentrate when there are people or other activities going on in the environment?

8. Quality of mood is related to how your child sees the world in his own eyes and understanding. Some react with acceptance and pleasure while other children scowl with displeasure just "because" they feel like it.

- Does he display mood changes constantly?

- Does he generally have a happy disposition?

9. Sensory Threshold is linked to sensitivity to sensory stimulation. Children who are sensitive to stimulation requires a careful and gradual introduction to new people, experiences, or objects.

- Is your child easily bothered by bright lights, loud sounds, or food textures?

- Is he totally undisturbed with such things and welcome them as such?

There are three main types of toddlers:

1. Active or Feisty Toddlers--These children have a tremendous amount of energy, which they show even while inside the uterus of their mothers, like lots of moving and kicking. As an infant, they

move around, squirm, and crawl all over the place. As toddlers, they climb, run, jump, and even fidget a lot to release their energy. They become excited while doing things or anxious around strangers or new situations.

They are naturally energetic, joyful, and loves fun. But when they are not happy, they will clearly and loudly say it. These toddlers are also quite obstinate and hard to fit in regular routines.

To help him succeed:

- Acknowledge his unique temperament and understand his triggers.

- Teach him self-help skills to get going if his energy is low or how to calm down when his activity level is very high. Some simple and effective ways to calm down are counting from 1 to 10, taking deep breaths, doing jumping jacks to get rid of excess energy, and redirecting him to other activities.

- Set a daily routine that includes play and other activities that enhance his gross motor movements. Provide him with opportunities to play and explore safely. It is necessary to childproof your home.

- Insist on nap time. An afternoon nap will refresh his body and mind, preventing mood swings and tantrums.
- Do not let him sit in front of a television or do passive activities. Break the boredom by taking him outside and play in the outdoors.

- Become a calming influence. Understand how your temperament affects his temperament and find ways to become a role model.

2. Passive or Cautious Toddlers- These children prefer activities that do not require a lot of physical effort, move slower, and want to sit down more often. They are slow-to-warm-up when meeting new people and often withdraw when faced with an unfamiliar situation. They also need ample time to complete their tasks.

To help him succeed:

- If your child is less active, set guidelines or deadlines that will prompt him to finish the given tasks.

- Invite him to play actively by using interesting noises, bright toys, or gentle persuasion.

- Always accentuate the positive. Be generous with praise and words of encouragement when they display efforts or achieve simple milestones.

3. Flexible or Easy Toddlers - These children are very adaptable, generally calm, and happy. But sometimes, they are easily distracted and need a lot of reassurance and love from you.

To help him succeed:

- Be realistic and expect mood changes when something is not smooth-sailing. Do not be too hard on the child when he displays unusual outburst.

- Provide him with interactive activities and join him. Sometimes, it is easy to let him play his own devices because of his good-natured personality. It is necessary to introduce other options to enhance his skills.

- Read the signs and find out the reasons for subtle changes in the behavior and attitude toward something. Be observant and have a special time for him.

14

Coach: State What Is Going on

Most of the time, there are underlining reasons for your child's uncooperative behavior; you are anxious, you are rushing, and you are suffering, and their pick on that. Reclaim that connection. Try to be funny about, get silly. Let go a bit of control if it is a minor issue.

If it does not work, comment that 'you are having a difficult time this morning. It's ok you don't want your shoes on' agree that is not put the shoes on, put them in your bag and try to break the drama by singing a favorite song, get silly, etc..

You need to act big ONLY when is actually needs it: stop at the end of the pavement, do not run into the road, etc.

How You Affects Toddlers

For kids, their parents are the live example and guideline. The very first role model of a kid is his or her mother and father. The kids observe how their parents are dealing with the people, issues, matter, and routine work as well. Other than the actions, your traits and personality do affect the kid and a kind of model for them.

Before getting started with how your personality affects theirs, it is necessary to know what defines your personality. Personality is the combination of behavior, reaction, treatment to the situation, and public dealing. If, as a parent, you are kind to others and have a polite nature, the kid will learn the politeness and kindness through observation. Same as on the other hand, if you have anger issues or are mostly confused in the decision making or taking a stance, then your child will end up with the same condition.

When it comes to making your kid learn the positive discipline, you need to work on the overall discipline as well. Something you want your kids to learn, you are supposed to do the same in front of them. As per the recent study of behavioral learning explains that kids are good at observation, and the visuals they have in daily life are the biggest source for them to learn everything. From the manners to behaviors and even the way of life, they learn from the environment and elders.

Watch Your Actions

If you want to bring change in your kid, the most important thing is to watch your actions. If you are lying to your kids, they will lie back to you. This is something that is learning from your behavior and action in the first place. You are supposed to give them reasons for everything that is happening.

Do Not Find the Easy Escape

Scolding a child on questions, giving lame excuses, or ignore their questions is the easy escape that parents have most of the time. This is something that can lead to adverse behavioral changes in the kids. They will adopt the habit of ignorance and anger when they are unable to sort out the problem or do not have answers.

Make Them Reasoning

If there is something you are unable to do for the kids, or some things are impossible or unmanageable, then you are supposed to reason that. When you give solid and measurable reasons for something that develop a habit and understanding of logic in the kid, they will know the way to say not is proper reasoning, not just running away. It seems to be a difficult task in the beginning, but eventually, you can make some real improvements in your kid's behavior and overall discipline as well.

Understanding Developmental Appropriateness

Developmental appropriateness is an approach to teach the kid. In this approach, the curriculum is designed according to age and individual needs. The basic objective of this program is that every kid fits in this program. In other words, it is a program for each kid. He should not need to fit in the program as the program will fit in him.

Best Curriculum Design Strategy

Designing the curriculum for preschoolers is a critical task. A teacher needs to keep various elements in mind. The appropriate development strategy helps the teacher to design the best curriculum concerning this approach curriculum designed according to the capabilities of a student. At a certain age, what he can do physically, cognitively, and emotionally. This strategy helps in all these perspectives.

Every Children's Need is Different

The teachers of preschool look at the whole child individually. They see his physical, intellectual, emotional, social, and creative growth. The growth of these different segments raised in every child at its speed. Some factors developed in some children at an early stage. On the other side, in some children, they develop later.

Every child has capabilities, but teachers need to recognize and polish them. Some preschoolers have strong intellectual skills. But he needs to develop those skills through socialization. Likewise, some kids have great speaking power. However, the only thing they need is the confidence to speak in public. Besides this, some common developmental patterns are there, too, the same for all kids.

Role of a Teacher

Through the developmentally appropriate approach teacher observe all the preschooler's behavior. By utilizing her experience, she will recognize the capabilities of students. According to their strength, teachers design and plan the activities. She tried that those activities should not be too easy or too tough for kids. The purpose of these activities is to help students to grow and learn.

Flexible Method

To make it feasible for all the student's development appropriate approach has flexible methods. These methods are open-ended and have limited chances of mistakes. The reason behind this strategy is to teach all the kids equally. With the fewer chances of mistakes, students learn with confidence.

Students Keep Themselves Active

For a child's positive discipline, he must remain busy in positive activities. The development appropriation keep.

The kid busy. If your preschooler is engaged in his independent activities, it is a sign. Yes, it is a sign of his appropriate development. He will not get frustrated or bored, rather than that, he will engage in the activities his teacher taught him.

The Miraculous Brain: In learning and Development

Your child has a miraculous brain like other kids. Even before birth till age 5, the child's brain develops with the highest speed. Brain development at an early age has a long-lasting impact on his ability to learn. This early learning remains with him for the rest of his life. His early childhood's positive or negative experiences play a key role in his brain development.

Strong Observation

The observation of a child at an early age is very strong. His brain picks up the information and actions at an incredible pace. His brain process that observation speedily, and he connects all his observations with observations.

He observes people around him and their behavior towards them. Along with this, he observes his physical environment, for instance, colors, food, fabric patterns, sounds, roof, walls, and so on. These observations play an important role in his early development and learning.

Strong Five Senses

The miraculous brain keeps all his five senses super active. His listening, speaking, seeing, tasting, and touching; all senses are really strong at this age. From a normal person, their brain absorbs more than these senses. His senses make him extra sensitive, especially about his physical environment. With these multiple strong senses, he learns various things in a short time.

Learn to React

As a child's brain works efficiently, he learns to react. Since the birth of a child, he starts his journey to learn how to react. When he should laugh or cry. How to tell he is hungry or in pain? He starts to understand the feelings of joy or sadness.

Similarly, he reacts to the situations. He learns who is her mother or to whom he feels protective? He learns all these reactions and feelings at high speed through amazing brain functions.

The Growth of Child's Brain Ability

According to the studies, initial years are really important for a kid's learning. You are thinking about how he digests lots of information at the same time. Yes, you are thinking right because adults, mostly can't digest more information at a time. But a kid's brain works differently. You will be surprised by the kid's brain ability development process.

A kid's brain ability not decreased but increased with increasing information. With the increased information, he started to connect and relate it with the information. It expands his imagination and learning canvas.

Excellent Memory

At an early stage of life, a kid has an excellent memory. He observes things and saved them in his brain. He tried to copy the actions of the people around him. Most of the kids didn't forget anything that they see only once. Therefore, parents need to behave well when kids are around them.

Strategies to Enhance Brain Function in Learning and Development

As mentioned earlier, every child has a miraculous brain. But the pace of learning of each child will be different from others. If you feel that your kid is going at a slow pace, don't worry. You and her teachers can deal with it. Some strategies will enhance his brain function to help him.

Active Their Mind

If you see your kid is not properly acting, help him in activating his mind. You can do this by engaging him in different healthy physical activities. These activities must be interesting and should be designed according to the kid's age. I must try to make them not too simple or too hard. Talk to his teacher and design an activity jointly so that he can do this in school and at home.

Social Gatherings

Man is a social animal and can't live without others. Similarly, kids also need to socialize for their development and mental growth. Take them to the parks and allow them to socialize with the kids. It will help them to make friends. On the other hand, his sadness or depression will vanish. You will observe the positive change in your kid's behavior with this simple action.

Besides eliminating his sadness, he will learn positive discipline. He will learn to share, cooperate, and to help others. In schools, teachers arrange parties or social gatherings just because of its positive impact.

Deal Him According to His Age

You need to deal with the child according to his age. If he is three years old and you feel he is weak in counting. Don't worry. Just leave him for some time. Four years is the age when a child's brain cortex is formed. That's the point that you were looking for. It is best for mathematics and logic.

At this age, gently start to encourage him to count. Give him small activities like collecting the objects. Likewise, labeling and comparing different objects. Teach him while playing. Don't force him and don't get angry. He will sometimes learn within minutes or sometimes within days.

Be Gentle

For kid's brain development and learning, your anger can be destructive. Kids only need your attention and love, whether you are a parent or teacher. Kids are sensitive in nature; thus, handle them with care and be gentle. It is possible he will take some time to learn, but it's ok. He is a child. Put yourself in his position or level and see what you will do?

15

How to Agree With Your Partner and Other Carers

The same process, connect with yourself, express empathy for their points, and say that you hear them and their concerns. How were you parented, and what you wish your parents did differently?

Communication is Vital

Communication is critical in any relationship, and the one you have with your baby is no different. The period from ages 1 through 4 is vital to your toddler's emerging language and social skills. Parent-child communication during this stage of development is all about effective interaction, modeling communicative behaviors, and fostering confidence, safety, and self-development.

The first thing to remember about communicating with your toddler is that it is a dynamic, two-way interaction. One reaches out, the other response. As you and your toddler learn to interact in increasingly responsive and effective ways, he will develop an increased sense of safety, confidence, empathy, and self-determination.

Let's consider some of the critical components of effective communication.

Effective Communication: Talking

The way that a parent speaks communicates much more than mere words. When you engage verbally with your toddler, you are modeling how a conversation works, including relevant skills such as listening, empathy, and turn-taking. As toddlers observe you talking to themselves and others, what they learn about human interaction contributes to their understanding of what it means to communicate effectively and exist in a social context.

But setting a good example isn't the only thing to keep in mind. The way that parents speak to their toddlers also impacts how effective the communication is (does the toddler understand in an actionable way?) and the toddler's developing emotional and social understanding.

Talking to your toddler in ways that are too aggressive or too passive can have negative consequences on their emotional and social development as well as detract from the potential benefits of teaching moments and healthy discipline. Instead, parents should speak firmly but kindly as they seek to communicate with their toddlers.

With these essential points in mind, let's consider some vital tips in talking in ways that your toddler can understand:

Use eye contact. When talking with your toddler, don't expect them to listen or know if you're just talking at them. Set aside any distractions, make eye contact, and let yourself connect fully with your little one.

Eye contact will help your toddler to pay attention to what you're saying and stay engaged in the conversation. It will also help bolster their sense of personhood by making it clear that you are interested in them.

Speak to them by name. Using your toddler's name while talking with them is another way to keep them focused on the conversation and give them a sense of importance as a co-communicator. It's especially useful to use names when validating or trying to let them know that you approve or disapprove. For example, 'Wow Jonny, that sounds so frustrating,' or 'I love how you shared with your sister, Alex,' or 'We don't throw food, David—please stop.'

Don't yell. Once you start yelling, the chances are that your toddler's behavior will become worse, either right then and there, or manifested tomorrow or a week. Yelling sets a poor example for your toddler and is likely to cause them stress that could become damaging. You may also frighten them, further adding to their anxiety and fueling further misbehavior as they try to cope. Instead, speak in a calm but firm voice. If needed, take a moment to breathe and calm down before speaking.

Be assertive but not aggressive. Be clear about the purpose of your communications by using a confident tone and body language when appropriate. However, do not mistake assertiveness for aggression. Assertiveness effectively communicates ideas and expectations; aggressiveness expresses anger, fear, and dislike.

Smile. Babies and toddlers are particularly responsive to facial expressions. As you undoubtedly discovered during the first year, sometimes a well-directed smile is all that it takes to brighten up a sad baby. The same holds for toddlers. Offering smiles during a conversation, let your toddler know that you enjoy talking with them and that the conversation is meant to be fun.

Minimize the use of 'no.' while some limits will undoubtedly focus on what your toddler should do, many will focus on what they should not do. Hearing 'no' over and over again throughout the day can be exhausting for your little one. Try to talk to him in favorable terms that model reasoning. For example, instead of saying 'No Michal! Don't throw your food,' you might try 'Hmmm, throwing our food makes the floor sticky. Let's try saving it for later instead.'

Don't talk too much. When speaking, keep it simple. Toddlers have short attention spans, and talking too much will likely cause your toddler to lose interest. For example, one day, 2-year-old Jimmy threw his toy car straight at the window. His mom responded by saying, 'Now Jimmy, you can't throw your toy car at the window because if you end up breaking the window we're going to have to buy a new one, and that costs a lot of money, and besides, throwing things is dangerous—what if you hurt someone? How do you think it would feel? Do you think it's nice to...' at this point, Jimmy has stopped tracking? His mother is using too many words, discussing people that aren't even present, and speaking in terms that a 2-year-old can't follow or relate to. Instead, she might say something like, 'Jimmy, don't throw your toys in the house. Throwing is for outside.' At two years of age, short, direct explanations of not more than 2-3 sentences are the most likely to result in understanding.

Use good manners. Using 'please' and 'thank you' will model proper behaviors for your toddler and help her see that kids and adults alike deserve respect in a conversation.

Ask questions. Asking open-ended questions is a great way to show interest in your toddler and encourage participation in the conversation. When trying to promote interaction, avoid problems that can answer with a short yes/no. Instead of asking, 'Did you go to the park with Grandma?' question, 'What did you do at the park?'

Don't limit the conversation to directions. Finally, don't just use talk to give your little one direction or feedback. Their language skills are growing a mile a minute at this age, and they are learning that language can use for all kinds of purposes. To support this growth and create positive interaction patterns by asking them about their day, their opinions, asking them to tell stories, solve problems out loud, etc. Responses will be limited at first, but need not be any less enjoyable. You will be astounded by how quickly your toddler's language develops in just a few short years.

Effective Communication: Listening

Listening goes hand in hand with talking. It's challenging to do one effectively without the other. Being a good listener will encourage your toddler to talk and help them develop excellent communication skills. Remember, effective communication with your toddler is dynamic and interactive, which means modeling both talking and listening abilities.

Listening serves several communicative purposes, including gathering information, opening the door for empathy, building relationships, giving respect, and gaining perspective. Listening will help you to understand what is going on in your little one's mind and heart, letting you relate to them better as you help them solve problems.

Tip 1: Ask for details. When your toddler tells you about what happened at church or that her baby doll feels sad, show that you are listening by asking for more information. What happened first? Second?

Third? Why is the baby doll sad? How will you make her happy? In addition to showing that you are listening and interested, such questions elicit a new language and help your toddler to practice critical cognitive functions such as recall, mental modeling, and problem-solving.

Tip 2: Pay attention. In today's world, multitasking has become a way of life, even when it's unnecessary. Show your toddler that you're listening and engaged, set aside devices such as phones or tablets, and give them your full attention.

Tip 3: Use active listening. Active listening refers to listening that is purposeful and fully engaged. During active listening, you entirely focused on what is said. Body language cues, including eye contact, mirroring facial expressions, and an attentive posture, all contribute to active listening. When you listen actively, your toddler will be more likely to feel that what they have to say is essential, and they will be encouraged to speak more.

Tip 4: Be physically interactive. High fives, hugs, and gestures are all great ways to show that you are listening and interested in what your toddler is saying. Getting bodies involved will also make the conversation more engaging and meaningful.

Tip 5: Give unconditional love. Toddlers seriously lack impulse control and often don't know how to express themselves in socially appropriate ways. They may speak out of anger and even say things like 'I hate you' or 'You're ugly.' Remember, don't take it personally! No matter how your toddler speaks to you or what the content of their message is, make sure that they always know that you love them, no matter what. Unconditional love creates a safe space where toddlers can speak freely and make mistakes without fear of losing your love or affection. This freedom will do wonders for their language skills, confidence, and trust in you as a parent.

How to deal with "I don't want..."

16

How to Coach Siblings' Relationship and Rivalry

Fights with Siblings

Siblings fighting with each other is another day-to-day experience a parent should expect. Fights can happen for literally any reason at all; kids can fight over toys, kids can fight for space, fights can even occur over who sits on daddy's lap, whatever it is, kids can fight over it.

Fights, sometimes, can be intentionally sparked by one child or the other; children can seek attention by any means possible, even if it is negative, and after all, half bread is better than none. Competition is another reason why siblings fight each other; fights can happen over who does what first, first to have a bath, who gets dressed first, until the end of the world, kids will compete and fight for supremacy. In the twinkle of an eye, playtime can turn into wartime between siblings.

Having a younger sibling can be frustrating for a toddler, which would cause them to express their anger by trying to start a fight. A toddler is yet to understand what it means to have a younger one; all he knows is that one new little creature has come to hijack all the attention, love, and care he's been getting.

It's not an easy job for a parent who, by the addition of a new member into the family, now has to add refereeing to the long list of parental tasks. In fact, some parents find it hard to the extent that they never even know what to do when the war begins, this war which happens, at least, about six times a day. The following are some tips that should be taken for the tackling and reduction of the daily inevitable sibling squabbles.

- Kids learn from what they see: Make sure you are not just telling your kids to do as you say, behave how you want them to copy; when your kids see that you handle everything that comes your way aggressively, you are only teaching them to be aggressive as well, how they see you treat and relate to people matters a lot, the kind of relationship they notice between you and your partner is another example they will learn from.

- Calmness in intervention: When fights erupt, and you want to intervene, be sure to show a high level of calmness; yelling never solves anything; it only brings about escalation; I know it is really annoying to see your kids getting in a brawl, but be sure to suppress your anger and not show your frustration.

- Try not to judge and take sides: When you hear your kids fighting over something (probably a toy), and you get there, with or without an idea of who had it first, try settling the fight regardless, putting blames can build grudges in the Kids' minds. It's normal to think about fairness, but trust me; the other kid will have the fault too some other time; there you have your balance.

- Ignorance: This will be needed at some point, when you find out that your kids start to fight in search of attention, then some amount of ignorance will help make them know that negative attention is not a way of life, because if they are always getting it anytime they fight, then they will keep on doing it anytime attention is needed. Well, a great way to prevent this is to make sure kids have a lot of equal time and attention.

- Assurance of importance: This is for an older toddler who is having a younger sibling, they believe that with the arrival of the new little one, their significance goes down the drain, they will do almost anything to make sure that doesn't happen; they'll fight for their right. This also requires a lot of attention to the older toddlers so that they can feel secure and not feel threatened by the arrival of the new one. Parents can prevent this by preparing the kid for the new baby, you create a connection even before the baby is born, having them talk to the baby, feel the baby kick, see images of the baby in the belly, can create the desired connection, making them through pictures of their baby days can also help prepare them for what is coming.

- Verbal lessons: Try explaining to your kids how bad it is to fight their siblings, show them how they can live together in peace and harmony; you can even encourage them to employ turn-taking; it helps reduce the rate of fighting as they know they will have their turns.

Fights Over the Table

Your toddler frequently gives you a hard time each mealtime; this can happen as a result of a variety of reasons. Below is a list of possible causes of toddlers' mealtime fight and their respective solutions.

- You show too much attention. When you concentrate too much on your kid at mealtime, showing too much concern about how much they eat, showing excitement when they eat well, or displeasure when they eat less. It puts pressure on them, which displeases them, and in turn, they lose interest, then the war begins.

- You can give them some amount of freedom and a sense of independence at mealtime. When they feel they are in control, then they don't get to feel that eating is an obligation.

- Transition problem. You have to work the transition into them before time; notifying them beforehand is essential so that when the time finally comes, they will be prepared. For example, when it's about ten minutes before mealtime, you say to them, "Amber, you have eight minutes until mealtime, you'll need the two minutes extra time.

- Tiredness. Kids, after so much unrest, become too tired to do anything, and yes, they can also be too tired to eat. Be sure to plan your kids' daily schedule well, with a balanced amount of rest and activity so that they don't eventually become over-worked or stressed out.

- Snack, eaten too close to mealtime. When your kid has a satisfying snack too close to mealtime, he becomes filled up, and digestion has not yet fully taken place when it is time for the meal, he, of course, would refuse to eat. Be sure to give snacks further from mealtime; there should be at least two hours interval between the snack and mealtimes.

- Taste disorders. Your kid might be having a condition of taste disorder, which can change how some foods taste. A specialist (pediatrician) should be consulted ASAP.

Helping Parents

When we think "toddlers," what comes after is "play," especially when we are busy, maybe doing some house chore or the other, we never believe our toddlers can be of help. Parents need to learn to understand their kids (even though it's easier to say than to execute); we also need to understand that toddlers too, apart from tantrums and other displays of anger, can be serious at times. When they see us doing some things, they also want to try, but parents always think otherwise. Sometimes, when we even recognize their willingness to help, we simply refuse and tell them, "no, you'll get to help when you're bigger." We also just prefer to do these things by ourselves just because, if we allow them to do it, they end up messing it up; It is true toddlers aren't yet perfect at doing these things, but stopping them from trying doesn't help either. Allowing kids to help in house chores aids in their growth and development into adults.

Benefits

Below are some good returns of allowing toddlers to help with tasks.

- Sense of belonging: When kids get involved in doing the household chores, they get the feeling that they, too, are recognized as an important part of the family.

- Confidence builder: Being allowed to a part in the house chores make them know that you have trust in their abilities (no matter how tiny it might seem); this, therefore, gives them a level of confidence, which eventually becomes part and parcel of their personality.

- Enhances their cooperation with others: Working together with your toddlers in doing house chores helps build their collaboration and cooperation skills. Working with other people won't be hard for them since it's what they've been doing since toddler-age.

- Promotes an appreciative spirit: When kids get appreciated for helping, they grow to become appreciative beings, since you are their role model.

- Builds self-discipline: Self-discipline and responsibility-taking are also portrayed by kids who are involved in carrying out house chores.

However, with all these being listed, it's not all kids that want to help at all time, and getting them involved when they are not interested initially can be exhausting, but they can be left alone because toddlers need to be taught to help with house chores for their personality's sake, so some tips have been developed in order to get them to help.

Tips for getting toddlers to help

- Not by force: As I have always said, kids, like adults, never like being bossed around or dictated to; there is no room for dictatorship if you want to get them to help out with house chores or other things, let them decide they want to, when they are forced, there is a very high tendency for refusal.

- Encourage collaborative work: Do not make tasks like clothes folding personal; instead of asking them to fold their own clothes while you fold yours, you can just allow them to fold anyone.

- Expect and allow the mess. It is true that help from toddlers can make things a little slower, sloppier and messy, but you have to learn to allow for the mess to happen; although you will take care of it, it shouldn't be immediately, so as to not give your kid the wrong impression.

- No task is too small: Be sure to expose your kid to every possible chore, give a wide range of tasks from helping while sweeping, to helping out in the garden, to helping with laundry and dishes. Do not limit their exploration; try and make them redirect their energy usage from throwing things, hitting, and all that show of power, into using it for useful work for the family.

- Sense of contribution: The chores you let them do, of course, can't be "big," but be sure that the tiny ones they do are significantly important that it gives them the impression that they are truly contributing.

Kids also develop gross and fine motor skills when they carry out certain tasks (with parents' help, of course), involvement in chores also help sharpen Kids' brain, which helps improve their problem-solving skills.

17

Parenting Requires Time. A Lot of It. And Patience, A Lot of It

O nly when you have started to coach your emotions and be aware of them you can now coach their emotions; they need connection with you to self-regulate. Communicate your disappointment. Comment what is happening, take away the child that is crying, and then go back to the child that has misbehaved, connect by commenting what has happened, and acknowledge their feelings of frustration and anger as the base for their wrongdoings. Start from where your child is. Kids don't know they are doing the wrongdoing. No shame, no blame, but comment by repeating what has happened and try to acknowledge their feelings behind the bad action. Help them figure out what they can do to be better, express their emotions, accept emotions. You need to help your child to repair their actions; this later, we lead them self-regulate and motivated to take care of others and take better decisions.

Never withdraw love and affection.

Managing choice and freedom, power struggle, and the need for self-determination and free will in small children.

Effective Positive Parenting Tips

Positive parenting helps you make the best decisions for your child. There is no such thing as an ideal parent who is confident all the time, but you can learn specific tips to help guide your children with more confidence toward a better life in the future. If positive parenting techniques are not applied, then chances are the child will automatically be inclined to focus on the negative side of life.

Parenting strategies work when the child is in the process of growing, and the brain is developing. A child learns by observing first and then receiving an explanation verbally, so it is always better to portray positive parenting in your daily actions. In other words, live the life you want your children to have one day, and they will be much more likely to have a healthy and well-balanced childhood because of it.

Tips for Positive Parenting

Be the Model

Children need guidance and a figure they can look up to and admire. Be that person in your child's life by giving them a clear example to follow. For example, if you ask your child to throw their trash in the trash bin, then you have to do the same. Show them through action, and they will learn. Children look up to their parents and imitate their actions more than anyone else. They also watch their parents closely, even when the parent may not be aware, so be vigilant and conscious of your actions at all times. You have to be the person you want your child to be. If you show them a positive attitude, they will learn from it and do the same.

Be Loving

Know that love is something that can never spoil a child. Please show your appreciation through hugs, kisses, spending time together, talking about mutually exciting topics, listening to the music he/she likes, and much more. Love does not have to be mundane, just meaningful--anything that can create memories for a lifetime. Showing love for a child can help them develop a sense of calm and contentment. It introduces them to the emotional side of nature, which brings resilience and creates a close relationship with the parent.

Staying Positive

Try not to influence your child with your negativity, even if you hit with a challenge that brings out negative emotions. Rather than expressing negativity, try to think of ways to approach the situation with a positive attitude. Share your positive personality with your child so their brain learns to have positive thoughts no matter what the circumstance may be. Share positive experiences with them so they can have hope and goodwill.

Be There for the Child

Always be available for the child no matter what the problem is. Do not underestimate their ability to handle the situation on their own, but at the same time, always be the safest spot for them. Please support your child when they need you because it develops trust and closeness. Be responsive to a child because it directly affects their emotional development, and the outcomes of this approach are always positive.

Always Communicate

Make sure you keep small conversations on the go every day and recognize the importance of communication with your child. Do not miss a day without talking to them. Always listen to your child and speak to him/her carefully with understanding and respect for his/her perspective. Ask about any event which happened and listen to how he/she dealt with it. You do not have to impose your opinion but quietly listen to their view and acknowledge what they share. Please keep an open dialogue, so he/she can talk about anything without hesitation or fear. Excellent communication between a parent and child makes the child more cooperative and friendly as they grow up.

Change Your Parenting Style

Do not follow the same route your parents took with you to deal with your child. While your parents may have been great, there is always room for improvement, and what worked for you may not be as effective with your child. Observe positive parenting techniques and take notes on how you can do even better as a parent. Change your behavior positively, and you are bound to see a good result come of it gradually, if not immediately.

Maintain Your Well-Being

To implement positive parenting solutions, you must have things sorted out on your end. You need to pay attention to your relationship with your spouse and the things that you manage like your house and finances so that your brain is calm. Once you are relaxed and everything is fine on your end, then you are in a better position to raise a child to the best of your ability. If the relationship with your spouse is weak, then it will surely hurt the child directly or unintentionally. Take care of yourself in the best way you can, so you are at peace mentally and physically and can give your very best self to parenting.

Keep a Goal in Mind

How do you want your child to be when he/she grows up? Every parent has a dream that their child will possess a particular kind of behavior which the parent appreciates. Keep that goal in mind while you are raising your child. If you want your child to be positive, kind, helpful, and empathic, then show them how to be those things so they can follow by example. It's easy to lose sight of what you want for your child amid daily challenges. That's why it is so important to take a step back from time to time, look at the bigger picture, and re-adjust your approach with your long-term goal for your child in mind.

Never Stop Learning

Approach parenthood with an open mind. Acknowledge that is a job you can only aspire to master while the challenges in front of you will keep changing at every stage, and you need to adjust your priorities and values. Read about it and keep yourself in check!

Ways to Become a Positive Parent

So, by now, you're on board to becoming positive parenting. Keep in mind these fundamental principles as you go through your days with your kids.

I believe that if you intend to parent positively and keep in mind these eight overriding principles, you will have much more success.

Children need to feel like they have some control over their lives. "Instead of telling children what to do, find ways to involve them in decisions, and to draw out what they think and perceive." When we involve our kids in our day-to-day lives, they feel like they have more control and power over their worlds. Over time, this builds their self-esteem and ability to make choices on their own.

Kids need routines, and by getting them involved by helping to choose their methods, they get to understand the natural consequences of their choices. We do need to provide limited options, however, for our kids. It is through repetition and consistency that they will learn new skills. We need to create opportunities for them to grow and learn every day. By providing opportunities to help us throughout the day, our kids will learn what it takes to be a "grown-up." Kids revel in learning; for them, it is an exciting adventure. Don't make these learning opportunities away from your kids by scheduling and doing everything for them. Sometimes the learning is slow and messy, but that's okay. Get used to dirty and quiet.

Teach respect by being respectful

Listen to your children. Figure out what their needs are and respect their little personalities. Some kids need lots of breaks and quiet time during the day. Some kids thrive when there is a lot to do and want to play with other kids. Know your child and respect who they are. Respect their timelines, their needs, their schedules, and unique temperaments. Our kids are special and learn and move in the world on their terms. Celebrate that.

Use your sense of humor

Sometimes parenting seems like such serious business. You are serious about wanting the best for your children and giving them the best start in life. Kids are kids, and they need to not only feel safe, but they also need to have fun. A child's life should be full of fun moments and lots and lots of laughter. Sometimes we take our parenting role so seriously; we just forget to lighten up and laugh with our kids. It can be a lot easier to get our little ones to do something if we make a game of it and have a sense of humor when things go wrong. And things will go wrong.

Positive Discipline is not about giving your child everything that they want. Permissiveness doesn't help your child develop initiative or other social skills that they need. What you need to do, instead, is offer clearly defined choices and follow through on these choices with kindness and firmness. And, yes, you need to be consistent with your efforts. If you give them two options, don't let them make up a third choice. Make positive decisions are appropriate, not only for their age and development level, but also for their personalities. Again, we need to get to know and respect our little one's unique place in this world and start from there when we proceed into each day.

Be patient

We all know that kids are not our little programmable robots. And, we don't want them to be either. They come into this world with their temperaments, personalities, likes, and dislikes. They won't always agree with us, and as they get older, they want to do things their way more and more.

If we can truly empathize with our kids--see the world from their perspective, through their eyes--we will automatically be more patient with them. The world is a big, scary, yet awesomely fascinating place for a little one. They always told what they cannot do, what they should be doing, and how they should act. At times, this can become overwhelming for them, and until they can learn how to cope and self-regulate all of the time, there will be meltdowns. And I can't think of a time when our patience tested than during a meltdown.

18

Peaceful Parenting: Mindfulness Tactics for Parental Stress Management

When working with or parenting a child, tween, or teen with any diagnosis, especially ADHD, we often undergo real feelings of immense pressures, marital strife, physical and mental health struggles, time and financial management, guilt, anger, sadness, loss, frustrations, stress, blame, and other adult challenges.

As mentioned, mindfulness is not a magical cure or pill to swallow, but it can certainly melt away stress and anxiety, like the Wicked Witch of the West was dissolved by the water in the movie. Once you master the basics and accrue practice over time, you will see the results in yourself and your kids! Experiment today with at least one of these Grateful 8 Strategies. They are not listed in any particular order of importance, so feel free to mix and match:

Under the Sea

Whether you are a wondrous water baby or a lovely landlubber parent, it is so necessary to deeply and truly connect with your inner parental mermaid/merman and maintain a parenting model that is not all about perfection.

Keep yourself afloat and your head above the waters. Recognize that like water freely flowing, parenting a child with ADHD is not stagnant and/or a perpetually picture-perfect or pretty pond.

Ride and let the waves and whirlpool of colorful emotions and evolving learning experiences exhilarate you and unveil your inner strengths amid the serious struggles (and sharks!). Do not forget to play and splish splash along with the way because humor will be your life vest as you surf steadily in life, teaching, coaching, and parenting!

Love Lingo

This technique is also imperative. Use your words, mindfully and compassionately. Do not fight fire with fire; do not allow words to become weapons when parenting kids, tweens, and teens with ADHD. Of course, this does not mean that you must speak in eloquent poetry and poise all the time, but learn love lingo.

Why? It can tenderly tame your tongue when we use love lingo instead. Following suggestions from Conscious Parenting experts, I have learned to take a moment literally since we as parents must really try and discern the difference between reacting to kids with ADHD from the central state of who they are and from our own proud, parental egotistical worlds.

While this advice might sound a bit harsh, love lingo roots us in reality and empathy, so it affirms that we as adults have already had our own time to grow up and learn the ropes of this world. Thus, love lingo is powerful because it reminds us not to make it all about us as the adults. What does this mean? It does not encourage you to be a pushover or a doormat, but try not to take everything, so personally, although I know it is much easier said than done.

It also forces us to stop comparing ourselves to other parents, the Kardashians, and everyone else out there. Who cares what others think about us as parents and people? Be authentic and live in love in your own skin! You are not in a pageant or parenting competition, so learn love lingo for confidence and empowerment.

One way to employ better love lingo is to have some handy dandy one-liners when tensions are high to diffuse your own adult egos. My favorite one, for example, is "I love you too much to argue." It works like a charm with my kids, spouse, and family members. What will be your love lingo line/lines be? Think creatively and practice, practice, practice. Live the love lingo when you are "Livin La Vida Loco!"

Pregnant Pause

No, this strategy is not advocating a plan to conceive another bun in the oven, foster an entire football team, or adopt triplets, but I assure you that it is one of the easiest ways to integrate mindfulness into your daily life routines and parenting approaches. Simply add a pregnant pause and breathe deeply when you feel overwhelmed, frazzled, angry, or ready to give up.

I love this idea so much that I actually suggest repeating it based on your age (or your kiddo's ages): so if you're 40, do it forty times! Words are so powerful, so "word up" with this holistic wisdom to cope with ADHD!

Slow Your Roll

Of course, you can order some yummy sushi when you are overly stressed and over the parental edge, but this mindful strategy is equally imperative.

Kids with ADHD can become overwhelmed so easily and over-stimulated. Don't let tons of back to back, crammed scheduled events, technologies, or rushing around every day exacerbate the ADHD triggers? In turn, slow your roll, ya'll! Take a minute and critically reflect upon this week's calendar. Talk to your kiddos about which ones to prioritize. Discuss together ones to possibly modify or delete in order to spend more face time with your kiddos, not Facetime, the app. Slow your roll before stress takes a toll!

Balancing Act

Parenting in a mindful manner does not mean being a cop or being a lenient buddy to kids 24/7. In actuality, it is truly about respectfully setting limits and reinforcing your authority with "I'm the adult here" (Southgate, 2002, p. 210). It does not always feel this way when parenting, so this helpful tip is one of my favorite pieces of advice for adults.

Similarly, the article, "Wonder Years," from Essence helps us to also realize that as early as 9 months, we must model and reinforce to children consistently which behaviors are acceptable and those that are not. If we are constantly frazzled and depressed when dealing with a kids' diagnosis, then we automatically model the negativity and toxic vibes that follow.

Think like a gymnast and find that proper balance; center yourself holistically and mindfully as a parent to keep your stress minimized and your confidence flying high amid ADHD!

Chillax

Taking a timeout is not just for kids. In reality, adults equitably need to take breaks in order to remain grounded and sane when parenting, coaching, mentoring, or treating kids with ADHD in any capacity or role. If your child is having a major meltdown, tantrum, diva session, or rebel without a cause chaos moment, I suggest using this technique on yourself called "Stop, breath, and chill" as (L., 2008) advises in "Peaceful Parenting" from Scholastic Parent and Child.

When attempting to take two sibling toddlers today to lunch at Panera Bread, sit with them on a small couch in the middle of a crowded mall while you are trying to order online, so you could skip the line and go straight to your table. Ask them to play calmly with their sticker together while you ordered. In less than 30 seconds, a circus ensued: they rambunctiously used the public couch as a trampoline, started pulling each other's hair, kicking, pinching, and sobbing loudly. You had to apply this technique to literally calm yourself first before attending to their mall mania. When do you need to chillax the most as a parent? What are you currently doing to distress less?

Pump It Up

Exercise is so essential and something that parents need to maintain mindfulness, health, and sanity. I know many experts recommend striving for roughly 10,000 steps per day, but my personal goal is 7500.

I swear I am not receiving any promotional or monetary compensation for suggesting them. They have literally toned and changed

296

my life and mental health. They are also free and readily adaptable to suit any level, or need. Pump it up for parental patience and power in whatever way suits your style and preference.

19

The Correct Way to Discipline a Child Based on Age

It doesn't matter how old your kid is. Each life part requires some teaching, and the discipline you give must be consistent.

Before starting the guideline, I want to tell you about the most important aspect you need to understand. If you, as a parent, don't stick to the rules and values that you set up, your children won't do it either.

But, let's take each period of your child's life of which you are fully responsible for mold and see what the correct ways to approach him or she is and how to teach them to become the best version of themselves.

Newborn to 2 Years Old

This is the time in which the babies discover the world, and with this discovery comes the curiosity and the desire to know more. During this period, the brain is exactly like a sponge that absorbs all the information surrounding them.

Because of this, the best thing you can do is eliminate attractions that can be dangerous, such as jewelry, medicine, or cleaning products, which can be ingested and produce harm. Also, I know that parents prefer leaving the child in front of a TV and do their house chores, but I highly advise the contrary. Video equipment at this age is just as toxic for the brain as chemical products are for the stomach.

Of course, crawling babies will tend to put their unacceptable hands-on objects. The simplest way to solve this is to simply but calmly say, "No." The worst thing you can do is to rush the child and yell at him or her. After gently saying, "No," try and distract the child with an appropriate activity. As I've said, at this age, they are really curious, so that a shiny suitable toy will captivate them, and they will forget about the forbidden gadget.

On the other hand, timeouts can also be a form of useful discipline for toddlers. Explain to your child how this kind of behavior is not acceptable and give him and her two minutes of a timeout to calm down. Always remember that you should not leave your child on their own during the time-out. You should stay with them, look at their eyes, connect and explain calmly why their behavior is not acceptable.

Whatever you do, don't spank your child. At this age, the child will not make the connection between the punishment and their actions. However, they will imitate you since you are their role-model and will tend to be even more offensive towards you and other kids.

From 3 to 5 Years Old

Your child is growing up very fast in this timeframe, and they start to understand more and more about life. Also, because during this interval, the child accumulates so much information, she or he will start making connections between their actions and the consequences that come from them. Due to this, it is the best time to start explaining the house rules.

So, it is important that you talk to your kid and explain the differences between right and wrong, how it is ok to behave, and what is forbidden.

For example, starting with the age of 3, whenever your child does something that you disagree with, such as throwing food on the floor; try not to yell. Remain calm and explain how wasting food is not acceptable in your house. Also, think of a suitable consequence for this action, like telling your kid that he or she does something like that, they will have to clean the mess.

The sooner you establish rules, the better it is for everybody. I know that sometimes it is always hard to express your dissatisfaction, but overlooking the violation of your own rules will not help your child grow up and turn into the person you want him or her to become. Empty threats will weaken your authority as a mother or father, and your kid will just test your limits.

The only thing that you should not forget about is that good deeds also have consequences, so be sure to offer your child a reward for every positive action. Tell your baby how proud you are of him or her with every occasion, but don't forget to specify the part of their behavior that satisfied you. By doing so, it is more probable for your child to repeat the gesture only to make you happy. This way, it will become a habit and will come to them naturally.

Of course, disciplining some kids will be an easier job than others. If you have a very stubborn kid with a very strong personality, you will need to try some other techniques. For example, give your kid a timeout whenever it does something bad. Be sure you send your kid to contemplate the things that have upset you, somewhere without distractions such as a TV or computer.

There is no exact time of how long the timeout should be. Try multiple time intervals and see what works for your child. Researchers say that for each year of life, you should add a minute, but again, you need to test and see what length is suitable for your case.

The last thing I want to talk about when it comes to disciplining a toddler is the necessity of giving clear commands, which are also self-explanatory when it comes to distinguishing right from wrong.

From 6 to 8 Years Old

This represents the period of time in which your child starts going to school and becomes more and more responsible for his life. Because of this, the education you give is very important, so let's see how you should act and how you shouldn't.

Even though your kid is older and knows more about what he or she likes or dislikes, it is still important to keep your rules standing and apply the necessary consequences.

Timeouts are still very effective, so don't be afraid to make use of them. One important thing is always to be consistent. It is very important that your child actually believes what you are saying. To be sure that your kid takes you seriously, don't start making unrealistic threats such as, "Do your homework, or you will not play PlayStation ever again in your life." Both of you know that this will not happen, so the child will just ignore you.

Lastly, remember that you are raising a child and not starting a military school. So, give your child not only the benefit of the doubt but also a second chance when he or she makes a mistake.

From 9 to 12 Years Old

You will notice that even though kids are growing up, it will not become easier to discipline them. However, if you follow the golden rule of natural consequences, then you should be able to educate your offspring without issues.

You will see that as they grow, they evolve and become more mature. With this, they will start requesting more freedom and trust. So, what you need to do is to teach them how to deal with the results of their behavior. By doing so, you will ensure an efficient and suitable method of discipline.

I propose to take an example and see exactly what I am talking about. Let's say that your kid has broken one of the school's windows, and you are called to the principal's office to discuss the issue. An inappropriate thing you can do is to rescue your kid from detention and not let him or her take the blame.

By letting your kid take the punishment, you will help him or her to learn a very important life lesson. They will learn that bad actions bring hard consequences, and even more importantly, they will acknowledge the fact that you, as a parent, won't always be there to save them.

Only by learning from their own mistakes, they will be able to keep themselves away from similar situations.

If you see that natural consequences don't have any effect on your child, remember that this age period is the best to use interdictions on electronic devices as a consequence of their actions.

Teenage Years

I consider this period to be the most difficult one because, during these years, your baby is no longer a child per se. They have their own desires and expectations and probably know what they want to do with their life. However, during these years, your child needs you just as much because they can make some very big mistakes that they will regret for the rest of their life. So, I advise you to pay great attention to what I have to say.

Until now, you already gave them the basis of the education they need in order to have a good life. Your kid is aware of what is good and what are the aspects of the life that should stay away from. Yet, they still need your rules and guardianship more than ever.

Therefore, set up boundaries even though most probably your child will hate them. Too much independence will not be good for your child, just as too much limitation will not prepare them for life.

This being said, let your kid have friends and go to parties, but be sure that those friends are not a bad influence, and curfew hours are set.

Don't forbid your child to date. It will just make them do it behind your back and do stupid things. Let them discover the meaning and implications of a relationship. Let your child know that you will always have an ear for their problems and a shoulder for him or her to cry on.

Most importantly, don't be afraid to talk about the sexual aspects of the life. This is exactly the age period when people are discovering their sexuality and become curious about their bodies. Talk to them about how starting their sex life is a very big deal and how they should wait for the right time and person. Explain to them the importance of protection and about the risks of contracting a disease or an unwanted pregnancy.

Even if your child will not feel very comfortable talking to you about these aspects, they need to know that you are open to discussion.

So, to wrap this part up, it is really important to establish the appropriate limits for your child at this age. The relationship you will have with your child will be influenced by this age period.

Last but not least, raising a teenager is not about control. It is about focusing on the positive aspects to help your kid discover their life path.

20

The Common Mistakes That Parents Make and How to Fix Them

Disciplining your toddlers alone is not alone. You must also avoid the common pitfalls of parenting. Many of these blunders do not just decrease the effectiveness of the discipline that you impose on your toddler but may even encourage your toddlers to misbehave. Here are the common mistakes that many parents make when disciplining their children.

Being Aggressive

Some parents simply give up and become aggressive. The problem with being aggressive is that the children learn nothing except fear. They do not get to understand the value that you want them to learn. Instead, they obey you out of fear. Studies also show that toddlers who have experienced, aggressive or abusive parents are likely to grow aggressive as well. Being aggressive does not just mean spanking your kids, but it also includes using highly offensive words and threatening words. It is important to note that you are dealing with a toddler, and being aggressive is the worst thing you can do.

Comparing Yourself with Other Parents

Stop comparing yourself with other parents. How they discipline their kids is their problem. If one of your friends tells you that slapping your kid in the face is effective, even if he could prove it, do not follow the advice right away. After all, according to various studies, slapping or hitting your kids is not an effective way to discipline them.

Comparing your Child with Other Children

It is wrong to compare your child with other children, except if it will be something that will make him feel good about himself. Would you like your child to compare you in terms of money with a parent who is much richer than you are? Of course not. In the same way, you should not compare your child with other children. Your toddler is unique in his way, and you should appreciate him as he is.

Lying

Some parents lie to their toddlers to make them obey. Although this may work from time to time; it also has bad consequences. In a case study of a mom from New Jersey with a 2-year-old daughter, it so happened that one day when her child did not want to get in the car, she pointed at her neighbor's house nearby and told her kid that it was a daycare center full of troglodytes from a scary TV show. She told her daughter that she had two choices, to get in the car or be left alone in the house with a threat of being attacked by creepy cavemen. Of course, her daughter finally gave in and entered the car. Now, if you look at what happened, it will seem that it was successful. There was no shouting or spanking or anything that took place. However, the problem here occurred after the incident. Following the case study, the mom's daughter began to have a fear of daycare centers, thinking that such places have scary cavemen. As you can see, although the mother was able to make her child get into the car, the consequence was worse. Therefore, instead of lying, the best way is, to be honest, and be emphatic.

Yelling

You do not have to yell at your toddler just to get your point across. According to Dr. Alan Greene, a pediatrician and member of the clinical faculty at Stanford University School of Medicine, if you lose control and start yelling, your kid will also do the same. Now, this does not mean that your kid is intentionally disrespecting you. This only proves that your child is having a hard time with you because you cannot understand each other. Therefore, you must keep your voice quiet yet firm. Eye contact also helps.

Thinking that You Understand Your Toddler

The truth is that you cannot always understand your toddler. This is simply because toddlers do not think the same way as adults do. You simply cannot tell exactly how certain things have an impact on your toddler's feelings and thoughts. More importantly, you do not know just up to what degree. Therefore, do not be too hard on your toddler.

Raising the Child, you Want

Do not impose your life or your will upon your toddler. Your child has his own life. Let him pursue whatever he wants. Let him paint his dreams and believe in them. Focus on the child whom you already have and not the idea of a child in your mind whom you would wish to have. Your child may not be wired the way you would want him to be, and this is normal. Let your child have his chance in life. Let him believe and live his dreams.

Correcting Everything at the Same Time

Many parents try to correct all the inappropriate behaviors of their child, and they expect a toddler to be able to do it within a short period. This is a very unreasonable expectation. Even you cannot change your bad manners and behaviors quickly, so do not expect your toddler to be able to do it much more than you can. Not to mention, most parents' complaints about their toddlers are normal behaviors (or misbehaviors) for a toddler.

You must learn to pick your battles, and do not even attempt to win everything at the same time. You may start with the behavior that you consider to be the most serious and requires attention. Once you have corrected it, then you can move to another. Of course, you should discipline your child with every opportunity that presents itself. But, learn to focus on a particular behavior, so you can also gauge the effectiveness of the technique or techniques that you are using.

Long Explanations

Long explanations do not work on toddlers. You will only seem like talking gibberish after a few minutes. Do not forget that toddlers have a short attention span; therefore, long explanations do not work well with them. For example, you do not have to lecture your toddler why eating cookies before bedtime is not good for her teeth. She will learn that when the right time comes. Instead, just say, "No cookies." You do not have to explain so much. After all, toddlers are not meant to be very logical. They do not care so much about explanations. Of course, this rule is subject to exceptions, such as when the toddler himself wants to know the reason behind something or when giving an explanation appears to be the best course of action.

Bribe

Do not bribe your toddler just to make him do what you want. Otherwise, he will always ask for it, which could be a problem in the long run. In a case study of a mom in Montclair, New Jersey, she offered her daughter a piece of chocolate if she (her toddler) would eat her meal. It worked well. Her daughter finished her meal quickly. Up to this point, it would seem that bribing is also effective. However, what happened here was that after that dinner, the daughter would always ask her mother to give her a piece of chocolate so that she would finish her meal.

Instead of bribing your child, the suggested way is to help her realize the importance of food. Using the case as mentioned earlier study, the better way would be to tell her child that she will get hungry late in the evening if she eats so little and that she will not be healthy, which could make her sick. If you face a similar problem with your child, you can tell her about the health benefits of the food, like it could make her skin more beautiful, make her taller or smarter, and others—but do not lie.

Not Asking Questions

Toddlers usually have so many questions. As a parent, you tend to answer your question as much as you can. It is worth noting that you should not lie to your child when he asks questions. However, you can make silly answers, but be sure that he knows that it is a joke when you do so. Also, avoid giving creepy answers or those that will tend to scare your child. So, avoid answers that relate to ghosts and other scary stuff. However, parents get too caught up with answering their child's countless questions that they miss another important thing to do: to ask their child questions.

If you can take the time to ask your toddler questions, even crazy and illogical ones, you might just be surprised by the answers that you might hear. Toddlers have a powerful imagination and are very curious and open to almost everything. By asking questions to your child, you will also get to understand how he thinks, and even appreciate how young he truly is—so all the more reason why you should never be aggressive or harsh on your toddler.

21

Screen Time and Discipline

As already introduced at the beginning of this book, an old say states: 'it takes a village to raise a child.' Well, where is everybody gone? In today's modern world, more often than none people tend to leave away from immediate family members and old friends. Not everybody is surrounded by supportive communities with free baby groups or parks and play centers. No to talk about been locked in with your children during a pandemic! While home-schooling, continuing working, child-rearing, and housekeeping.

What about screen time? Some Parents feel guilty of giving any amount of screen time to their children. In a world of mostly full-time work, parents away from immediate family, and extremely expensive childcare. So, let's get a grip! Yes, all day tv is detrimental for your child/dren learning experience and often for the effects that tv can have on their behaviors. But it also is detrimental for your children to be around extremely tired, hungry, frustrated parents that are pressured from daily chores like preparing a healthy meal, pay bills, or answering emails.

Is there a chance for a happy middle?

Screen time should be treated like dessert plus try not to give their own screen, so you control them. Select contents, check the time, and so on.

It is difficult to stay happy and positive when stressed. You need to reconnect with yourself. Children won't develop self-control until 4 or later. So, this is your choice: reconnect with yourself, organize your home, control nap time and mealtime, and be happy. Or chaos.

There are so many things our kids do that can be regarded as a bad habit, but my focus is mainly on the one that affects modern kids the most, regardless of how he/she was brought up or what country they live in. Yep! You guessed it, their bad habits with technology. Every child today knows how to use a phone, the internet, computers, applications, and whatnot. One moment you are celebrating your child's first steps and words, then you blink, and they already know how to download a video game.

Ever since the inception of technology, parents, or should I say adults, in general, have been worried about how technology would impact their children—socially, academically, physiologically, and psychologically. These are all big words, but the bottom line is that there is a fear about how so much dependence on technology could affect our children's lives negatively.

These days, our kids are doing one thing or the other on the internet. The truth is, the internet is very addictive, and almost anything relevant to the social world these days is happening on the internet or on a screen. The question is, are you going to decide to cut off your kids completely from the use of technology, or look for ways in which we could use it to the advantage of our kids? I would recommend that we opt for the second option.

It may seem tricky and scary at times, but as a parent, you should not worry, because there are always old and new methods that can be applied for the children of today. Perhaps you have a long list of your worries and struggles (especially when it comes to technology and your kid using it), but in the following lines, you will read handy tips and information.

When your child is still young, it is quite easy to keep them under control towards everything, even for the use of technology. Doctors warn and parents worry that extended screen time can seriously affect a child's health (posture, sight, night rest, anxiety, excitement, aggression, and so on). Not all screen time is bad, and naturally, your child will want to watch cartoons or play their favorite game. Just bear in mind that screen time can be constructive, passive, or interactive.

Passive screen time is defined as spending time on a device (tablet or cell phone) or in front of a big (TV or computer) screen. Constructive screen time includes actual work and creating something new, such as web development, writing codes, designing websites, creating music (digital), drawing, and so on.

Passive time, as the name suggests, means watching a film, TV show, or a video. Interactive screen time involves playing video games, finding or downloading apps, and on-screen activities (sports or fitness).

Parents must be willing to control each type of screen time, because too much of anything is not good.

Here are a few tips for your child's screen time:

• Spend time talking to your children about their favorite online programs. Make sure it is not their only source of entertainment. Find a balance between their screen time and physical activities, play dates with their friends, learning, dining, and relaxation, but also creative and strategy games.

• Avoid commands because they usually never work. Pick nice words to encourage your kid to take breaks from their screen time. Once they realize that taking breaks in between watching TV feels nice for their eyes and entire body, they will willingly do it on their own.

Internet Access

The Internet is an upgrade in your child's technology life. The moment they get access to the network, they will realize that only the sky is the limit. No matter how useful and easily things can be found online, the Internet will make everything more challenging. At this point, every parent starts to worry about what their kids watch, read, play, and so on.

Video Games

I know you were probably thinking about it: "Oh yeah, Sandra plays games too much."

So, let me start with the positive aspects of gaming for your kids. Many types of research have been carried out concerning games, and many parents would like for it to be conclusive that all that video games do is make your kids anti-social. The results of the research have actually been the opposite of that; here are some of the advantages of letting your kids play games.

- Better hands and eyes coordination

A lot of games that your kids get to play could involve them having better coordination of their hands and eyes. By playing these sorts of video games, your kids will develop habits that are fundamental to helping them better their coordination as well as their puzzle-solving ability. The overall advantage of this is that they are able to easily solve complex problems when confronted with them in the real world.

- Higher cognitive function

Usually, it has been found that when something is done repeatedly for a long period of time, the brain works like the supercomputer that it is and finds a new way for it to perform those functions even faster. Basically, what the brain does is create new pathways and structures to help your child solve similar problems faster, and this also spills over to real life, of course.

- Health problems

It is true that too much of anything is detrimental, and this is true for video games too. One of the health issues that has been associated with playing video games is obesity. Due to the long hours spent sitting in one place and not doing any physical activity, your child can become prone to being obese. Another condition is the development of weak bones, weakened muscles, numb fingers, and weakened eyesight. All of these issues are prone to affect your child if he/she spends to0 many hours playing video games.

- Social isolation

Video games are mostly played indoors, and if your kid turns out to be a hermit in the first place or has a personality that makes him enjoy isolation instead of social mingling, playing video games might just be the right excuse that he or she needs to stay all day and all week indoors. The truth is that even without video games, a shy kid would still not prefer to interact with the outside world, but at least they can be more easily persuaded to go out and have some fun. However, with video games made available to them, trust me: there is no getting that kid out of the new Razer gaming chair you just bought for him/her.

- Declining academic results

Anything fun has a way of making itself seem more appealing than listening in class, doing homework, or studying for a test. Even just doing an activity like skipping rope after school can be more interesting than the impending doom of a test that your kid has to study for.

- Moral issues

Most of the games out there are geared towards teenagers and adolescents. This is because it is believed that at least a teenager is able to distinguish between what is right and wrong. However, kids who are still in their preadolescent ages might find it hard to distinguish between what is okay to do in a video game and what is not okay to do in the real world. This is where the choice of the kind of video games that parents allow their kids to play actually matters.

Tips for Growing Children with Mobile Devices

As your child grows, he or she will ask for a phone of their own. Everyone else has it, so they must have it too; you already know that story. This isn't bad per se; you would feel safer knowing that you could call them and ask where they are or if they need something. We are talking about the age when they are old enough to go to school alone, visit friends, have sleepovers, prepare simpler meals – you get the picture.

Part of today's kids' socializing is using social media.

So once your child (no matter if he or she is an adolescent) creates an account on social media, it is your responsibility to check what is going on there. Forbidding, it will not work, but, again, limiting the time spent on their phones can ease things up. If you see that they spend too much time using their social media and chatting with friends, you can easily pick an internet policy with limited mobile data.

22

Nutrition

S imilar to the sentiment expressed in Woolf's quote, mindfulness also targets this notion of mindful eating as a link to better holistic health.

Recent studies by (Yunus, 2019) from the renowned Exceptional Parent have asserted how there is a possible link between ADHD and high sugar, salt, and fat intake when kids receive diets with only minimal whole grains, fruits, and vegetables intakes (p. 24). Many findings specifically herald the benefits of a whole-food plant-based (WFPB) diet with minimal or no processing for protection against ADHD, cancers, heart disease, osteoporosis, and other chronic conditions (Yunus, 2019, p. 24) as well.

While I am not suggesting a rigid Biggest Loser style diet or any particular dietary model. I also want to arm you with research and resources, so you can explore and take it to the other level as far as what is best for your particular family's needs.

Are you ready for some yummy suggestions? Let us find those aprons, ok?

- **Snack Attacks:** Make snack attacks healthy with fresh fruits and veggies. Make healthy smoothies together with your child and add some chia and flax seeds to balance moods. MasterChef Junior, anyone?

- **Mr. and Ms. Clean:** This advice does not mean operating a pristine household free of dust bunnies and flawlessness, but it is about eating as clean as possible to avoid unnecessary additives and food colorings. Of course, kids are attracted to the colorful, marshmallow, vibrant products that are often so full of crap.

- **Diggity D:** There is "No Diggity" about it that Vitamin D is the superior sunlight vitamin that most kids, tweens, and teens often lack from excessive indoor gadget time, nutritional voids, etc. As a result, Laliberte's (2010) "Problem Solved: Winter Blues" from Prevention insists that we must all ensure that our family members are digging it with vitamin D proactively since it is closely linked to keeping our serotonin levels elevated and balanced (p. 48). This connection is something that is super important in kids, tweens, and teens with ADHD for critical brain balance and overall wellness.

Are you excited to dig it with D? Take a family hike, jog, stroll, or skate around the block. Find a local park and dive into the D!
- **Straight from the Hive:** Try warm milk with Manuka honey for a natural relaxer before bedtime with your kiddos. Other girls really love it on bananas with peanut butter and chia seeds, too. You can also add it to evening herbal teas to evoke some sweet dreams and deeper sleep.

As a slight disclaimer, because of honey's sugary contents, be sure to just use a small amount, roughly the size of a poker chip. Just do not try to karaoke Lady Gaga's "Poker Face" song, or you might lose face with older kids! BEE holistic, BEE well, and BEE wonderful when you try honey with your honey!

- **Sugar High:** As adults, we really need to embrace the "You are what you eat" mindset with all kids, but especially those who have ADHD. In turn, closely monitor sugar intake with their candies, sodas, caffeinated beverages, and all those ooey-gooey treats and desserts. Carefully monitor the amount of fast foods that you are serving to your families, no matter how tempting or timesaving it may seem. Studies encourage us to eat "clean" as clean as possible as opposed to relying on the fatty, greasy, over-processed foods. Clean eating will naturally "eliminate unnecessary food additives such as artificial colors, flavors, sweeteners, and preservatives that do not add nutritional value and may contribute to ADHD symptoms. Limit sugar intake to 10% of total calories daily (roughly 6 teaspoons for children aged 2 to 19 years)" (Rucklidge, Taylor, & Johnstone, 2018).

A female toddler recently attended a birthday party with tons of sugary cakes, candies, and fruity drinks. Then she began bitterly bickering in the car on the ride home to no avail from all the junk in the trunk (literally). Are you eager to crush that sugary rush and move toward mindful eating? You have been baking and cooking with dates as a natural sugar alternative when you make muffins and other goodies lately. While you are not a professional cook or baker by any means, you are encouraged to freely consult at the local library or online that focus on mindful and natural ingredients to curb those high sugar sensations that tend to exacerbate ADHD! Be mindful when dining out, and always looks for healthier family options.

Putting a freeze on fast food addictions can be so instrumental. (Valles, 1998) Pioneering article from Drug Store News also indicates how high sugar intakes can cause low blood sugar and chromium depletion. The fast-food frenzy is really taking a toll on our kids as "The average American now consumes an average of 152.5 pounds of sugar in a year. That large soft drink at the drive-through window contains roughly 22 to 27 teaspoonfuls of sugar. It is reported that increased sugar intake actually increases urinary chromium excretion. Over time, this could have an impact on behavior."

- **Move Over:** Dairy overload can often cause major digestive issues. When kids are literally plugged up, they can act out even more. To counter these tummy troubles, consider some new dairy alternatives like almond, soy, coconut, cashew, and oat milk. I also suggest adding probiotics to your kiddos' diets with more kefir, Greek yogurt, and other mood foods. In a toddler's case, they have been extremely helpful to tame tummies and boost moods. Let us Move over mindfully!

- **Veg Heads:** You can opt for a Meatless Monday approach for more mindful family eating. Try to replace traditional noodles with veggies such as asparagus, zucchini, carrots, etc. Indulge in Brussel sprouts, cauliflower pizza crust, corns, asparagus, etc. Be a vicious veg head and also add more veggies to morning egg dishes, especially omelets.

Make the Jolly Green Giant proud and be a veg head of household more often to facilitate holistic health and happiness in all kids, but especially ones with ADHD! Some toddler adores making and eating kale chips with me. She has also recently been trying the freeze-dried snap peas, too. We never know what they will like until we experiment, right?

Go beyond broccoli and green beans on your grocery run!

In essence, it is also highly advantageous to ensure that your kids, tweens, and teens are getting enough B vitamins in their diets: B1 is linked closely to many key functions like immunity, heart support, and mental processing; B2 offers energy, hair, skin, and eye health; B 3 stabilizes our memories, moods, and hearts; B5 can keep cholesterol levels in check; B6 is a sleep reliever. Are you ready for some "Sweet Dreams" by Queen Bye?

Finally, buzz with B-12 for increased mood and energy management. My young kids love the "classic ants on a log" snack with peanut butter, cashew butter, sunflower seed butter, or almond butter slathered onto celery with raisins, dried cherries, or cranberries.

- **Beanie:** While I am not talking about the cool, fashionable hats, try to eat more mindfully against ADHD with beans and legumes. Make black beans burritos, hummus with chick-peas, serve up some edamame, and add lentils or sunflower seeds to beam up your families' diets!

- **Magnesium Magnets:** Strive to add more magnesium into your family's overall dietary routines, especially in cases of ADHD. Studies describe how the average American is often highly deficient in magnesium "by about 70 mg daily. Magnesium is the calming mineral, since it is the principal mineral used to control the parasympathetic nervous system. There is also the potential for calcium deficiency. Many children complain of aching legs and will see positive results with the initiation of a well-formulated multiple mineral supplement" (La Valle, 1998, CP13.). Get your magnesium magnets via food or supplements today!

- **Finding Nemo:** Set a goal to serve a fatty fish to amp up those Omegas and vitamin D 2-3 times a week. Yunus (2019) reminds us of compelling research that depicts how those with ADHD may also have "lower levels of omega-3 fatty acids and higher levels of omega-6 that may lead to inflammation and oxidative stress."

Accordingly, Evidence by Rucklidge, Taylor, & Johnstone, (2018) also suggests that supplementation with omega-3s and/or a broad spectrum of micronutrients (for those not taking medication) may be beneficial for ADHD symptom reduction, but it is so important that all "Patients should consult with their primary care provider before starting any supplement and with a dietician before changing their diet" (p. 15). Get your rod and reel in some fishing action during family meals and snacks for more mindful eating.

In fact, salmon nuggets and fish sticks are always a major hit with the little one. Give it a try or more. They also can enjoy coconut shrimp with fun and tasty dipping sauces. How can you get your Nemo and Dory on and blast more fish in your weekly menus?

- **See for Yourself:** Fruits like pineapples, grapefruits, tomatoes, berries, mangoes, oranges, and kiwis, are a definite self-care saver for the blasts of vitamin C. I also recently discovered passion fruit, a rich source of beta-carotene and vitamin C, as recommended by the recent article aptly called "Mood Food" (DailyMail, 2019)

- **Zing with Zinc:** Assist your kids with ADHD in the culinary department to better zing against mood swings, common colds, flus, and other physical problems. Simply add more fruits and vegetables rich in zinc to their diets daily.

23

Sleep Routine

As a toddler is learning, you need to introduce behaviors that he recognizes as being part of the going to bed process and a winding down of another day. Your toddler's body clock is not yet set, and all of the steps I have outlined will help you to help your toddler to establish those links. You can say that "Mr. Clock" says it's time to put the toys away, for example, so that the child does not feel that it's the parent's fault that the play has come to an end for the day. Here is the ideal schedule for putting toddlers to bed in ideal circumstances. Bear in mind that you will have to make adjustments when you are traveling when the child is not in his own home and at times of illness, but apart from that, the routine should become something the child becomes familiar with.

Toys Get Put Away

This is a good habit. It clears up the play area and leaves the house tidy. In some homes, this may be on the ground floor, and it's important what the house looks like. Invest in a huge toy box instead of expecting a child to sort through things and put them into certain cupboards as that may be a little difficult for the child to grasp. If you have drawing tools, these can all be placed into a plastic box so that they don't stain other things, but at the end of the day, all of the playthings are to be put into the box. Mom can help with the clearing up because toddlers love to mimic adults and will be happier to join in rather than be expected to do all of the work themselves.

Bath and Pajamas

This gets the child into the routine that he needs to be clean and relaxed at the end of the day. If you want to encourage your little ones to enjoy this time, invest in some floating toys and even bubble bath that is suitable for their delicate skin. This is a time when the child is preparing for what he knows lies ahead, and parents should supervise the bathing process and wash the child's hair. It can be a fun time, but don't make it too rowdy as you are also getting ready to wind down for the day.

Supper

It is known that kids who have supper, sleep better relating to this. You will see the kind of supper that is usually at this time of night. It is a light something just to stop hunger pangs and a drink but not too large. This is enough food for the night and will stop the child complaining about being hungry five minutes after being tucked in for the night. Supper should be a time spent sat down eating, rather than being active. If parents can sit down with the kids, this gives them the impression that they are not alone. After supper, make sure that one of you goes upstairs and draws the curtains to the nursery so that the bedroom ambiance is correct for sleeping. Check the bed and go back down to the children to encourage them to go to the bathroom and clean their teeth and have one last try at going to the toilet.

Tooth Brushing and Toilet

It's a very good idea to make sure that your little one has a clean diaper for the night, and this is the ideal time for that. Make sure that your toddler is encouraged to clean his teeth properly and to ready himself for bed. You may find that the child likes a little bit of independence, so I encourage parents to have a stool that the child can stand on. The more grown-up a child feels at this age, the more the child feels in control of learning things like potty training and hygiene, so encourage your child to

321

enjoy this part of the evening.

Choosing Your Reading Material Together

You want to avoid any hurry at this stage. Take your time with your child and choose suitable reading material before placing the child into bed and tucking him in. The story should never be something that is going to wake him/her up but should be read in a low voice, so that the child can hear, but also so that he relaxes while the words are read to him. He may enjoy looking at the pictures, but at bedtime, make this kind of interaction minimal because you don't want to wake him up. You can promise him that you can look tomorrow at playtime, but make sure that you keep the promise as he/she will remember that you made it.

Getting The Room Ready For The Night

The room light should already be subdued, so when the reading is finished, tuck teddy into bed with your little one and ask him/her to look after teddy because teddy needs lots of love. Never skimp on a cuddle before you place the child into bed because, after the reading, all that is left is a little bit of affection and a goodnight kiss. The child knows that you are going to leave the room, and this may prove to be a difficult time with boys and girls. If it is, an extra cuddle won't go amiss, but the child does have to understand that bedtime is bedtime, and there is no negotiation.

Dealing with Crying

It is quite normal for a child to whimper before they go off to sleep. They are tired, probably a little grouchy, and now you are leaving them on their own in their bedroom, and that makes their little hearts a bit anxious. However, although you may be monitoring the sounds, be aware that this may die down very quickly if the child is left to it. Some systems have been devised whereby you are told by experts to ignore crying. However, if the crying gets too forceful, the child can get extremely distressed, and I would never recommend that to anyone. Go in and cuddle the child if you have to calm him, but remember that placing the child in his bed for sleep is very important. Any other reaction will encourage the child to keep on trying to win your favor when it comes to being moved into the grownup's bed.

You need to remember that psychological damage can come from fear and that this battle is about fear, not about wits. If your child is a little uncomfortable with the level of light, perhaps you can adjust the light a little so that he feels more comfortable. Sit on the chair beside the bed. Sing a lullaby if you want to, and you will notice that the child will gradually go to sleep. It may take a little bit of training, but the idea is that you gradually move away from the side of the bed. You are still there to reassure, but the distance between you should become more so that you can leave the room and carry on with your evening without too much problem.

Safety Considerations in the Bed Area

Make sure that the bed is not crowded in with toys and that there is nothing that can harm the child within the area of the bed. This should be a cozy place where the child can relax without turning over and hurting himself on sharp toys. You will know from the level of dribbles whether the child is teething, and this may give you a clue about the discomfort of the child. If you pop in before you go to bed and notice that the pillowcase is particularly wet, you can change it so that the wetness does not disturb your little one while he sleeps.

Catering for the Bodily Needs of a Toddler

On average, a toddler needs a total of 11 to 12 hours of sleep in 24 hours. Keep a diary note of the times that the child slept in the day, and you will get a much better idea of how to adjust the daytime schedule to encourage more tiredness at night. This will change as the child grows, but for the time being, it's important that you respect that need and that during the hours of being awake, the child eats food that is nutritious and gets plenty of outdoor exercises. This helps the child to get the most of healthy nutrition and fresh air, and all of this contributes to how well the toddler sleeps. A happy child who has a well-balanced life will be easier to train than one who is not given sufficient exercise and has excess energy to burn when it comes to bedtime. That excess energy could be the reason for lack of sleep, so adjust the daytime schedule accordingly.

Remember, there is no bargaining when it comes to bedtime. Many parents do barter with their children by saying, "Okay, one more story" or "Okay, you can come downstairs for another half hour" or by letting the child dictate the rules for bedtime. It has been proven time and time again that this isn't the end of the problem but is the beginning. A child who knows that a parent will bargain will be even more angry and upset when the parent decides that bargaining is not possible on certain nights of the week. Thus, you need to instill that just as a child eats his breakfast, he also needs to learn that certain actions are not negotiable. The ideal steps are ones that will get you off to a good start. Involve the toddler in every single step, including putting the toys away, sitting very still and quietly for his/her supper, going through the hygiene things like cleaning the teeth and going to the toilet, and the child will have a better understanding of what is to be expected at bedtime.

The things that will sidetrack you are:

- Illness and how to deal with it

- Crying that seems irrational

- Signs that something is wrong and getting to the bottom of it

- Insecurity was shown by the child in the way he/she acts out.

Most of these are common sense things to deal with. For example, if you suspect illness, then a visit to the doctor can reassure you. Crying that seems irrational can be dealt with by sitting by the child's bed and trying to work out what it is that is upsetting the child, without taking the child out of the bedroom environment. Sometimes, the child just needs to settle down with teddy and have the reassurance that mom or dad is there listening to them. You can also go through the different areas of the room to reassure the child that there is nothing to be afraid of.

24

Establishing Boundaries for Your Toddler

Make a Plan

You must be strategic and come up with plans about how you want to handle your toddler. As a parent, you must assume an active role instead of a passive role when it comes to parenting. You must always be a step ahead of your toddler. Well, the good news is that, as an adult, your prefrontal cortex is quite developed, unlike your little one. You are capable of strategizing and thinking rationally. Now, it is time to put these traits to good use. By paying little attention to your child's behavior, you will come up with various triggers or circumstances that cause your little one to fall apart. It might probably be a transitional activity like shifting from playtime to mealtime, or even a specific activity like bedtime. Spend some time and think about all these triggers. Once you are aware of his triggers, it becomes easier to deal with them. You can easily come up with certain limits well ahead and use them when the situation arises. It also helps you understand what your limits are, and the kind of behavior you expect from your child.

Mindful of Your Language

Whenever you are giving directions to your child or are setting limits, you must never use weak language. You must be firm and avoid using ambiguous words. Try to avoid using sentences like, "I don't think you should do that." Instead, you can say something like, "You must not do that!" or "You will be in trouble if you do that." Do you see the difference between these two sentences? Even if they convey the same meaning, the way you convey it matters a lot, especially while dealing with a toddler. If you want to become mindful of your language, here's a simple exercise you can try. The time you are conversing with your toddler, record it on video. When you have time, watch this video, and make a note of the language you use. If you notice any verbal habits you wish to break, then you can start working on them. Using wishy-washy language is a strict no-no. Using weak language will enable your child to think that he can test your limits. You must re-establish authority and make him understand that you are the leader of the pack, and he must follow you. Keep in mind that you are dealing with a toddler and not an adult, so the way you talk to him must be different from the way you converse with other adults.

Non-Verbal Communication

Non-verbal communication is as important as verbal communication. Most of the communication that takes place is usually through our body language and facial expressions. Therefore, it is quintessential that you start paying attention to these things whenever you communicate with your child. Non-verbal cues must never be ignored. If your words say one thing while your face says something else, you will only end up confusing your child. For instance, if you use a jovial tone while talking about any mistake a child makes, it will only confuse him. Never use a serious tone when you are praising your child. There are a time and a place for the different tones you use. Maintain a neutral facial expression and don't allow extreme anger to show on your face. After all, you are not trying to scare your toddler away now, are you? Don't use threatening body language and make yourself open. If you maintain a neutral facial expression, crouch down, and place yourself in close proximity to your child, you can effectively convey that you mean business. From a child's perspective, your presence is often huge and intimidating. So, get down to his level while explaining any limits or boundaries to him.

Your Tone Matters

Another aspect of non-verbal communication you must pay heed to is the tone you use. Always make sure that your tone is warm and welcoming, but firm. When you use a sharp tone, you will end up scaring your young child or even over stimulating him. When this happens, his flight or fight will be triggered, and his ability to understand you will dwindle drastically. Another trigger you must be aware of is yelling at your child. Never yell at your child while trying to discipline him. You can calmly explain any rules you wish to set without scaring him away. It is quite difficult to get a scared child to listen to you. He might comply momentarily but will get back to doing what he was doing once again. While setting boundaries, you must have long-term goals in mind and not just momentary compliance. If you don't want him to repeat any dismal behavior, then you must effectively convey the message to him. Don't startle and scare your child.

Immediate Compliance

Adults often have a tough time accepting a "no." So, expecting a child to comply with whatever you say without putting up a fight is not realistic. You must have a realistic view of your expectations while dealing with toddlers. Whenever you set a limit, establish a limit where it is a limit for you. Once you do this, then make sure that there is a little space left for feelings. It is highly unrealistic to expect a child to reply with an "okay, sure" when you say "no" to him. If you talk to him in a calm and reassuring tone, the chances of him understanding and respecting your "no" without putting up a fight will increase. If you don't want to give him another cookie, then say, "I said no more cookies. I know you want it, but you've had enough." By acknowledging the fact that he wanted something, and by denying it, you are helping him process his emotions. The only way to deal with and work through tough emotions is by handling disappointment. Have some faith in your little one and his ability to process his emotions. Keep yourself in check whenever you are dealing with your child's big emotions.

Reasonable Expectations

You must set certain expectations related to your child's behavior. As he grows, the way he behaves will change, so must your expectations. You cannot expect a one-year-old to behave the way a six-year-old does. For instance, a two-year-old might have a tough time-sharing his things with others without putting up a fight, whereas a five-year-old might find this quite sassy. A four-year-old might constantly ask you, "why?" whereas it is normal for a three-year-old to keep saying "no." Understand that as your child ages, he is developing--not just physically, but mentally and emotionally too. It is a lot to take in for him, and you must be happy that he is as pleasant as he often is! Dealing with change is overwhelming, and you must manage your expectations while dealing with your toddler. You must hold it all together and be his support system. Don't get frustrated with him if he doesn't behave the way you expect him to.

Decisiveness

You must always be decisive while setting limits and boundaries for your child. The slightest hint of indecisiveness will give your child the confidence to take you for granted. Even if you do change your mind about a decision, you must be decisive. It is not just about setting a rule, but you must be decisive while following that rule. Let us assume that you tell your child, "You can watch TV for a while longer," on Monday because you are busy with some work, and then on Tuesday, you tell him, "You cannot watch TV today," because you are tired and want to sleep. You cannot change a rule according to your convenience. Being a parent is seldom about convenience. Remind yourself that you are doing something for the wellbeing of your child. Being consistent and decisive about a rule is almost as important as the rule itself. Children respond well to consistency. When your child knows how he is supposed to behave and what you expect from him, it becomes easier for him to act accordingly. If you keep changing the rules, you will only end up confusing him.

Using Humor

Humor is an effective tool that can diffuse tension and help convey your message easily. Using humor is a great parenting tool. You can start animating an inanimate object like a toothbrush or a rubber ducky and use a silly voice to convey your message. For instance, saying something like, "You better get dressed before I count to five," in a funny British accent will get your message across without scaring your child. A little humor every now and then helps lighten things up and motivate him to behave better.

Good behavior must come from within, you can teach it, but you cannot force him to behave like you want him to. If he starts doing something only because he fears punishment or because he knows he will be rewarded, then you are not teaching him good behavior. Fear of punishment and rewards might work for the time being, but you aren't teaching him the importance of good behavior by doing this.

25

Roles of Parents

The most powerful desire or drive in a man is often his physiological need to fulfill the act of procreation.

Modern society and families have changed drastically from generations. The new attitude towards sex (right or wrong) has led to an increase in the number of unplanned pregnancies.

Anyone can be a sperm-donor and be the biological father of a child, but it takes more to be a dad. It takes a lot more also to be a mom than carrying a child for nine months.

We often assume parenting should come automatically and that we will be better parents than the parents that raised us. Relationships are like rose gardens when well-kept. They are beautiful. But if we leave our relationships un-kept, we will end up with dysfunctional relationships that bring us nothing but stress.

Roles That a Parent Must Focus On

There are six main roles that a parent must focus on: Love, Guidance, Provision, Security, Friendship, and Development.

Each child is different, and some children need more attention than others, especially strong-willed children, but we must fulfill our role as parents regardless of the difficulty. One thing all parents must learn is that having children is undoubtedly a life-changing event.

No matter how many children we have, each child is different and unique with a different set of challenges.

Love

Some parents believe that loving a child will come easy, and for the most part, it does. However, there are moments when love becomes strained, and tempers flare. Maybe the child is not on your schedule and not allowing you to sleep (which happens the first few months of life).

Strong-willed children may often test the boundaries of love. They may often leave you exhausted and even depressed with their antics. If you are at your wit's end, you are not alone. The trick is to get help.

When you become challenged in raising a strong-willed child, try and get help. If you have a partner, you can both take turns in dealing with your difficult child. If you are a single parent, you may need to reach out for assistance in raising the child, from siblings or the grandparents, but don't try and do it alone.

Even when you are stressed-out from parenting, you still have a responsibility to love the child. If you start to feel the strain, seek help, and try to take a break if you can.

But when we talk about love in relationships, we are not just talking exclusively about some sense of mutual endearment or fondness.

Parenting a strong-willed child will require what is referred to as "tough love." As children learn about the world they live in, and they will often do make choices they shouldn't. As parents, if we love our children, then we must encourage them to do what's right. Sometimes we have a misplaced sense of what love is in parenting, and we focus too much on endearment in times when we are required to show tough love.

When we focus on being liked or loved by our children rather than on encouraging them to do what's right for their good, then it's not them that we love but ourselves.

You must ask yourself, are you sacrificing their long-term fulfillment and happiness in life for your short-term sense of peace and endearment.

When your child takes a jar of jam from the supermarket aisle and smashes it on the floor because you refused to buy a toy for them, what do you do?

However, you choose to correct the behavior is down to you, but you must correct this behavior. If we willingly allow them to develop a sense of self-entitlement and lack of respect for authority, we are not showing love, as we are facilitating and encouraging behavior that will prevent them from developing into well-rounded adults.

Some parents result in yelling to correct bad behavior. But shouting does not help at any stage during development. When tempers flare, and words are spouted out, there is no telling the damage those words can cause.

Sometimes it might be better to leave the child if possible and allow things to cool down, and for clear heads to prevail before dealing with the situation.

Many parents get upset with toddlers who simply don't know any better because they have not learned the difference between right and wrong. This lack of emotional control will only exacerbate the situation.

Love is the ability to look past mistakes and guide your kid regardless of the emotional toll of doing so.

Guidance

It is often said that the first five years are the most formative of a child's life. It is the parent's responsibility to teach them and build up the child emotionally. Praise the child when they have done a good deed and correct them when they have done something not so nice or pleasant.

Guidance is more than teaching extremes or polar ends of morality. Guidance is about helping them develop a moral compass, direction, and the noble traits and qualities we want them to have in life without indoctrinating them and stealing their ability to come to their conclusions.

A child does not understand the word "no," and unfortunately, that one particular word is the most familiar word a child will hear growing up.

During a child's exploration, a parent may look over to discover little Jane is digging in the dirt of a flowerpot. The mess, of course, is easy to fix, and the enjoyment of the soft squishy dirt between the fingers is new. However, it is the mess, not the action, that causes a resentful "NO!" from the parent. It is not as if the parent doesn't want Jane to play in the dirt; it is the mess she is causing.

The child may not see the difference in playing with this sandbox inside the house to playing with it outside. Yet, many parents may flare up and even spank the child as they lose emotional control. Understanding that your child does not understand the difference and taking the time to explain may be more beneficial than shouting at them in anger.

Many parent's sources of frustration stem from them repeating their bad parenting habits and expecting different results. Yelling and spanking are not always effective and can serve only to re-enforce your child's strong will.

In situations like above, it would be wiser to remove the child from the sandbox outside and explain the difference. Redirection is one form of guidance. Although it is simple to remove the child and explain the difference between the sandbox and the flowerpot, there will be times when it is not so easy.

Security

One of the most important roles of a parent is to provide security. As our children are developing, it is our duty not only to guide them but also to protect them from harm. There are many dangers in the world they are growing up, in particular, those brought about by the

Very choices our children may make.

But regardless of the source of danger, it is the parent's duty as a responsible adult to stand up for their child. If the child is bullied at school or if the child feels pinned against various odds, it is the parent's job to step up and fight for their child. Many parents these days leave the child to battle on their own with the mentality of the survival of the fittest. This mentality, however, may work in nature, but as humans, this concept is flawed. To build trust with a child, the parent must prove to the child that they will fight for them.

It is, however, the parent's responsibility to provide the child with a safe environment free from verbal, emotional, and physical abuse. Even if that does mean taking away a new phone so that the texts stop, or the computer, so the hate mail ends.

Friendship

Inwardly most parents desire to be best friends with their kids. At one point in their lives, we may have been the center of their world, but as time goes on, kids will often become disinterested in their parents.

This is why it is important where possible to foster friendship with our children at an early age. But friendship with our children should not be used as an emotional crutch if we are unfulfilled in our own lives.

Becoming friends with our kids is about fostering a loving relationship, where the child knows we are their parent, but still feels they can talk to us, hang out with us or share with us without always having the obstacle of the type defined role of parenthood.

New every day.

Mindful Parents go within and get quiet to access their power.

Mindful Parents practice presence, create their experience, embrace imperfection, and love themselves.

Mindful Parents are motivated, knowing that with every step they are changing things for the generations that follow.

I am a Mindful Parent.

Conclusion

Toddler discipline is not a negative concept, but one filled with the methods to teach your child how to cope, to use the left brain, and work quickly to stop the right-emotional mind from taking control. You learned twenty strategies, starting with child development knowledge and parental behavior through practical advice and examples to help you deal with specific situations.

Knowing when to discipline your child is very important, and it is essential that you take the time to examine your child before giving them a punishment. Are they just acting out, or is there a deeper reason why they are doing what they are doing?

Here are some times when you need to discipline your child:

When their actions put them in danger--If your child is walking up to a stove and you tell them not to, their instinct is to do it anyways. This could cause them to be injured, and this could put them in danger. The point of discipline is to help them to learn the difference between the right and wrong actions, and you should take steps to discipline if your child continues to do things that put them in danger.

When their actions put others in danger--If your child is covering the baby's face with a pillow, playing with matches around big sister and her long hair, or doing something else that could put someone else in danger, this is another time to punish. First, you have to explain to them why it is wrong, but once they have been warned, you need to follow up on the punishment to help them to avoid hurting others.

When their actions cause harm to someone or something--If they are running around the house, they can smash into something and break it or knock into you can cause you to drop the baby.

When their actions have the potential to harm someone or something, it is important that you follow up on any promised discipline in order to help them realize how important it can be.

When they purposely do the opposite of what you tell them––If you tell your toddler, "Don't do this," and they immediately do it, that is direct disobedience, and they should be disciplined to help them learn to obey. It is important that they learn that obedience is essential, as it can help to save their life or prevent serious harm from coming to them or others.

It is important that you save discipline for the moments when it is really important, and that you don't just go around spanking or punishing your child because they act out. Make sure that the actions are extreme enough to warrant discipline, and that will help you to not spend all your time punishing your child.

You now have the tools in your box to be the parent your tot needs. You can start implementing all the strategies in the various situations when they arise, so you know you are raising a happy, healthy tot with confidence, responsibility, respect, and curiosity intact.

Remember the golden steps to listen, repeat, offer a solution, and correct the behavior over the long term rather than hoping one lesson will do. Your toddler is fantastic and deserves respect in everything you do, even if there are times when you need to use a kind-ignoring to reset the brain into a calmer one that listens to you as much as you listen to your toddler.

You have the power to shape your child or hurt your tot. Reading through the information and strategies, you must be the one to implement what you learned positively, even using reverse psychology to keep your child interested and learning. Whether you are looking to teach moral values, respect, good ways, or confidence, the tools are within these pages for you to continue referring to as needed.

Enjoy this time in your toddler's life, where anything and everything can be exciting, fun, and entertaining. As your child grows, they will calm down, stop getting into everything, but will still need your love and affection. Love and respect are the two things you should never withhold, even in the throes of upset.

Thank you, and good luck on your journey with your beautiful toddler.

We're here
because of you

If you have found any value in this material, please consider leaving a review and joining the Author's Mission to give the most resourceful start to all children around the world

By scanning the QR-Code below ♥

★ ★ ★ ★ ★

References

Bayley, C., (19 Nov 2019) Why kids need good-mood food. DailyMail.

Baumrind, D. (1966). Effects of Authoritative Parental Control on Child Behavior. *Child Development, 37*(4), 887-907. doi:10.2307/1126611

Hart, R., (2017). Toddler Discipline. La Vergne: Editorial Imagen LLC.

Hargis, A., and Sylvester B., (2018) Toddler Discipline for every age and stage. Effective strategies to tema trantrums, overcome challenges and help your child grow. Rockridge Press.

Montessori, M. (2004). The Montessori method: the origins of an educational innovation: including an abridged and annotated edition of Maria Montessori's The Montessori method. Rowman & Littlefield.

Montessori, M., (2010) The Montessori Method, Schocken.

Montessori, M., Hunt, J. M., & Valsiner, J. (2017). *The montessori method.* Routledge.

Rucklidge J, Taylor M, Whitehead K. (2011) Effect of micronutrients on behavior and mood in adults with ADHD: evidence from an 8-week open label trial with natural extension. J Atten Disord. 15(1):79-91. doi: 10.1177/1087054709356173. Epub 2010 Jan 13. PMID: 20071638.

Sanders, M. R. (2008). Triple P-Positive Parenting Program as a public health approach to strengthening parenting. *Journal of family psychology, 22*(4), 506.

Seay, A., Freysteinson, W. M., & McFarlane, J. (2014, July). Positive parenting. In *Nursing Forum* (Vol. 49, No. 3, pp. 200-208).

Made in the USA
Middletown, DE
05 October 2023

40322376R00203